Ted Naman

The Book of Revelation Verse-By-Verse

A Commentary on The Book of Revelation

www.christinrevelation.org

Revelation 1:3

"God blesses the one who reads the words of this prophecy to the church, and he blesses all who listen to its message and obey what it says, for the time is near"

Table of Contents

Revelation Verse-By-Verse

A Commentary on The Book of Revelation
By Ted Naman

Printed in the United States of America

ISBN 9781075528323

Revised February 2023

Scripture quotations in this book are taken from the New Living
Translation (NLT), New King James Version (NKJV), New American
Standard Bible (NASB), New International Version (NIV) and King
James Version (KJV), www.biblegateway.com, Bible Gateway, a
division of The Zondervan Corporation, 3900 Sparks Drive SE, Grand
Rapids, MI 49546 USA. All Rights Reserved.

Preface

In 2013 I was inspired by the Holy Spirit to begin writing my first book "**Revelation Through My Eyes**", a study guide for Sunday school teachers and students on the last book in the Bible, the Book of the Revelation of our Lord and Savior Jesus Christ.

In 2018, I was inspired by the Holy Spirit to begin writing my second book "**Are We The Generation That Will See Christ's Return**", which was published in June 2019.

You are now reading my third book "**Revelation Verse-By-Verse**", a commentary on the book of Revelation. It is organized verse-by-verse to help the reader better understand each passage of scripture. I pray that the Lord will bless you as you read my book, and I thank you for giving me the opportunity to share with you my teachings and commentary from my discipleship classes at our church in Owasso, OK.

I want to thank Pastor Linzy Slayden and his staff at Friendship Baptist Church Owasso and Pastor Chris Wall and his staff at First Baptist Church Owasso for entrusting me and giving me the opportunity to serve the Lord by teaching Bible Prophecy classes on Wednesday evenings.

If you put your trust and faith in Jesus Christ and accepted Him as your Lord and Savior, then praise the Lord for that! But If you are not sure about your faith, and you want to know Jesus Christ as your Lord and Savior, then all you have to do is repeat this simple prayer with a sincere heart: "Dear Lord Jesus, I believe in my heart you died on the cross for me, and three days later you rose from the dead and ascended to heaven. You are the Son of the One and only true God who created this universe. I confess my sins and ask for your forgiveness of my sins. Please come into my heart, and I make you my Lord and Savior".

The time of His return is near, as we are told in Matthew 24:32-33 tells us the time for Jesus' return is near: "*Now learn this parable from the fig tree: When its branch has already become tender and puts forth leaves, you know that summer is near. So you also, when you see all these things, know that it is near—at the doors*!

Some people believe if they are born into a Christian family, they will automatically go to heaven after death. This is simply not true. Just because you are born into a Christian family does not automatically guarantee you eternal life in heaven. You must ask Jesus to come into your heart and be born again of the Holy Spirit as Jesus told Nicodemus in John 3:5-7: "*Jesus answered, "Most assuredly, I say to you, unless one is born of water and the Spirit, he cannot enter the kingdom of God. That which is born of the flesh is flesh, and that which is born of the Spirit is spirit. Do not marvel that I said to you, 'You must be born again*".

In this passage of scripture, Jesus is contrasting our physical birth (born of water) to our spiritual birth (born of the Holy Spirit). In other words, He is telling us without being born again of the Holy Spirit we cannot enter the kingdom of God, which is the only way to eternal life.

The apostle Paul tells us in Romans 10:9: "*If you confess with your mouth the Lord Jesus and believe in your heart that God has raised Him from the dead, you will be saved*". Romans 10:13: "*For whoever calls on the name of the Lord shall be saved*".

If you say this prayer with a clear conscience and a sincere heart, you are now a born-again believer, saved and guaranteed eternal life in heaven. You may ask what evidence is out there about my salvation. The answer is simple. Three things must happen if you are sincere about your prayer and salvation:

1.   **There is a change in your heart**. Once you are saved, the Holy Spirit indwells in you. Your heart changes and you become a new and changed person. 2 Corinthians 5:17 tells us: *"Therefore, if anyone is in Christ, he is a new creation; old things have passed away; behold all things have become new". Jesus said to His disciples in the Sermon on the Mount in Matthew 5:8 "Blessed are the pure in heart, for they shall see God"*.

2.   **There is a change in your mind**. Romans 12:2 says this: *"And do not be conformed to this world, but be transformed by the renewing of your mind, that you may prove what is that good and acceptable and perfect will of God"*. Studying and memorizing God's word transforms our minds. It changes the way we think, the way we act toward other people and guides us towards the will of God for our lives.

In Philippians 4:8, the apostle Paul tells us what to meditate on: *"Finally, brethren, whatever things are true, whatever things are noble, whatever things are just, whatever things are pure, whatever things are lovely, whatever things are of good report, if there is any virtue and if there is anything praiseworthy—meditate on these things"*. Studying the Bible and memorizing verses are two ways we can meditate on the Word of God.

3.   **There is a change in your character and your behavior**. The old things you used to do and say in your sinful nature before you were saved will all be things of the past.

Your new behavior reflects the fruit of the Spirit given to us in Galatians 5:22-25: *"But the Holy Spirit produces this kind of fruit in our lives: love, joy, peace, patience, kindness, goodness, faithfulness, gentleness, and self-control. There is no law against these things! Those who belong to Christ Jesus have nailed the passions and desires of their sinful nature to his cross and crucified them there. Since we are living by the Spirit, let us follow the Spirit's leading in every part of our lives"*.

I encourage you to start reading the Bible daily using a devotional book and draw close to God. James 4:8 says this: *"Draw near to God and He will draw near to you"*. Find a Bible-based church whose pastor preaches the Gospel of Jesus Christ with emphasis on His second coming. Get involved in small Bible study groups. Then get baptized before your congregation by declaring your faith publically.

This is important because Jesus said in Matthew 10:32-33: *"Therefore whoever confesses Me before men, him I will also confess before My Father who is in heaven"*, but whoever denies Me before men, him I will also deny before My Father who is in heaven"*.

About the Author

I emigrated to the United States of America from Beirut, Lebanon at the age of twenty-two in August 1970 to pursue my bachelor's degree in Mechanical Engineering at the University of Oklahoma (OU) in Norman, OK.

Little did I know back then that was God's plan for me. He wanted me to take that leap of faith, leave my family and my native country, and come to the U.S. to become His servant and ambassador. The apostle Paul tells us in 2 Corinthians 5:20 *"We are therefore Christ's ambassadors, as though God were making his appeal through us"*. Looking back at my journey, the Lord was with me every step of the way.

I was born in Damascus, Syria in 1948. This is the same year that Israel became a nation in the Middle East on the fourteenth day of May. This fulfilled the prophecy of Isaiah 66:8-9: *"Who has ever seen anything as strange as this? Who ever heard of such a thing? Has a nation ever been born in a single day? Has a country ever come forth in a mere moment? But by the time Jerusalem's birth pains begin, her children will be born. Would I ever bring this nation to the point of birth and then not deliver it?" asks the Lord. "No! I would never keep this nation from being born," says your God."*

I recall when I lived in Damascus, my mom and dad frequently traveled between Damascus and Beirut to visit my mom's relatives. It gives me goose bumps knowing that the apostle Paul had his encounter with our Lord Jesus Christ appearing to him as a blinding light on the road to Damascus travelling from Jerusalem. He was converted from Saul of Tarsus to Paul, from persecuting Christians to becoming the second most outspoken preacher of the gospel after our Lord Jesus Christ. His conversion is given to us in Acts 9:3-19.

My dad was diagnosed with pancreatic cancer in Lebanon at the age of forty-seven, and soon after, the Lord called him home. My mom was ninety-two years old when she was diagnosed with terminal esophageal cancer while living in Orlando, FL. Two months later she went to be with the Lord. Both my mom and dad were godly people who knew the Lord as their Savior. They instilled Christian values in me. Someday I will be reunited with them in heaven in the presence of my Lord and Savior Jesus Christ. What a wonderful and joyful day that will be!!

After finishing my high school education in Beirut, I was able to work for a couple years at a local French bank. I saved my money and was able to come to the U.S. to pursue my college education. My older brothers Ghassan and Nabil and my older sister Lina helped me financially to get me started in the U.S. I am grateful to them because without their financial help, I would not have been able to accomplish my goal.

I had considered pursuing my degree in Mechanical Engineering at the American University of Beirut, but political conflicts among the students and repeated rioting convinced me to go abroad for my college education, so I took that bold leap of faith and I applied at the University of Oklahoma (OU) where I was accepted, and I became an "OU Sooner" football fan. OU has had a reputation for outstanding education, especially in Engineering and Science. I graduated with a Bachelor of Science degree in Mechanical Engineering in 1974, and I became a U.S. citizen in 1976.

Over the years OU college football teams captured seven national championships in 1950, 1955, 1956, 1974, 1975, 1985 and 2000; fourteen Big 12 conference championships including four in a row in 2015, 2016, 2017 and 2018; seven Heisman Trophy winners, including ten Heisman finalists and two successive Heisman trophy winners in 2018 and 2019, Baker Mayfield and Kyler Murray. This has never happened before in collegiate football history. Furthermore, OU holds the longest winning streak in college football at 47 under head coach Bud Wilkinson between 1953 and 1957, which still holds to this date.

My wife and I have been blessed with three children, eight grandchildren and three great grandchildren. Prior to relocating to Owasso, a suburb north of Tulsa, we lived in Ponca City, OK where we were members of Northeast Baptist Church. I was a Sunday school and Bible Prophecy teacher, and Jacquetta was the greeter, hostess and "coffee maker". I taught Sunday school, discipleship classes and Bible Prophecy classes for nine years to adult members of our church. I also led a small group of adult men in Bible study at our home on Monday nights, and I was active in various committees within our church.

Before I made my decision to retire early from my job, my wife and I joined with thirty people from our church, and we visited the Holy Land of Israel in March 2011. We were there for ten days, and we walked where Jesus and His disciples walked. We visited many holy sites where the Old Testament prophets walked, and the highlight of our trip was our baptism in the Jordan River.

Despite the cold water of the Jordan River, I cannot put into words the rejuvenation I experienced after this baptism. I was renewed spiritually, and I had indescribable peace and joy in my heart knowing that our Lord Jesus Christ was baptized in this same river by John the Baptist.

We also visited the Nabatean city of Petra in southern Jordan and many other historical and Biblical sites in Israel. This trip changed our lives forever. I was energized afterwards to share what we saw and learned during our trip with members of our Sunday school class, friends, and family.

The Bible Prophecy conferences I attended provided the foundation for my knowledge about biblical prophecy and subsequent teachings at our church on this topic. If you believe Jesus is coming back soon based on the scripture Jesus gave us in Matthew 24 and 25,

17

please have a sense of urgency and reach out for the lost, share the Good News with them, and encourage them to turn to Jesus Christ before it is too late.

I personally enjoy public speaking on biblical prophecy topics, and the game of golf. Playing golf relaxes me especially when I shoot low scores! I was able to lower my handicap from twenty to fifteen primarily by taking online lessons, practicing what I learned, improving my approach shots, and working on my chipping and putting. My goal is to reach a single-digit handicap, and I know that is achievable because with God all things are possible (Matthew 19:26).

After working for a major oil company for thirty-one years, I made it a matter of prayer every day with my wife during our devotional time in the morning to pray and ask for the Lord's wisdom, guidance, and to reveal His plan for us. The Holy Spirit revealed to me that it was time for me to retire and take that leap of faith to pursue what God wants me to do. I did just that. I retired in May 2011, and we relocated from Ponca City to Owasso in 2013. We attended First Baptist Church in Owasso, OK for a few years, and then transitioned to Friendship Baptist Church in Owasso in 2022 where I currently co-teach Sunday School to adult members and Bible Prophecy classes on Wednesday nights.

I recall during the last few years of my career in the oil business, as I started to walk with God, I began to experience spiritual growth and I drew closer to Him. I also began a daily routine of spending my lunch hour when I was in the office laying the groundwork for my first book and preparing my Sunday school lessons from the books of Daniel and Revelation. I noticed my days were always peaceful and not as stressful once I got into that routine.

As I look back at the years of my life since I left my native country of Lebanon, I can clearly see now how the Lord had a plan for me as He promised us in Jeremiah 29:11: *"For I know the plans I have for you," says the LORD. "They are plans for good and not for*

disaster, to give you a future and a hope".
The Lord had a plan for me and my wife to bring us together form one corner of the earth to the other to serve Him and to let people know about the second coming of His Son Jesus Christ to this earth. He did so through my Sunday school class and Bible prophecy teachings, and by guiding me to write my first two books: **"Revelation Through My Eyes"** and **"Are We The Generation That Will See Christ's Return"**.

I pray that the Lord will bless you and your family, as we await His return at the glorious Rapture as we are told in <u>Titus 2:13</u>: *"Looking for the blessed hope and glorious appearing of our great God and Savior Jesus Christ"*.

Acknowledgments

-Google.com

-Gotquestions.org

-Cdc.gov

-The Masterpiece, Dr. Joseph Chambers

-Escape the Coming Night, Dr. David Jeremiah

-The Revelation Record, Dr. Henry Morris

-Revelation Through My Eyes, Ted Naman

-Life Application Study Bible, Tyndale House Publishers, Inc.

-Focus-economics.com/blog/the-largest-economies-in-the-world

-Biblegateway.com

-Biblestudytools.com

-en.wikipedia.org

Overview of Revelation

When people I know ask me about my book and want to know what topic I am writing about, I tell them the book is about the last book in the Bible. Most would say "Revelations" is a difficult book to read, and when I read it, I need a commentary or someone knowledgeable about Bible prophecy to be able to interpret it for me. They do not realize that the name of the last book in the Bible is singular "Revelation", and its purpose is to unveil or reveal the full identity of our Lord Jesus Christ in His glory and to give hope to all Christian believers.

I was also told by many Christian believers the books of Daniel and Revelation are difficult to understand because they are apocalyptic in nature and they contain many symbols and numbers, so they shy away from reading them, not realizing they are probably the two most important books in the Bible. Daniel and Revelation give us a panoramic view of the events of the last days which culminate with the second coming of our Lord Jesus Christ to defeat Satan and his followers and to reclaim this earth as His own.

As we study Revelation, we notice right away the book contains many symbols and numbers. It portrays good angels and fallen angels in battles in the heavenly realm. It portrays the Holy Trinity (God the Father, God the Son and God the Holy Spirit) engaged in a battle against the unholy trinity, the evil rulers and authorities of the unseen world: Satan the dragon, the antichrist, referred to as the beast out of the sea, and the false prophet, referred to as the beast out of the earth in Revelation 13.

In the first chapter of Revelation, we are introduced to our Lord Jesus Christ revealed in His glory addressing His letters to the seven churches in Asia Minor. His Word is depicted as a two-edged sword coming out of His mouth, which is depicted again in Revelation 19 as a triumphant warrior riding on a white horse ready to defeat the antichrist and his followers at the battle of Armageddon. The seven churches in Asia Minor symbolize all the churches in our world, from the first century church, Ephesus to the church of the last days, Laodicea.

Throughout Daniel and Revelation, we see numbers, such as three-and-a half, seven, ten, twelve, twenty-four, forty-two, four hundred and ninety, twelve hundred and sixty, twelve thousand, one hundred and forty-four thousand. But the most prominent number in the Bible and in Revelation is the number seven, which is indicative of completion by God's divine standards. Are you surprised? You should not be, because God created the heaven and the earth and everything in between in six days, and He rested on the seventh day. The number seven and its multiples, seventy and four hundred and ninety are frequently mentioned throughout the Bible.

When God gave Moses the Ten Commandments on Mount Sinai in Exodus 20, He specifically instructed him and the Israelites to observe the seventh day of the week, the Sabbath Day, as holy and a day of rest. He further instructed the Israelites in Leviticus 25 and 26 to observe the seventh year as a year of rest, and if they did not, they would be punished seventy times for each year they did not observe the Sabbath week. This came to fruition when the Israelites were exiled to Babylon for seventy years after the Babylonians under the leadership of king Nebuchadnezzar invaded Judah and destroyed Jerusalem in 586 BC.

Depending on the Bible translation, and not counting repetitions, the number seven is found forty-nine times in Revelation (seven times seven). This shows how important the number seven is to God: There are seven churches, seven-fold spirit, seven stars, seven lampstands, seven seals, seven horns, seven eyes, seven angels, seven trumpets, seven thunders, seven heads, seven crowns, seven plagues, seven hills (mountains), seven kings, and seven years of tribulation.

You may ask yourself these questions: Why does the Apostle John describe what our Lord revealed to him in symbols and numbers and not in layman's terms so the average person can understand them? Why does it seem difficult for us to figure out the meanings of his visions? The answers to those questions are:

What the Apostle John saw in his visions while exiled on the Isle of Patmos was indescribable in layman's term, so he used symbols and illustrations as revealed to him by our Lord, which live on forever, and they never lose their meanings over time.

We should also accept the fact that our Lord does not reveal to us all the details in the Bible. Our Lord wanted us to dig deeper into this amazing book of truth to understand its meanings and applications to our personal lives. By doing so, we draw closer to Him and our faith grows stronger in Him. James 4:8 tells us *"Draw near to God and He will draw near to you"*.

The Apostle John was told to share his visions with God's other servants and with all the people that John encountered. Just like the Apostle John, we are told if we share Revelation with people we encounter, especially the ones who have not read it or are hesitant to read it, we will be blessed.

Often, I hear people say, "I believe in Jesus Christ and He is my Savior, but I do not want to know about these apocalyptic events that will come upon the earth, and certainly I do not want my kids to know about them". They do not realize they are missing out on God's promise of blessing to them by reading this book, listening to its words, and doing what it says.

This last book in the Bible is about the revelation of our Lord Jesus Christ in His glory and about His triumph over evil. I certainly want my children and grandchildren to know what God's plan is for them. I also want them to know if they do not put their trust and faith in

Him and accept Him as their personal Savior, the consequences are devastating.

When I taught Sunday school at Northeast Baptist Church in Ponca City, OK, I made it a point to teach in detail Daniel in the Old Testament because it parallels and compliments Revelation in the New Testament. I also taught the Full Armor of God the Apostle Paul gave us in Ephesians 6:10-18 before we began our study of Revelation.

I wanted to prepare the students in my class for Satan's deceptions and accusations, and certainly about the fiery darts that he throws at us during our moments of weakness. More importantly, I wanted my students to understand the full meaning of the Armor of God and the importance of equipping ourselves with it as we live for Christ.

By doing so, when Satan throws his fiery darts at us, he will never succeed. You see, Satan hates this book. One of his deceptions is to keep millions of people away from it, because it reveals his identity, his accomplices his defeat, and his final destination, which is the Lake of Fire.

Satan is bitter about being expelled from heaven and thrown down to earth after he boasted about his pride (Isaiah 14:12-19 and Ezekiel 28:12-17), and he took one third of the angels with him who became known as fallen angels or demons (Revelation 12:4).

Furthermore, Satan does not want people to learn that he will be locked up in the bottomless pit for one thousand years, and shortly thereafter permanently cast into the Lake of Fire (Revelation 20:10).

But now that we know about his doom, we become targets for his attacks, deceptions, accusations, and temptations just like he did when he tempted our Lord Jesus Christ in the wilderness as we are told in Matthew 4:1-11 and when God allowed him to tempt Job in Job 2. So, it is more important now than ever that we clothe ourselves with the full Armor of God described in Ephesians 6:10-18 to fend off Satan's attacks. The Biblical tools to use against Satan's attacks are summarized in this table:

Scripture	Application
The Belt of Truth	Jesus is the Foundation of our Faith
The Breastplate of Righteousness	Jesus is our Righteousness
The Shoes of Readiness & Peace	Jesus is our Preparation & Peace
The Shield of Faith	Jesus is the Focus of our Faith
The Helmet of Salvation	Jesus is the Way to Eternal Life
The Sword of the Spirit	Jesus is the Word of God

Chapter One
The Vision of the Glorified Son of Man

Near the end of his life, approximately 95 A.D., while exiled on the Patmos, a small rocky island in the Aegean Sea about fifty miles offshore the city of Ephesus in Asia Minor (the country of Turkey in modern geography), the apostle John, received a vision from our Lord Jesus Christ, which he recorded for the seven churches in Asia Minor and for all the churches and all the Christian believers throughout history. Revelation 1 begins with the first of seven beatitudes in Revelation:

1. God blesses the one who reads the words of this prophecy to the church, the body of Christ. It does not have to be a large gathering in church. It can be a small gathering during Bible study at home, during Sunday school hour, or even during Sunday evening service.

2. God blesses people who listen to the words of Revelation. We are instructed to read Revelation so others will listen to it. At Northeast Baptist Church our pastor led a small group in Bible Study on Wednesday evenings and occasionally I filled in for him leading that group. On Sunday afternoons and during the week we had Discipleship or Bible study classes at church. I had on-going Bible study at home for the men in my Sunday school class that   on Monday nights, so the study of Revelation is right for this type of gathering.

3. God blesses people who obey the words of Revelation because the time is near when the events described in this book will take place. I want to point out a scripture in Revelation that our Lord repeats repeatedly, which is not found anywhere else in the Bible.

It is in <u>Revelation 2:7</u> in the message to the church in Ephesus; in <u>Revelation 2:11</u> in the message to the church in Smyrna; in <u>Revelation 2:29</u> in the message to the church in Thyatira; in <u>Revelation 3:6</u> in the message to the church in Sardis; in <u>Revelation 3:13; 3:22 and 13:9</u>. The scripture is: "*Anyone who is willing to hear should listen to the spirit and understand what the spirit is saying to the churches*".

What does our Lord want us to know and understand? What He is telling us is this: If we read, hear, and study this book as He instructs us to do, we should apply it to our own personal lives and put it in practice, and not just read it and set it aside on a shelf and forget about it.

In <u>2 Peter 3:11-14</u> the Apostle Peter tells us because of what Revelation is saying about the end times, we are to be different and changed people and seek personal and practical applications to our lives: "*Since everything around us is going to be destroyed like this, what holy and godly lives you should live, looking forward to the day of God and hurrying it along.*

On that day, he will set the heavens on fire, and the elements will melt away in the flames. But we are looking forward to the new heavens and new earth he has promised, a world filled with God's righteousness. And so, dear friends, while you are waiting for these things to happen, make every effort to be found living peaceful lives that are pure and blameless in his sight."

If you stop and think about it, if the year when Apostle John wrote Revelation while he was exiled on the Isle of Patmos was 95 A.D., think how much closer we are today to the Day of the Lord, which is the day all these events described in Revelation will begin to take place.

In <u>Daniel 12:4</u> when God finished giving Daniel the prophecy about the last days, He told him to seal this prophecy and not share it with anyone, because it would not mean anything to the people of that generation, and they would not understand its meaning. The Lord wanted the apostle John to reveal that prophecy to us, because the time is right for our generation.

In <u>Revelation 22:10</u> Jesus told the apostle John *"do not seal this prophecy; share it with everyone as the events are close at hand"*. What does this scripture mean? It means we should spread the Word and tell everybody to read this book. It was written for our ancestors, our forefathers, our grandparents, our parents and now for our generation and for future generations while there is still time before Jesus comes at the Rapture to take his bride, the church.

We need to let them know about it. That is why the Holy Spirit led me to write this book. I want everyone to know about it. <u>2 Peter 3:9</u> tells us: *"The Lord is not slow in keeping his promise, as some understand slowness. He is patient with you, not wanting anyone to perish, but everyone to come to repentance"*.

The Apostle Paul wrote in his second letter to the believers in Thessalonica to clarify some of the confusion and misinformation that was circulating among them. The believers in Thessalonica thought that the tribulation period had already begun, and they were living in the midst of it. Paul wrote to tell them they were not living in the tribulation, and certain events will have to take place before the seven-year tribulation begins, which he refers to as the day of the Lord.

Here is the passage in <u>2 Thessalonians 2:1-4</u>: *"Now we request you, brethren, with regard to the coming of our Lord Jesus Christ and our gathering together to Him, that you not be quickly shaken from your composure or be disturbed either by a spirit or a message or a letter as if from us, to the effect that the day of the Lord has come. Let no one in any way deceive you, for it will not come unless <u>the apostasy</u> comes first, and the man of lawlessness is revealed, the son of* *destruction, who opposes and exalts himself above every so-called god or object of worship, so that he takes his seat in the temple of God, displaying himself as being God".*

Then Paul goes on in this chapter to answer two particularly important questions that were in their minds and are on many people minds today: Paul said certain things would have to happen in the sequence of events of the last days before the day of the Lord, which is the beginning of the seven-year tribulation period, which culminates with the second coming of Jesus Christ. They are:

1. There must be an apostasy, falling away from the faith, or great rebellion against God. Depending on the Bible translation, the words "fall away, turn from the faith, offended, stumble or rebel", are translated from the Greek word "Apostasia", which literally have dual meanings. The primary meaning is defection, revolt, rebellion or turning away from the faith. Most students of the Bible understand that to mean that the tribulation period will follow a period in the last days when many in the church will walk away from the faith or stumble.

   We see that often in our society today, where many people do not come to church on Sundays, because they are pre-occupied with worldly events such as shopping and outdoor sports (golfing, fishing, boating, football, baseball, soccer, and auto racing). That is one of Satan's deceptions, to keep people away from church on Sunday instead of observing it as holy commemorating the resurrection of our Lord Jesus Christ when He rose from the dead on the third day.

   The secondary meaning of Apostasia in Greek according to well-respected Bible prophecy teachers is departure or disappearance. In other words, what they say the Apostle Paul is referring to in 2 Thessalonians 2:1-4 is the Rapture of the church and not the falling away from the faith.

I personally do not agree with this view, because I believe the biblical meaning of apostasy here is departure from the faith and not a physical departure of the church at the Rapture. This is confirmed by our Lord Jesus Christ and the apostles Paul and Peter who specifically told us in the following verses there will be a falling away from the faith in the last days:

Matthew 24:10: "*And then many will fall away and betray one another and hate one another*".

1 Timothy 4:1: "*But the Spirit explicitly says that in later times some will fall away from the faith, paying attention to deceitful spirits and doctrines of demons*".

2 Peter 1:10-11: "*So, dear brothers and sisters, work hard to prove that you really are among those God has called and chosen. Do these things and you will never fall away. Then God will give you a grand entrance into the eternal Kingdom of our Lord and Savior Jesus Christ*".

2. The man of lawlessness (the antichrist) is revealed. The antichrist has not been revealed to us by our Lord Jesus Christ, and he will not be revealed until after the rapture of the church. The apostle John tells us the spirit of the Antichrist is alive in our world today in 1 John 4:3: "*and every spirit that does not confess that Jesus Christ has come in the flesh is not of God. And this is the spirit of the Antichrist, which you have heard was coming, and is now already in the world*". The Antichrist will be revealed to the world by our Lord Jesus Christ at the appropriate moment at the beginning of the seven-year tribulation.

3. The Tribulation Temple would have to be rebuilt in Jerusalem. Once this Jewish Temple is allowed to be rebuilt by Satan's right-hand man, the Antichrist, he will declare

himself to be God (2 Thessalonians 2:4) and Satan's false prophet will build a statue of the antichrist in the Temple and will try to force everyone to worship it as God (Revelation 13:15). It is interesting to note that plans are underway today in Jerusalem today by the Sanhedrin to rebuild the Temple north of the Islamic sites of Al Aqsa Mosque and the Dome of the Rock.

The other question we may ask ourselves is what happens to the believers after the Rapture? The answer is we will all stand before the Judgment Seat of Christ (2 Corinthians 5:10). He will judge us like a silver refiner (Malachi 3:1-3) to determine our rewards in heaven. Our eternal rewards will be determined based on how we lived our life for Him here on this earth since we were saved.

The Apostles Paul, James and Peter specifically talk about five different crowns that will be given to God's people when they enter heaven and stand in presence of our Lord on Judgment Day:

1. **The Victor's Crown** (1 Corinthians 9:25-27). This is also called the imperishable or incorruptible crown. This reward is given to believers for the sacrifices they are willing to make for God to successfully complete the call and mission God had called them to do. This includes sacrificing all the amenities and luxuries they have in their own homes, such as food they eat at home, clothes they wear, their money, possessions, and lifestyle they are accustomed to living.

2. **The Crown of Rejoicing** (1 Thessalonians 2:17-19). This reward is given to believers who witness to people in their community and win souls to Christ. This crown is also called the **soul winner's crown**.

3. **The Crown of Righteousness** (2 Timothy 4:8). This reward is given to those who anxiously await and look forward to the day

when our Lord will return for His saints. This crown is given to those who have lived a good and righteous life for God while living down here on earth.

4. **The Crown of Life** (James 1:12). This crown is for those believers who endure trials, tribulations, and severe suffering even unto death. Revelation 2:8-11 tells us this crown is also referred to as the **martyr's crown**, which is applicable to Paul and Jesus' disciples who were martyred for their beliefs spreading the gospel of Jesus Christ.

5. **The Crown of Glory** (1 Peter 5:1-5). This reward is for the elders of the church including, pastors, deacons, and possibly Sunday school teachers and other faithful leaders.

In Revelation 4:10-11, we will see the twenty-four elders sitting on their thrones around the Throne of God with their crowns on their heads worshipping Him. These crowns are incorruptible and will last for eternity.

If you are a new believer, I encourage you to start reading the Bible daily and participate in small Bible study groups. You will draw near to God, and He will draw near to you. The Holy Spirit will begin to guide you in your spiritual walk with our Lord, and as you want to know more about the character of our Lord, He will lead you to study the Books of Daniel and Revelation. I have experienced that myself in a big way and the Lord has blessed me and my family.

Revelation 1:1-2

The apostle John opens with a vision that God the Father revealed to him about our Lord and Savior Jesus Christ in His glory standing among seven churches in Asia Minor (the country of Turkey today). The purpose of this vision is to show us the events that must take place soon on earth before the second coming of Jesus. Unlike how God communicated His message to His people, the Israelites, in the Old Testament, in this last book of the Bible God sent an angel to present this revelation to his servant John, who faithfully reported everything he saw. This is John's testimony of Jesus Christ and of what was revealed to him by this angel.

Note here that God did not chose Peter, Paul, Matthew, Mark, Luke or one of His other disciples to carry on this monumental task. Instead, He specifically entrusted His apostle John for a specific reason. Let us go back to the gospel of John and examine what Jesus said. John 21:20-23: *"Peter turned and saw that the disciple whom Jesus loved was following them. (This was the one who had leaned back against Jesus at the supper and had said, "Lord, who is going to betray you?)". When Peter saw him, he asked, "Lord, what about him?"*

Jesus answered, "If I want him to remain alive until I return, what is that to you? You must follow me." Because of this, the rumor spread among the believers that this disciple would not die. But Jesus did not say that he would not die; he only said, "If I want him to remain alive until I return, what is that to you?"

Based on this passage of scripture, Jesus had specific plans for John, which He revealed to him in this book. John was the only disciple whom Jesus loved. He was the only disciple kept alive by Jesus to receive this revelation. All the other disciples were martyred for their faith.

Revelation 1:3

As we read this verse "for the time is near when these things will happen", it indicates a certain sense of urgency. In other words, it is approaching quickly, and there is nothing left that must happen before the events take place. This brings up this question: What does it mean to us? It means we are to live our lives with this in mind in anticipation of the return of our Lord Jesus Christ for His bride, the church.

My wife Jacquetta and I are awaiting the imminent return of our Lord Jesus Christ. We live each day anticipating His return to take us to be with Him in heaven. He can come at any moment. There is nothing left that must happen, no single prophetic event that has to take place before the Rapture. He can come tonight, tomorrow, next week or next month.

Revelation 1:4

The Apostle John tells us this letter is specifically addressed to the seven churches in the province of Asia, which were founded by the apostle Paul in the first century. Then he goes on to tell us his greeting is from our Triune God: God the Father, God the Son and God the Holy Spirit:

God the Father. He is referred to as: Who is, Who was and Who is to come. He is our Eternal God whom we know in Hebrew as "YHWH", meaning "The One Who Existed". In Hebrew "Elohim" means "The Creator" and "Adonai" means "The Master" (Appendix A). John is emphasizing to us God is the same yesterday, today and tomorrow. The Apostle John tells us in John1:1: *"In the beginning was the Word, and the Word was with God, and the Word was God.* This is consistent with how our Lord describes Himself in an incredibly special way in the Old Testament in Exodus 3:11-14. God said to Moss, *"I AM WHO I AM". This is what you are to say to the Israelites: "I AM has sent me to you".*

God the Holy Spirit. John tells us *"Grace and peace to you from the sevenfold Spirit before his throne"*. What is the meaning of the sevenfold spirit that John is referring to? This has to do with the seven characteristics of the Holy Spirit given to us in the Bible in Isaiah 11:1-2: *"Out of the stump of David's family will grow a shoot-yes, a new Branch bearing fruit from the old root. And the Spirit of the LORD will rest on him-the Spirit of wisdom and understanding, the Spirit of counsel and might, the Spirit of knowledge and the fear of the LORD"*.

What Isaiah is telling us in these verses is from a tree stump a new shoot would grow, and that shoot is the Messiah. He would be greater than the original tree and would bear much fruit. So, the sevenfold Spirit describes the characteristics of our Lord Jesus Christ in perfection. They are:

1. Spirit of the Lord
2. Spirit of wisdom
3. Spirit of understanding
4. Sprit of counsel
5. Spirit of might
6. Spirit of knowledge of the Lord
7. Spirit of the fear of the Lord

God the Son. John tells us in vs.5 *"and from Jesus Christ. He is the faithful witness to these things, the first to rise from the dead, and the ruler of all the kings of the world. All glory to him who loves us and has freed us from our sins by shedding his blood for us."* We should remember this book that John is writing about is the Revelation of the glorified Jesus Christ. So, he is describing Him to us as the Faithful Witness, the First to rise from the dead and the Ruler of all kings of the world. Let us look at all three titles.

A Faithful Witness is someone who preaches the Gospel and salvation by faith through Jesus Christ without concern for his or her life. We see a great example of that in the Bible with Joseph, the son of Jacob. When he was sold by his brothers into slavery to the Ishmaelite traders, and when he was imprisoned in Egypt, he always spoke the truth about God even though it could have cost him his life on more than one occasion.

Another example is John the Baptist. His life was dedicated to witnessing the coming Messiah. It cost Him his life when he was beheaded. Just like Joseph and John the Baptist, Jesus spoke the truth to

38

the Jews and to the Romans, but it cost Him His life. That is why the Apostle John refers to Him as the Faithful Witness, and Revelation is the only book that refers to Jesus Christ in this title.
A third example is the Apostle Paul. After his conversion on the road to Damascus, he became the greatest apostle to preach the Gospel to the Gentiles. He dedicated his life to witnessing about our Lord and Savior, and established several first-century churches in Greece, Cypress, Crete, and Asia Minor. He was martyred for his faith in Rome by Roman Emperor Nero in 67 A.D.

Revelation 1:5

The Apostle John says Jesus was the first to rise from the dead. This is the truth of the Gospel. Without the resurrection of our Lord after His crucifixion, Christianity would be meaningless. Jesus was the first to rise from the dead to show us the way to receive eternal life. Colossians 1:18 tells us: *"Christ is also the head of the church, which is his body. He is the beginning, supreme over all who rise from the dead. So, he is first in everything."*

But notice the third title, the Ruler of all the kings of the world. The Bible often speaks of our Lord as a King because there is no one higher in authority. Take a look at the scripture describing our Lord as King:

King of Glory	Psalm 24:7
King of Heaven	Daniel 4:24-26
King of the Jews	Matthew 2:1
King of Israel	John 1:49
Eternal King	1 Timothy 1:17
King of the Nations	Revelation 15:3
King of kings	Revelation 19:16

Revelation 1:6

In this passage, the Apostle John tells us by the death and resurrection of our Lord and Savior Jesus Christ, who loves us and has freed us from our sins by shedding his blood for us on the cross, He has made us a Kingdom of priests for God the Father: *"He has made us a Kingdom of priests for God his Father. All glory and power to him forever and ever! Amen.*

Revelation 1:7

The Apostle John tells us this book is about the coming again of Jesus who will ultimately be victorious and will establish His Kingdom on earth. Matthew 24:30 (NLT) tells us: *"And then at last, the sign that the Son of Man is coming will appear in the heavens, and there will be deep mourning among all the peoples of the earth. And they will see the Son of Man coming on the clouds of heaven with power and great glory"*.

We should not lose perspective this letter is from the Apostle John to the seven churches in Asia Minor. The believers in Asia Minor were being severely persecuted in the Roman Empire. They began asking themselves, is Jesus really the awaited King, which is one of Satan's deceptions, to plant doubt in their minds. They questioned if He is King, then why are we still being persecuted by the Romans?

The answer to these questions is they were looking at Jesus as an earthly king while they lived in bondage to the Law of Moses, and not as a heavenly King who frees them from slavery and bondage to the Law with promise of grace and eternal life.

When we study the Bible, we discover every time there is an appearance of our Lord in the clouds, it is always an expression of His judgment. In Exodus 19:1-16 during the giving of the Ten Commandments on Mount Sinai to Moses, God descended in a thick pillar of cloud over the mountain when He spoke to Moses.

When the Israelites worshipped in the tabernacle in the wilderness, the pillar of clouds of God hovered over the tent. At the mount of transfiguration in Matthew 17:1-9, Jesus and his disciples were overshadowed by a cloud. In Daniel 7:13-14, Daniel saw in his vision the Messiah coming with the clouds of heaven.

Revelation 1:8

Jesus is presented to us as the King in control of this world. He says I always was, I am, and I always will be. When he uses the words Alpha and Omega, He takes the first and last letters of the Greek alphabet translated into English from A to Z. He is eternal. He precedes the beginning of creation and He will be at the end of man's day on this earth. He is the All-Sufficient Omnipotent God.

Revelation 1:9

The Apostle John tells us he is our brother in Christ and our partner in suffering for being faithful to our Lord, while he was exiled on the Isle of Patmos by Roman emperor Domitian for his outspoken testimony of Jesus Christ. Under these conditions when he was isolated from his fellow believers, the Apostle John received a panoramic vision of future events that will take place, far exceeding Daniel's vision in the Old Testament.

We must remember, around 95 A.D. the Roman Empire was getting more and more powerful, and the Romans were persecuting Christian believers. This happened because the Empire declared Caesar to be their god, and everyone in the entire Empire was required to go before the Roman Emperor and declare he is god. Therefore, Christians were considered enemies of the Empire. The result is they became target for terrible persecution.

The Apostle Paul persecuted Christians before his conversion on the road to Damascus. When Paul was in Antioch, Syria he tried to prepare the Christians there for a life full of hardship and persecution by encouraging them to strengthen their faith (Acts 14:21-22). Paul told us in 2 Timothy 3:12-14 that all who live a godly life for Jesus Christ will suffer persecution. He lived to experience that and in the end, he gave his own life for that in which he believed.

Revelation 1:10

The Apostle John received this vision while he was in the spirit on the Lord's Day. What does it mean to be in the spirit? The phrase "I was in the Spirit" means he was worshipping in the realm of the Holy Spirit and was transported in the Spirit to heaven.

Think about it when you hear of people who have near death experience, they often describe being temporarily lifted away from their bodies and transported in the Spirit to heaven. The Apostle John moved in two directions: Upward in the Spirit to see things in heaven which he has never seen, and forward in time to view the future events yet to come.

John 4:23 tells us: "But the time is coming - indeed it's here now - when true worshipers will worship the Father in spirit (realm of the Holy Spirit) and in truth (knowledge of the Word of God). The Father is looking for those who will worship him that way".

What does John mean when he says, "It was the Lord's Day"? There are two views of the Lord's Day. The first view, which is taught by Dr. Robert Jeffress of First Baptist Church in Dallas, TX, is the first day of the week, Sunday. The second view, which is taught by Dr. David Jeremiah of Shadow Mountain Community Church in San Diego, CA is the Lord's Day, which is the same as the Day of the Lord, is the day God's wrath is poured on this earth in judgment for seven years of tribulation.

There are problems with the view of the Lord's Day as Sunday. How could John receive the entire book of Revelation in one day on

42

Sunday? It is humanly impossible to document all the events in Revelation in one day.

In the New Testament, we do not find any reference to Lord's Day mentioned as being on Sunday. The rest of the time when the apostles and other believers talked about Sunday, they always referred to it as the first day of the week. Acts 20:7: "*On the first day of the week we gathered to observe the Lord's Supper*".

1 Corinthians 16:2: "*On the first day of every week, each one of you should set aside a sum of money in keeping with his income, saving it up, so that when I come no collections will have to be made.*" These passages indicate that first century Christians were probably meeting regularly on Sunday (the first day of the week) because it is a day of rest and Christ rose from the dead on the first day of the week.

The second view and better alternative to understanding this verse is to take it literally as it means: The Lord's Day or the Day of the Lord is the day God's wrath is poured on this earth for seven years. It culminates with His second coming at the battle of Armageddon, and that makes the most sense, because this whole book is about end-times prophecy.

The scripture tells us so in Zechariah 14:1-2: "*Watch, for the day of the LORD is coming when your possessions will be plundered right in front of you! On that day I will gather all the nations to fight against Jerusalem. The city will be taken, the houses plundered, and the women raped. Half the population will be taken away into captivity, and half will be left among the ruins of the city*".

The Apostle Paul spoke about the day of the Lord and the last days' events in 1 Thessalonians 5:1-4: "*I really don't need to write to you about how and when all this will happen, dear brothers and sisters. For you know quite well that the day of the Lord will come unexpectedly, like a thief in the night.*

When people are saying, "All is well; everything is peaceful and secure," then disaster will fall upon them as suddenly as a woman's birth pains begin when her child is about to be born. And there will be no escape. But you aren't in the dark about these things, dear brothers and sisters, and you won't be surprised when the day of the Lord comes like a thief".

So what I believe the Apostle John is telling us here is this: I was worshipping in the Spirit, and in truth, I was lifted upward to heaven to see the universe from God's heavenly point of view, and I was carried forward and given a sneak preview of the time when the church age comes to an end, a preview of the beginning and the end of seven years of tribulation on earth, and a preview of the second coming of our Lord which he refers to as the Lord's Day.

Now keep in mind John was the only Apostle alive at that time. The persecution of the church by the Romans was so terrible that many believers needed a lot of encouragement and reassurance. This is really the purpose of this Revelation to give encouragement and hope to those who are suffering and struggling in this life, whether it is an individual, a family, or a nation.

Revelation 1:11

The Lord instructs the Apostle John to write down what he sees and to send it to the seven churches in Asia Minor which we know today as the country of Turkey which is 96% Muslim (http://en.wikipedia.org, the free encyclopedia).

Revelation 1:12-16

The Apostle John describes our Lord and Savior Jesus Christ in His glory standing among the seven churches in Asia Minor. John tells us *"When I turned to see who was speaking to me, I saw seven gold lampstands. And standing in the middle of the lampstands was someone like the Son of Man".*

44

Then he goes on to describe our Lord in his glory as King of kings and Lord of lords: *He was wearing a long robe with a gold sash across his chest. His head and his hair were white like wool, as white as snow. And his eyes were bright like flames of fire. His feet were as bright as bronze refined in a furnace, and his voice thundered like mighty ocean waves. He held seven stars in his right hand, and a sharp two-edged sword came from his mouth. And his face was as bright as the sun in all its brilliance".*

√ LIGHT

When you stop and think about a lampstand, what picture comes to mind? It is a picture of light shining in the dark. In this scripture it represents the church as the light in a dark world. During the day, lampstands are worthless, but at night they are needed to show us the path, so we do not stumble and fall.

Jesus told us in His Sermon on the Mount in Matthew 5:14-16 that we are the light of the world: *"You are the light of the world -- like a city on a mountain, glowing in the night for all to see. Don't hide your light under a basket! Instead, put it on a stand and let it shine for all. In the same way, let your good deeds shine out for all to see, so that everyone will praise your heavenly Father".*

In John 8:12 Jesus said *"I am the light of the world. If you follow me, you won't be stumbling through the darkness, because you will have the light that leads to life."*

I want you to know our world will continue to be dark until Jesus comes back to take us to be with him, and then we will have light again. But in the night in the absence of our Lord Jesus Christ, He has lifted the seven lampstands in front of the Apostle John to show him that he will bring light to this world again. Those seven lampstands were the first century churches that John was familiar with at that time. They were the first churches to rise after Jesus ascended into heaven. John was instructed to write letters to them.

As the Roman government stepped up its persecution of Christians, John must have wondered if the church could survive and stand against the opposition. But our Lord Jesus Christ appeared in His glory and splendor reassuring him that he and his fellow believers have access to God's majesty and strength through the Holy Spirit to face these trials.

If we are facing difficult problems in our lives, we should remember that the power of God that was available to the Apostle John and to the first century church is also available to us. 1 John 4:4 tells us: *"But you belong to God, my dear children. You have already won your fight with these false prophets because the Spirit who lives in you is greater than the spirit who lives in the world".*

Revelation 1:17-18

Our Lord reminds us of His omnipotence and majesty. He holds the keys of death and the grave. He alone has the power to free us from bondage to sin. Believers do not have to fear death or the grave because Christ holds the keys to both. All we must do is confess our sins to Him; ask for forgiveness of our sins; ask Jesus to come into our heart and put our faith and trust in Him as the Son of the living God.

Revelation 1:19

The Lord tells John to write down what he has seen, the things that are happening now and the things that will happen in the future.

Revelation 1:20

This first chapter in Revelation ends with Jesus telling the apostle John the seven lampstands are the seven churches, and the seven stars he saw in Jesus' right hand are the angels of the seven churches. Who are these angels to the seven churches? Some say they are the guardian angels to the churches; others say that they are the elders or pastors of the local churches who are accountable to God for the churches they represent.

The Messages to
The Seven Churches in
Asia Minor

Introduction

In Revelation 1:19 the Lord told the apostle John to write down the things that he saw. Between Revelation 1 and Revelation 4 are the things which are happening now in John's lifetime. They are the messages to the seven churches in Asia Minor. These messages contain a divine revelation pertaining to past and present age churches. Between Revelation 4 and Revelation 22 are future events yet to come.

The letters written to the seven churches in Asia Minor are actual letters written to first century congregations, and they form the foundation for all the congregations in our world today. Those churches to which the letters are addressed are given to us in Revelation 1:11: Ephesus, Smyrna, Pergamum, Thyatira, Sardis, Philadelphia, and Laodicea.

The seven churches represent the chronological growth of the church. To illustrate, Ephesus represents the first century church in the days of the Apostles John and Paul, and the church of Laodicea is the last church that will be on the earth before Jesus comes back. I personally believe the church of Laodicea is represented in many of our churches today. Our Lord with His infinite wisdom chose these seven churches in Asia Minor as representatives of all the churches in our world today.

There are similarities in all seven letters the way they are written. Each of the letters begins with a glorious description of our Lord Jesus Christ, which is applicable to that church. Each of the letters begins with *"I know all the things you do…"* Each of the letters has a special promise at the end: *"Whoever is victorious…"* Each of the seven letters has the same concluding sentence: *"Anyone with ears to hear must listen to the Spirit and understand what he is saying to the churches."*

As we read the seven letters, we see how our Lord tests the churches on where they stand compared to what the Lord envisioned them to be. God is not interested in the outward appearance of His churches. God wants to know what is going on within the hearts of the congregations in the churches.

In the previous chapter of Revelation, we saw our Lord Jesus Christ depicted as the glorious King standing in the midst of the seven churches with eyes like a flame of fire penetrating through and beyond the externals of the churches into their very hearts and exposing the churches for what they really are.

Many of the problems modern churches face today can be solved by careful adherence to the contents of these seven letters. We are privileged to read those letters, so we can understand how a church should function based on God's directions. Let us look at the first church, the church in Ephesus.

Chapter Two

The Messages to the Churches in Ephesus, Smyrna, Pergamum, and Thyatira

<u>Church in Ephesus</u>

In <u>John 13:34-35</u> our Lord told His disciples: *"So now I am giving you a new commandment: Love each other. Just as I have loved you, you should love each other. Your love for one another will prove to the world that you are my disciples."*

When Revelation was written, the city of Ephesus was the most prominent city in the Roman province of Asia, much like Tokyo, Paris, London, or New York today. What do we know about that city?

It was the religious and commercial center of the Roman Empire. It was a cosmopolitan city of the rich and the poor filled with the educated and ignorant. It was populated by artists and merchants. In that great city was the Temple of Artemis, the Greek goddess often depicted as a huntress carrying a bow and arrows, also called the Temple of Diana by the Romans. It was considered one of the seven wonders of the ancient world (<u>http://en.wikipedia.org</u>).

The Apostle Paul visited this city on his way from Athens to Jerusalem. This was during his second missionary journey around 60 A.D. He left Priscilla and Aquila there as we are told in <u>Acts 18-19.</u> Jews and Greeks who dwelled in the province of Asia heard Paul's message and the Word of God. When Paul was returning home from his third missionary journey (<u>Acts 20:17-38)</u>, he met the elders of the city of Ephesus at Miletus, and he said his final goodbye to them. The letter which we know as Ephesians was written by Paul to this church.

After Paul finished his ministry in Ephesus, he appointed Timothy as the pastor of that church, and when he wrote the two letters to Timothy, Timothy was the Pastor of the church in Ephesus. Bible scholars believe when Timothy finished his ministry, John the Apostle whose book we are studying, was the Pastor in Ephesus continuing the work that Timothy started. While John was living in Ephesus, he was taken captive and exiled to the Isle of Patmos and received the Revelation of Jesus Christ.

Revelation 2:1

As our Lord addresses the congregation in Ephesus, He identifies Himself to this church as the One who holds the seven stars in His right hand and as the One who walks among the seven gold lampstands.

Next Jesus performs a diagnosis of this church. Just like a physician who gets ready to examine a patient looking through a magnifying glass and listening to his stethoscope, Jesus takes an in-depth look at the church in Ephesus and diagnoses its health, its strengths, and weaknesses. He examines the heart and the lungs of its congregation. He checks its heartbeat and its blood pressure. He checks its pulse to see if the willingness to serve Him is still there. We will see later, after the diagnosis of each of the seven churches, a verdict is given to each one of them.

Revelation 2:2

Our Lord begins by describing the characteristics of the church in Ephesus. He says I know all the things you do, and I have seen your hard work and patient endurance. In other words, the church in Ephesus was doing the work of the Lord, i.e., spreading the gospel and bringing the lost to Christ. Doing God's work is an important part of the Christian life. However, we need to understand it is not by our works that we are saved. We are saved by grace through faith in our Lord Jesus Christ as the apostle Paul tells us in (Ephesians 2:8-9): *"For by grace you have been saved through faith; and that not of yourselves, it is the gift of God; not as a result of works, so that no one may boast."*

The church congregation in Ephesus did not love Jesus Christ or His followers as they first did. In other words, they had lost their first love and are not as caring as they once were. Then the Lord commends the church in Ephesus for not tolerating evil people within their congregation. They did their homework by examining the claims of those who say are apostles, but they are not.

Apparently, there were church leaders in the first century who professed to be successors to the apostles, and they were not. The church members discovered they are liars and not who they pretend to be, so they expelled them from their church. They would not allow evil to infiltrate the church. They cared about the purity of its doctrine.

Revelation 2:3

The Lord says you have patiently suffered for me without quitting. The word patience here has to do with serving and suffering. What the Apostle John is telling us here the believers in Ephesus were patient, they suffered, and they endured. They were despised and persecuted for their faith in Jesus Christ, but they endured and kept on proclaiming the truth in the gospel. In other words, they took a stand for Christ. We should do the same when facing persecution for our faith in Christ.

Revelation 2:4

Here we come to the point where our Lord Jesus Christ tells the church in Ephesus that He has a complaint against them. First, He tells them all the good things they are doing, and then He gives them a corrective plan of action. The members of the church in Ephesus had stopped loving Christ and stopped loving each other the way they once have. They were doing all the right things outwardly, saying all the right words, but they had lost their heart for Jesus and for each other.

53

Love is the foundation of the Christian faith as the Apostle John tells us in 1 John 4:7-8: *"Dear friends, let us continue to love one another, for love comes from God. Anyone who loves is born of God and knows God. But anyone who does not love does not know God -- for God is love"*.

Revelation 2:5

There are key words we should discuss in this passage. They are: Remember, look how far, or look back depending on the Bible translation. Do you know how to get back the love and excitement you once had for Jesus Christ? Just take some time off and get away from it all.

Recite Psalm 46:10: *"Be still and know that I am God"*. God speaks to us in a still soft voice, and if we are too occupied with worldly events, we cannot hear His voice. Sit down and contemplate what it was like when you were on fire for the Lord. Recreate in your mind the events which took place right after you were saved, when you came forward in church and accepted Jesus in your heart as your Savior.

Do you remember when you first opened the Bible, asked the Holy Spirit to guide you and the Word of God jumped right at you? Remember when you looked forward to going to church to fellowship and participate in Bible study? Can you get back that burning desire you used to have?

Then the Lord gives a warning to the church in Ephesus at the end of this verse, and the same warning applies to our churches and to all of us. When Jesus looks into the heart of a church and sees how far they have fallen from their first love, He says let me tell you how to fix that. He says I am giving you one more chance, or else, if you do not, I will come and remove your lampstand from its place among the churches. What does He mean by that statement?

The lampstand is the light of the church which spreads around it in this dark world. What Jesus is saying to the church in Ephesus is this: If you don't do what you need to do to get your love life with Christ back the way it used to be, then I will come to you and take your light away, and you will have no influence in the world for Christ anymore, and you will be called "A church that used to be instead of a church that is".

Do you know any churches in your community that fit the pattern of the church in Ephesus? Churches that once were beaming with light for Christ in their community, and because they got so committed to political correctness and personal interests, they did not want to offend anyone with their teachings that they stopped loving Jesus and stopped loving one another. The missionaries are gone, the outreach in their community is gone; the warmth and love they once had for visitors are gone.

You see a lot of churches like that in Europe today where church attendance once was standing room only, now only a handful of people attend church on Sundays. Sunday school classes are non-existent. They had abandoned their first love for Christ.

So how do we prevent our churches today from abandoning their first love for Christ? We keep the lights of our churches shining in our community by showing love for one another and show willingness to serve with open hearts without showing favoritism and without being judgmental of others. If we do that, the lampstand that our lord Jesus lit in this church will never have to go out.

Revelation 2:6

Our Lord commends the church in Ephesus for hating the deeds of the immoral Nicolaitans, just as he does. Who are these Nicolaitans? Some Bible commentators believe they were a heretical sect who followed the teachings of Nicolas referred to in the Bible as a proselyte, a newcomer to the Jewish religion whose name means "one who conquers the people".

He was possibly one of the elders or leaders of the early church mentioned in <u>Acts 6:5</u>. Nicolas became an apostate, denying the true faith and became part of a group holding "the doctrine of Balaam," who taught Israel "to sin by eating food sacrificed to idols and by committing sexual immorality (<u>Revelation 2:14-15</u>)."

The apostle Peter compared false teachers in Israel to Balaam in <u>2 Peter 2:14-16</u>: *"They commit adultery with their eyes, and their desire for sin is never satisfied. They lure unstable people into sin, and they are well trained in greed. They live under God's curse. They have wandered off the right road and followed the footsteps of Balaam son of Beor who loved to earn money by doing wrong. But Balaam was stopped from his mad course when his donkey rebuked him with a human voice".*

The word "Nicolaitan" is a combination of two Greek words put together. The word "Nico" means to conquer or subdue and "laitan" means the laity or congregation. In other words, it means "to subdue the congregation" (<u>www.google.com</u>). This is the first evidence we have in the church in Ephesus about the division between the clergy and the laity. The term applies to those who created division in the first century church between the clergy and the laity.

Apparently the Nicolaitans were wealthy and influential. They thought they were a class above their congregation and dictated what they should and should not do. We see a lot of that today in the Catholic, Lutheran, Presbyterian, and Anglican churches. According to the scripture, the church in Ephesus took a stand against the Nicolaitans. They did not let them infiltrate their church, and the Lord commended them for recognizing a false doctrine and preventing it from infiltrating their church.

The message to the church in Ephesus ends here with a word of wisdom and encouragement from our Lord: *"Anyone who is willing to hear should listen to the Spirit and understand what the Spirit is saying to the churches".* In other words, pay attention and listen up! And a promise by our Lord: *"Everyone who is victorious will eat from the tree of life in the paradise of God".*

The tree of life in the paradise of God is first mentioned at the beginning of the Bible in Genesis 2:8-9 in reference to the Garden of Eden and again at the end of the Bible in Revelation 22:2 in reference to the New Jerusalem. Our Lord is telling the church in Ephesus if you obey my commands and persevere, you will have eternal life in the New Jerusalem, which will descend on our new and renovated earth at the end of the Millennium Kingdom of Christ.

Church in Smyrna

Smyrna was probably reached as a result of Apostle Paul's ministry in Ephesus. Acts 19:8-10 tells us after Paul preached the Gospel in Ephesus, he began preaching daily at the lecture hall of the school of Tyrannus in Ephesus. This went on for two years so that people throughout the province of Asia, including people in Smyrna, both Jews and Greeks, heard the Lord's message.

The congregation at Smyrna, unlike the one at Ephesus, was facing persecution and imprisonment. As we read the scripture in Revelation 2:8-11, we see the encouraging words of our Lord to those who are going through suffering, and we can apply those words to any suffering church in our community.

Smyrna was a port city about thirty-five miles northwest of Ephesus. The seven cities formed a triangle in the province of Asia Minor up the coast of Aegean Sea from Ephesus to Smyrna and

Pergamum, and from there inland to Thyatira, Sardis, Philadelphia, and Laodicea.

The city of Smyrna was founded in 1100 B.C. It was captured and destroyed by Lydian soldiers in 600 B.C. It was rebuilt between 301 and 281 B.C. by General Lysimachus, one of the four generals of Alexander the Great after the collapse and division of the Greek Empire (Daniel 8). Some people called Smyrna the glory of Asia (https://en.wikipedia.org). The city is alive today in Turkey, but its name has changed to a Muslim name, Izmir meaning the Pearl of the Aegean. Izmir today is Turkey's third most populous city with 4.3 million and the country's largest port on the Aegean Sea after Istanbul.

Revelation 2:8

As our Lord addresses the congregation in Smyrna, Jesus refers to Himself as the First and the Last, who died and is alive, which is given to us in Revelation 1:17-18. Smyrna was a church suffering in poverty, and it needed to understand that Jesus is First and Last, He was dead and now He is alive, and they should not worry about suffering because Jesus Himself suffered on earth and now He is in heaven in control of what is happening on earth.

This is a parallel verse by Jesus to this verse in Revelation 1:8: *"I am the Alpha and the Omega -- the beginning and the end," says the Lord God. "I am the one who is, who always was, and who is still to come, the Almighty One."*

Smyrna got its name from its Commiphora Myrrha tree, one of the primary trees from which myrrh is harvested. It was an aromatic extract from a thorny tree which was a spice used by ancient Egyptians in embalming their dead (https://en.wikipedia.org, the free encyclopedia).

The word myrrh occurs three times in the New Testament in connection with our Lord Jesus Christ:

58

(1) At the birth of Jesus, when the wise men arrived from eastern lands to open their treasures, they presented Jesus with gold, frankincense, and myrrh (Matthew 2:11).

(2) At the crucifixion of Jesus at Golgotha. The Roman soldiers offered our Lord wine drugged with myrrh (Mark 15:21-23) to help deaden the pain and ease the suffering, but He refused it.

(3) At the burial of Jesus, Nicodemus came with Joseph of Arimathea, a secret disciple of Jesus because he feared the Jewish leaders, and they took the body of the Lord down from the cross. They wrapped his body with linen, and in the linen, they placed seventy-five pounds of perfumed ointment made from aloes & myrrh (John 19:39).

So, Smyrna is synonymous with myrrh. It was exported all over the world. It was used in embalming the dead and as an anesthetic to deaden pain. It is interesting to note Isaiah the Prophet in Isaiah 60:6 omitted myrrh, one of the three commodities associated with the birth of our Lord Jesus Christ for a specific reason: *"Vast caravans of camels will converge on you, the camels of Midian and Ephah. From Sheba they will bring gold and frankincense for the worship of the LORD"*.

In this passage of scripture, the Prophet Isaiah describes what it will be like when Christ rules on this earth during the Millennium Kingdom in His glory. Isaiah mentions two of the commodities that were there at His birth, gold, and frankincense, but myrrh is missing. Why is that? Because myrrh is associated with the suffering and death of Jesus Christ; it was offered to Christ to deaden the pain he suffered. It was put in a linen shroud and He was buried in it.

But when Jesus comes back again to reclaim this earth as His own, Isaiah says a multitude of people will bring gold and frankincense to worship Him, and there will be no myrrh, because He is not coming to suffer when he comes again, He is coming to reign as King of kings and Lord of lords. Isaiah made that omission on purpose when he was inspired by God.

In this letter, which is the shortest of the seven letters, there is no condemnation of the church. Of all seven churches, Smyrna and Philadelphia are the only two churches where there is no condemnation from our Lord. All the things said to the church in Smyrna are positive, encouraging and strengthening. Before we go on, we need to ask ourselves an important question regarding this letter. Why was the church suffering and why was it poor compared to the other churches?

First, it was despised and hated for its beliefs. The first century Christians did not have a church of their own where they could worship. They did not meet in churches as we know them today. Instead, they gathered in groups, hiding in small rooms quietly worshipping our Lord. Perhaps the real reason for their suffering is the fact that Smyrna was the place where the worship of Roman Emperors as gods began.

By the time the Apostle John wrote Revelation around 95 A.D., Roman Emperor Domitian worship was mandatory. John was then exiled to the Isle of Patmos, and the churches in Asia Minor were under pressure because they would not bow down to the emperor and declare their loyalty to Rome. They refused to burn incense on the altar dedicated to the emperor and confess "Caesar is lord". Because Christians refused to burn that incense, they became target for persecution and assassination.

How were Christians persecuted? Here are some examples, but I must warn you the descriptions I am about to give you are gruesome.

Christians were tortured in public on a Roman-designed rack which was about two feet wide & eight feet high (http://en.wikipedia.org, the free encyclopedia). The ankles of the Christian believers who would not worship the Roman Emperor as their god were tied to the floor, their wrists were tied to the top of the rack, and Roman soldiers would get behind the rack and turn a wheel and crank that ratchet down until the man's arms and legs would be literally pulled out of their sockets and eventually die a slow painful death. That is how gruesome it was.

Historical records tell us Christian believers, including the apostle John, who refused to bow down to Caesar and declare "Caesar is lord" were thrown into boiling hot oil in the Roman Colosseum, and literally boiled alive until death. The apostle John was one of them. He was miraculously protected by God when he was thrown into boiling oil.

As a result, Romans in the Colosseum were converted to Christianity upon witnessing this miracle. Other Christian believers were crucified. Roman crucifixion was one of the cruelest ways of treating a person. We saw how cruel and graphically displayed the crucifixion of our Lord Jesus Christ was depicted in many Christian movies.

Another cruel and common way of dealing with Christians because they would not declare Caesar as their god was to take them to the Roman Colosseum, and after they had starved the lions for days, they would put the Christians in the middle of the Colosseum and they would let the hungry animals loose, and thousands of Roman citizens would come to watch and scream for the blood of Christians, and they would be literally torn to pieces among the cheering crowds (https://en.wikipedia.org).

Revelation 2:9

In the letter to the church of Smyrna, Jesus tells the believers He knows about their suffering and poverty. They took a stand for Him and did not compromise their faith.

A great parallel to that testimony is the story of the Prophet Daniel when he took a stand for the Lord in Babylon by refusing to compromise his faith. He continued to kneel three times a day, praying and giving thanks to God as he had done many times previously (Daniel 6:10-13). In Daniel 3, Shadrach, Meshach, and Abednego took a stand for the Lord by refusing to bow down to the statue of king Nebuchadnezzar.

The Lord tells the believers in Smyrna not only He knows about their poverty, but He also tells them they are rich. What does He mean by that? The riches of the church at Smyrna were stored up in heaven by their works. In Matthew 6:19-20 Jesus tells us: *"Don't store up treasures here on earth, where moths eat them and rust destroys them, and where thieves break in and steal. Store your treasures in heaven, where moths and rust cannot destroy, and thieves do not break in and steal"*.

If the believers in Smyrna remain faithful to the point of death, Jesus promises He will give them the crown of life (the Martyr's Crown). Have you experienced poverty in your life when you reached a point when you could no longer pay your bills and put food on the table for your wife and children? That is how the Christian believers in Smyrna lived, suffering and in poverty.

We have been blessed beyond measure in the U.S. by the way we live, the houses we own, the cars we drive, the jobs we have, the food we have on our tables, in our pantries, in our refrigerators and freezers, and how we always help each other in time of need.

Our country has been blessed for years for the missionaries our churches send all over the world, for the help we immediately provide when disasters strike, and most of all, for our historical support of the nation of Israel. This blessing is the result of God's promise to Abraham in Genesis 12:3: *"I will bless those who bless you and curse those who curse you"*.

Notice the word slander (or blasphemy) in vs. 9: *"I know the slander of those opposing you. They say they are Jews, but they are not, because their synagogue belongs to Satan. Don't be afraid of what you are about to suffer. The devil will throw some of you into prison to test you. You will suffer for ten days. But if you remain faithful even when facing death, I will give you the crown of life."*

The word slander has to do with persecution. It refers to a group of Jews who converted to Christianity but were drawn to Smyrna because of the opportunities generated by the Myrrh business. These Jewish converts did not want to abandon their Jewish traditions, and they tried to marry their works of Judaism with Christianity. They were false priests who formed a cult within the church.

Remember when we studied the letter to the church in Ephesus, there were men in that church who said they were apostles but were not? Well, the church in Smyrna had a group of people who said they were Jews but were not. In fact, our Lord refers to their synagogue as a synagogue of Satan. Here are two churches we studied so far, and we found cults within both churches.

Revelation 2:10

Our Lord has two simple commands to the suffering church in Smyrna. The first one is "do not be afraid because of your suffering". The second one is faithful even if you are facing death or martyrdom, because I will give you the Martyr's Crown, the Crown of Life.

Revelation 2:11

The message to the church in Smyrna ends with the same message given to the church in Ephesus. First, with a word of wisdom and encouragement from our Lord: *"Anyone who is willing to hear should listen to the Spirit and understand what the Spirit is saying to the churches"*. In other words, pay attention and listen up! Second is a promise by our Lord: *"Whoever is victorious will not be harmed by the second death"*.

The second death is about the spiritual death unbelievers will experience at the Great White Throne Judgment after the thousand-year reign of our Lord Jesus Christ on earth as we are told in Revelation 20:6: *"Blessed and holy are those who share in the first resurrection (the rapture). For them the second death holds no power, but they will be priests of God and of Christ and will reign with him a thousand years".*

Church in Pergamum

Revelation 2:12

As our Lord addresses the congregation in Pergamum, Jesus is described as the One who has a sharp two-edged sword, which is given to us in Revelation 1:16 and it is mentioned again in Revelation 19:15.

As we continue our study of the letters to the seven churches in Asia Minor, always picture our Lord standing in the middle of the seven lampstands which represent the seven churches and holding in his right hand the seven stars which represent the seven angels to the churches.

When these letters to the seven churches were written in Revelation, Pergamum was the capital of the Roman Empire in Asia for almost 400 years. It was built on top of a hill overlooking the Mediterranean Sea and the Aegean Sea. Some translations have the city listed as Pergamum as in my New Living Translation Bible; other translations have it listed as Pergamos. It was a cultural center famous for its library located at the top of the Acropolis, which held about 200,000 manuscripts second only to the library in Alexandria, Egypt (http://en.wikipedia.org, the free encyclopedia).

In the first chapter of Revelation, we were introduced to Jesus ready to execute judgment with a two-edged sword coming out of His mouth, and that two-edged sword represents the Word of God (Revelation 1:16). In the letter to the angel of the church in Pergamum our Lord identifies Himself by these same words.

Hebrews 4:12-13 pictures this sword as the Word of God, so sharp, that it penetrates down deep into our innermost thoughts and desires: *"For the word of God is full of living power. It is sharper than the sharpest knife, cutting deep into our innermost thoughts and desires. It exposes us for what we really are. Nothing in all creation can hide from him. Everything is naked and exposed before his eyes. This is the God to whom we must explain all that we have done"*.

How do we know that He is ready to execute judgment? Revelation 19:11-21 tells us this sword is going to be used to strike down the nations that have rejected Christ at the battle of Armageddon. In other words, when the armies of the world gather at the battle of Armageddon, all our Lord has to do is speak His Word, and the nations who rejected Him and oppressed Israel will be defeated. And guess what? We the Saints will accompany our Lord Jesus Christ riding on white horses to witness His power and glory.

I want you to compare this scripture to when you take your car to a tire shop to have the tires replaced or rotated. The first thing the mechanic does is check the pressure in the tires. Then he inspects your tires to check for uneven tread wear. He then asks you if you are experiencing any problems like vibration, pulling in one direction, or noise from the tires. He next puts your car on a lift in his shop, and does a thorough inspection of the brakes, shocks, bushings, struts, and tires. He then summarizes his findings in a brief report and gives you his recommendations to extend the life of your tires.

Another way to illustrate this would be if you went to your doctor for your annual physical exam, and when the results come in, the doctor calls you to his office to discuss them. He says overall you are in good health, your cholesterol level is low, your blood sugar is normal, your heartbeat is normal, but your blood pressure is high, and if left untreated it can lead to a stroke, heart attack or even death, so I am putting you on a daily dose of blood pressure medication.
In the same way, our Lord performs diagnosis of the church in Pergamum. His findings reveal two things that are good and two things

that are bad. Let me ask you this question: If our Lord decides to perform a diagnosis of your church today, what would He find?

Revelation 2:13

Our Lord has the first good thing to say to the church in Pergamum. He says: *"I know that you live in the city where that great throne of Satan is located, and yet you have remained loyal to me"*. In essence, the Lord is saying to the Christian believers in Pergamum, I know that you live in a sinful city, you are part of that culture, and there is no place for you to go. I know what it is like to try to live for me surrounded by satanic influences.

There are many cities in the U.S. and around the world which fit the mold of Pergamum. One example is Las Vegas, NV known as sin city. Another one is New Orleans, LA, and yet there are missionaries who walk its streets preaching the Gospel of Jesus Christ to the lost.

Where Satan's throne is and where Satan dwells illustrate the darkness of this city; and in the midst of that city with satanic influence, there was a small group of Christian believers who were trying to live for our Lord Jesus Christ. This surely reminds us of Sodom and Gomorrah in the Bible where Lot and his family lived.

According to Dr. David Jeremiah's book "Escape the Coming Night", people in Pergamum were deeply entrenched in another kind of worship, the worship of Asclepius, the pagan god. Asclepius, the son of Apollo, was practitioner of medicine in ancient Greek mythology. To the people of Pergamum, he was the god of healing, and if you study the history of Pergamum, you will learn that the temple of Asclepius was the closest things to a hospital in the ancient world. From all over the Roman Empire people flocked to Pergamum for healing. priests and doctors worked together to try to bring about healing in the temple of Asclepius.

The emblem on the temple of Asclepius was the snake coiled around a rod. It is known as the Rod of Asclepius. On the coins of that time, you could see in Pergamum serpents coiled around a rod, which the Christians identified with Satan. In the scripture, we are told Satan is that old serpent who tempted Eve in the Garden of Eden. Today, two coiled snakes around a rod continue to be the symbol of healing adopted by physicians. It is called the Caduceus, which you see on diplomas, license plates, doctors' offices, and hospitals.

The second good thing the Lord says to the church in Pergamum is. *"And you refused to deny me even when Antipas, my faithful witness, was martyred among you by Satan's followers"*. Nothing is known about Antipas except that he stood by his principles, and he did not compromise. He was faithful to our Lord, and he was martyred by Satan's followers just like Jesus' apostles were martyred for preaching the Gospel.

Notice Antipas is referred to as "my faithful witness" by our Lord. Back in Revelation 1:5 Jesus described Himself as the faithful witness *"and from Jesus Christ He is the faithful witness to these things, the first to rise from the dead, and the commander of all the rulers of the world"*.

Revelation 2:14

Jesus looks down at the church in Pergamum and He says this: *"And yet I have a few complaints against you. You tolerate some among you who are like Balaam, who showed Balak how to trip up the people of Israel. He taught them to worship idols by eating food offered to idols and by committing sexual sin"*.

This reference to Balaam goes back to the Old Testament in Numbers 22-24. This scripture tells about a story of a man by the name of Balaam son of Beor, who was living in his native land of Pethor near the Euphrates River. He professed to be a prophet by resorting to divination, but in reality, he was a false prophet.

He professed to be able to influence the pagan gods for or against men by his rituals of magic. He had a reputation of getting favors from pagan gods. He would negotiate with any god, as long as the price was right. So, pagans would go down to his shop and ask for favors from their gods.

Balak, who was the king of Moab (which we know today as the country of Saudi Arabia) at that time, was one of Israel's enemies. He wanted to see Israel destroyed just like Haman did in Esther 3, and just like former president of Iran, Mahmoud Ahmadinejad, a radical Sunni Muslim, who wanted to wipe Israel off the map. He heard about Balaam's talents, so he went to him and he offered him a bribe, and he said, "Curse Israel for me" and I will pay you this sum of money.

Balaam responded and thought that was a good deal for him. He tried many times to curse Israel, but every time he opened his mouth a blessing came out instead of a curse. That made Balak who paid him all this money very mad and upset.

So Balak offered him a larger some of money, but each time Balaam tried to curse Israel, again blessings came out of his mouth. This shows how awesome our God is. He uses anyone He chooses to accomplish His purpose. He made a donkey speak when he saw the angel of the Lord with a drawn sword standing in the way of Balaam in Numbers 22:23, and he changed Balaam from relying on divinity to a prophet speaking on behalf of Israel.

The fourth part of the diagnosis of this church is the sin the church in Pergamum committed. It was the toleration of evil and evil men who are like Balaam within its congregation.

In each of the churches we have examined so far, Satan had a different strategy to undermine the church, and I want you to know he continues to do this today in our churches. Satan develops a strategy for every church to try to trip up the congregation, and as the Apostle Paul told us we need to be on the lookout for it so we can diffuse it quickly by putting on the Full Armor of God (Ephesians 6:10-18).

Satan knows our weaknesses and he knows how to trip us. 1 Peter 5:8 tells us *he prowls around like a roaring lion looking for some victim to devour*. His strategy is carefully worked out. He knows when to pull his trigger at that moment when he throws his fiery darts at us and causes disruption in our lives.

Sometimes he attacks the husband or the wife; sometimes he attacks the children; sometimes he attacks our closest friends to derail us off our tracks. It is how well we defend ourselves by putting on the Full Armor of God that day that we can deal with his fiery darts and deception.

Revelation 2:15

Our Lord mentions the deeds of the Nicolaitans again, which we saw in Revelation 2:6 in the message to the church in Ephesus. Apparently, some of the people in the church in Pergamum held on to those same deeds by imposing their false doctrine and authority on the rest of the congregation. As a result, they compromised their Christians values and began to implement a hierarchy of priests that ruled over the congregation, which consists of the priests of the temple and the Nicolaitans.

They ignored the fact that Jesus Christ is overlooking everything that goes on within their church, and there was no need to establish these levels of priesthood. We all are brothers and sisters in Christ. Today we see a great example of that in the Vatican, where the Pope is the Pontiff or the head of the Catholic church, and below him is a hierarchy of priests starting with the cardinals, archbishops, bishops, priests, nuns, and laity.

As a Sunday school teacher in our church, I am just like every member of our church in the eyes of God, and I have no other privileges or authority over anyone. Our church leaders have entrusted me to teach the Word of God, which is my ministry, and the gift of teaching is given to me by the Holy Spirit.

There is nothing special about our church leaders. They are my brothers and sisters in Christ, and that is how it should be. The only difference is we are held accountable to our teachings in the eyes of God as we are told in James 3:1: *"Dear brothers and sisters, not many of you should become teachers in the church, for we who teach will bejudged by God with greater strictness"*.

Revelation 2:16

At the end of this letter our Lord gives a warning to the church in Pergamum. He says *"Repent, or I will come to you suddenly and fight against them with the sword of my mouth"*. Ephesians 6:17 tells us *"Put on salvation as your helmet, and take the sword of the Spirit, which is the word of God"*. The sword of our Lord is His Word in the scripture. All He has to do is speak the Word and He will bring judgment on the Nicolaitans.

Revelation 2:17

Our Lord says, *"Anyone with ears to hear must listen to the Spirit and understand what he is saying to the churches"* and then He makes two promises: He says *"To everyone who is victorious I will give some of the manna that has been hidden away in heaven. And I will give to each one a white stone, and on the stone will be engraved a new name that no one understands except the one who receives it."* In other words, if you do not conform to the doctrine of Balaam and to the cult of the Nicolaitans, you walk the walk and talk the talk by living out your Christian faith, I promise to give you two things:

The first thing Jesus says is I want to give you some of the manna that is hidden in heaven. What does that mean? God gave manna, the miraculous food from heaven to Moses and the Israelites during the Exodus from Egypt. They did not have anything to eat, so

70

He promised to give them just enough manna for each day and warned them not to stockpile it for the next day otherwise it will spoil and rot. When they reached the Promised Land, the High Priest took the manna and put it in the Ark of the Covenant and laid it before the Holy of Holies of the tabernacle, so it became known as the hidden manna.

What the Lord is saying to the church in Pergamum, in this world you cannot compromise your faith & beliefs by copying the behavior of the pagans. You cannot participate in their sacrifices to their idols; and if you do what I tell you to do, I have something special for you. I will give you the hidden manna, which is symbolic of eternal life in heaven.

Notice the second thing our Lord says: "*And I will give to each one a white stone, and on the stone will be engraved a new name that no one understands except the one who receives it*". Again, what does that mean? If you are a student of the Bible, you probably noticed the stone, cornerstone or rock is always a reference to our Lord Jesus Christ.

Ephesians 2:20 tells us: "*We are his house, built on the foundation of the apostles and the prophets. And the cornerstone is Christ Jesus himself*".

Psalm 18:2 says this: "*The LORD is my rock and my fortress and my deliverer, My God, my rock, in whom I take refuge; My shield and the horn of my salvation, my stronghold.*"

1 Corinthians 10:3-4: "*And all of them ate the same miraculous food, and all of them drank the same miraculous water. For they all drank from the miraculous rock that traveled with them, and that rock was Christ*".

The white color is a reference to the righteousness of our Lord and His followers. Revelation 3:5 tells us: "*All who are victorious will be clothed in white. I will never erase their names from the Book of*

71

Life, but I will announce before my Father and his angels that they are mine".

Church in Thyatira

Revelation 2:18

As our Lord addresses the congregation in Thyatira, Jesus is described as the Son of God with eyes like flaming fire and feet like polished bronze, which is given to us in Revelation1:14-15.
If you read through the scriptures, you will see repeatedly illustrations of the piercing eyes of Jesus Christ bright like flames of fire. Then our Lord adds the third description as He speaks of Himself: Not only is He the Son of God and the One who has eyes who pierce like flames of fire, but His feet are like polished brass or bronze.

The letter to the church in Thyatira is the longest of the seven letters. We do not know very much about Thyatira from the Bible, except what Luke gives us in the book of Acts. There was a woman by the name of Lydia, a merchant of expensive purple cloth (Acts 16:11-15). That was one of the major exports from the city.

On his second missionary journey into Macedonia, Paul made his first evangelistic contact with a small group of women by a riverside outside the city of Philippi (in modern day Greece). Paul preached to these women and Lydia, who was an influential businesswoman, became a believer, and the Christian believers began to meet at her house (Acts 16:38-40). Not only did this open Lydia's heart, but it opened the way for ministry in that region.

In the Old Testament and in the early church, God often worked in mysterious ways through women to accomplish His will. Let us look at some examples.

In Genesis 17:15-21, Sarah, the wife of Abraham miraculously became pregnant at the age of ninety so that Isaac can be born to start the lineage of the Abrahamic covenant.

In Joshua 2, Rahab the prostitute in the city of Jericho helped the two Israelite spies scout the city and let them stay with her that night. After the destruction of Jericho, Joshua spared her life and her family's life.

In Esther 2, Esther (also known as Hadassah by her Jewish name) miraculously saved the Jews in exile in Persia from Haman's plot to assassinate them.

In Ruth 1-4, our Lord allowed a Moabite, gentile woman by the name of Ruth to have her blood mixed with the blood of the Hebrews when she married Boaz to make up the lineage from which His Son Jesus Christ would be born.

In Philippians 4:2-3, the Apostle Paul appeals to two women in Philippi, Euodia and Syntyche, to resolve their disagreements, because they worked hard with Paul in spreading the Gospel of Jesus Christ. In the same way, in the first century church, God used Lydia to help start the church in Thyatira.

Here Jesus looks right through the outward appearance of the church piercing into its heart with his eyes like flames of fire, and He starts off by telling them the good news about their church before he points out what is wrong within them.

He then offers a corrective action plan to get back on the right track. Think of it this way. When your boss comes to you on the job for your annual performance appraisal, he basically tells you several good things you are doing and commends you for that. He then follows up by telling you there are certain areas that need improvement, and if you do not try to change and improve in those areas, there will be negative consequences, such as no raise, no bonus, or no promotion for you.

Revelation 2:19

Our Lord has three positive observations and one negative observation to say to the church in Thyatira. The three positive observations are:

1. He says, *"I know all the things you do"*, your service, your love, your faith, your patient endurance, and the constant improvement in all these things. By those words, Jesus acknowledged their ministry. They had love and compassion for those who were in need. They raised money for the poor and needy. They ministered to those in their community, and they showed concern for others. So, Jesus said to the church in Thyatira you have something good going for you. You are a serving or ministering church.

2. Then the Lord says you are a loving church. Wouldn't you like to hear these words about your church from visitors that come to your church on Sunday? The word love is simply the love that Christ sees in the church. Despite all the faults this church has, Jesus found love in this church, which is high on our Lord's priority list. If you recall, the congregation in the church of Ephesus had left their first love, but the church of Thyatira still had all their first love.

3. Then the Lord says you are a hard-working, faithful church with patient endurance. Their members were persistent in their faith and did not quit when persecuted by the Romans. That is what Christ is talking about. He is saying you stayed the course when the pressure and persecution were on.

So far, we learned about the three good things about the church in Thyatira but notice the fourth negative characteristic of this church.

<u>Revelation 2:20</u>

Our Lord says: "*But I have this complaint against you. You are permitting that woman—that Jezebel who calls herself a prophet—to lead my servants astray. She teaches them to eat food offered to idols and commit sexual sin*". The church of Thyatira had everything God wanted her to have except one important characteristic: Holiness. What do I mean by that? Christ wanted that church to be holy, but instead, it allowed evil, sin and sexual immorality to infiltrate into its congregation.

Through the Lord's piercing eyes, there is a woman in the church in Thyatira who was teaching that sexual immorality was not a serious matter for the Christian believers. Her name may have been Jezebel, or the Apostle John may have used the name Jezebel to symbolize the kind of evil she was promoting.

If you recall from 1 Kings 19-21, Jezebel a pagan queen of Israel and the wife of king Ahab, was considered the most evil woman in the Bible, and that is why the Lord used her name here, a symbol of evil in the church in Thyatira.

In the Old Testament Jezebel was a princess, identified in 1 Kings as the daughter of Ethbaal king of Sidon (a city in southern Phoenicia or modern-day Lebanon) and the wife of Ahab, king of the northern kingdom of Israel. Sexual immorality was part of pagan worship. So, a priestess in the worship of Asherah was a prostitute.

When Jezebel married Ahab, he was out of the will of God, and he should have never married her. Jezebel brought her wicked religious and evil practices with her into Israel. She persuaded Ahab to build a temple for Baal and an altar to Asherah right in Samaria where Ahab was. She supported eight hundred and fifty false prophets of her immoral cult, 450 prophets of Baal and 400 prophets of Asherah. She systematically went through Israel trying to kill all of God's prophets that she could find including the Prophet Elijah.

As we know from 1 Kings 18-19, Elijah stood on Mount Carmel, and he challenged all four hundred and fifty prophets of Baal and four hundred prophets of Asherah who were supported by Jezebel to a contest. We all know the end of the story.

Elijah won the contest on Mount Carmel. He defeated all the false prophets and went on to kill all eight hundred and fifty of them with courage and faith in his God YHWH. Jezebel was singled out by Elijah in a prophecy that she would die, and her body would be eaten by dogs. This prophecy was fulfilled in 2 Kings 9:33-35. So, Jezebel in the Bible is the symbol of corruption, immorality, and idolatry.

Apparently, the church in Thyatira committed sexual sin, the kind of sin people thought they could get away with and cover up, just like David tried to do with Uriah, husband of Bathsheba in 2 Samuel 11. The Lord's anger came upon David and He disciplined him in a harsh way by taking the life of his first newborn son, by creating chaos and rebellion in his family, and by allowing his older son Absalom to turn against him.

We learned in Revelation1 that bronze in the scripture and especially feet of bronze are symbols of judgment. They speak of the Lord ready to execute judgment on those who rejected Him as we are told in Revelation 19:15 "*From his mouth came a sharp sword, and with it he struck down the nations. He ruled them with an iron rod, and he trod the winepress of the fierce wrath of almighty God*".

Here we see our Lord Jesus Christ presented with eyes that penetrate the hearts of the congregation of the church in Thyatira who are knees deep with idol worship, eating food offered to idols, and sexual sin associated with Jezebel. His feet are ready to trample them in judgment.

We should stop for a moment here and remember that the same Jesus Christ who died on the cross for our sins is the same One standing among the seven lampstands whom you and I will bow down to on Judgment Day when we pass away from this earth.

When we stand in front of our Lord on Judgment Day, there will be no lawyer defending us by some clever manipulation or deception, and there will be no jury to decide if we are guilty or not guilty. We will be judged by Jesus Who will determine our heavenly rewards, and for how we lived our lives for Him since He saved us.

I do not know what it means to you when you hear these words, but when I hear them, I get goose bumps, and I want to make sure my heart is right with God in everything I do. I want my family to be right with the Lord in everything they do.

I want to remind you of the power of Satan in our world. If Satan cannot conquer the church by deception as he tried to do in Smyrna when the Romans tried to persecute the Christian believers away from their faith, he will try anything he can, including infiltration of idol worship and sexual immorality into the church congregation. This was Satan's strategy in the church in Thyatira, to introduce evil into the church through a woman by the name of Jezebel who taught in the church that idol worship and sexual immorality were acceptable.

Now when Jesus writes to the church of Thyatira, Jezebel had been dead for a thousand years. But what He is saying to that church is there is a woman like Jezebel who calls herself a prophet in Thyatira who was luring the Christians to indulge in immoral practices, attend pagan ceremonies dedicated to some pagan god, and eat food offered to idols.

These followers of Jezebel boasted about these acts, and they thought they could keep them as secrets among themselves. The followers of Jezebel were basically following the same path the prophets of Baal took in 1 and 2 Kings, the same path as the Nicolaitans took in Ephesus. Their practice was two-fold: Idolatry and immorality.

Remember the people in the church in Ephesus? They would not tolerate the works of the Nicolaitans. The church in Pergamum had members who practiced both the doctrine of Balaam and the doctrine of the Nicolaitans. The church in Thyatira tolerated Jezebel by permitting her to lead God's servants astray.

Today we see the same thing happening in our churches. It starts when wealthy and dominant members of the church begin to impose their secular views on the rest of the congregation, then gradually the church gives in to satisfy their demands, and then they begin to tolerate it. A great example of that is when liberal congregations in our country have allowed same-sex marriage to infiltrate their churches and now they tolerate it. Other churches have allowed gay priests to serve.

The Christian believers in Thyatira either had poor conscience or weak faith. They did not see anything wrong with what they were doing, so they assumed it is OK to worship Jezebel's idols and practice sexual immorality.

This is one of Satan's deceptions. He blinds people who are weak in their faith and convinces them to do things normally they would not do. This is exactly what happened to the Israelites when they were waiting on Moses to come down from Mount Sinai. They fell into idolatry, engaged into sexual immorality, and worshipped an idol in the form of a golden calf.

Another possibility is the Christians in Thyatira saw something was wrong, but they did not have the courage to do something about it. They were probably afraid to speak out about this woman Jezebel just like Ahab was afraid to speak out about his wife Jezebel. So, Jesus saw that with His piercing eyes and let them know that they were deceived by Jezebel to commit sin, and He gave her time to repent.

Revelation 2:21-22

Jezebel was given time to repent, but she had not turned away from her immorality. Our Lord declared a terrible judgment on her that she would be thrown onto a sickbed of suffering, and those who shared her evil deeds will suffer the same consequences. Jesus is saying to this woman you are going to pay for what you have done. You brought immorality into the church and taught the people it is OK to conform to the patterns of this world and participate in this world's pleasures and idolatries, and at the same time act as a Christian.

Revelation 2:23

Our Lord says He will strike Jezebel's children dead. It will be done in such a way that all the churches will know that He is the One who searches out the thoughts and intentions of every person. And He will give to each of you whatever you deserve. In this passage Jesus is saying I know your hearts; I have seen what you have done, and I am going to judge you based on what I have seen.

Then our Lord tells the whole church in Thyatira He is going to do this if they do not repent. This reminds us of the story of David and Bathsheba, when King David committed adultery with Bathsheba and Prophet Nathan confronted him and told him the Lord's judgment will come down on his household and on your firstborn child (2 Samuel 11-12).

The Apostle Paul in his letter to the Ephesians gave a similar message in Ephesians 5:10-14: *"Try to find out what is pleasing to the Lord. Take no part in the worthless deeds of evil and darkness; instead, rebuke and expose them. It is shameful even to talk about the things that ungodly people do in secret. But when the light shines on them, it becomes clear how evil these things are. And where your light shines, it will expose their evil deeds. This is why it is said, "Awake, O sleeper, rise up from the dead, and Christ will give you light".*

Revelation 2:24-25

Jesus delivers a message to the Christian believers in Thyatira who did not follow Jezebel's false doctrine. He says, "I will ask nothing more of you except that you hold tightly to what you have until I come". What a great promise and comfort knowing that Jesus is coming again soon for His church.

Revelation 2:26-27

Our Lord delivers a message to those who are overcomers and victorious. At the end of each letter to the seven churches, there is a word of encouragement and promise from our Lord to the overcomers. Here is what Jesus said to those within the church of Thyatira, if you live above all that, then God will bless you for doing it. Then He promises them two things: He promises them the authority to rule with a rod of iron and the promise of the morning star.

Then Jesus says, "if you keep my works and endure to the end, I will give you power to rule the nations". What does He mean by that? This is about the future when the raptured Christian believers are going to reign and rule with Christ on earth during the Millennium Kingdom (Revelation 20), and we are going to have power to rule over the nations as our Lord Jesus is going to reign on this earth.

Now let us stop and think about this for a minute. We are going to rule over nations with our Lord! Think about Daniel when he was appointed to a high position under king Nebuchadnezzar. Think about Joseph when he was appointed to be the Prime Minister of Egypt, second highest in command to Pharaoh. That is how we will be rewarded. Are you ready for this assignment?

After the rapture of the church, we are going to be rewarded for putting our faith and trust in Jesus Christ and for serving Him while on this earth. People who have administrative and government responsibilities in our world today like our president, senators, congressmen, governors, mayors, and CEO's of major corporations will be nobody during the Millennium Kingdom if they have not put their faith and trust in Jesus Christ. By comparison, the poor, the faithful and servants of our Lord Jesus Christ will be given authority to rule with a rod of iron.

Revelation 2:28-29

In these verses Jesus says: *"They will have the same authority I received from my Father, and I will also give them the morning star!"* To the overcomers, our Lord has given the promise of the morning star, who is our Lord Jesus Christ Himself. There are different explanations of this scripture, but the one I personally adhere to is what is given to us in Matthew 2:9-10: *"Once again the star appeared to them, guiding them to Bethlehem. It went ahead of them and stopped over the place where the child was. When they saw the star, they were filled with joy!"*

In Revelation 22:16 Jesus said: *"I, Jesus, have sent my angel to give you this message for the churches. I am both the source of David and the heir to his throne. I am the bright morning star."*

The message to the church in Thyatira ends with the same message given to the church in Ephesus, a word of wisdom and encouragement from our Lord: *"Anyone who is willing to hear should listen to the Spirit and understand what the Spirit is saying to the churches"*. In other words, pay attention and listen up!

Chapter 3
Church in Sardis

W hen our Lord instructs the Apostle John to write this letter to the church in Sardis, He designates Himself in this way: *"This is the message from the one who has the sevenfold Spirit of God and the seven stars"*.

Revelation 3:1

When we studied Revelation 1:4 we learned of the seven spirits of God as explained to us in Isaiah 11:2, and I mentioned this is about the Holy Spirit in His perfect work symbolized by the number seven, a symbol of our Lord's perfection. The seven stars are the seven angels to the churches as we learned in Revelation 1:20.

It is interesting to point out here there is a parallel between the seven spirits of God as stated in Isaiah 11:2 and the seven churches in Asia Minor. It is a reminder to us that the Spirit of God was present in all the seven churches, and He is still present in our churches today.

The city of Sardis is located east of Smyrna (modern day Izmir). It was the capital of the kingdom of Lydia in the seventh century B.C., and it was the first city where gold and silver coins were minted. It fell to the Persians in 546 B.C. and became part of the Roman Empire in 129 B.C. It was destroyed by an earthquake in 17 A.D., and it was rebuilt and remained one of the great cities of Asia Minor until its capture and destruction by the Mongolians in 1402 (http://en.wikipedia.org, the free encyclopedia).

Jesus is saying to the church in Sardis I have the Holy Spirit, and I am in control of the seven churches. Did you know that our Lord is in control of all our churches in our world today, and He knows everything that goes on within each church? Immediately as we begin to read this letter, we notice it is different from the other six in that it is a letter of condemnation. In other words, there are no encouraging words at the beginning of the letter by our Lord to this church. It begins with two condemnations by our Lord in vs.1.

He first condemns the church for appearing to be alive as their outward appearance projects, but then He says you are spiritually dead. Basically, what he means when He says that is the church had a good reputation in their society, but it was dead on the inside. To put it in other words, the church in Sardis had among its members what we call today "Nominal Christians" or Christians by name only. The church in Sardis apparently was filled with people who claimed to be Christians, but they were spiritually dead.

When we compare the church in Sardis to the one in Smyrna, the church in Smyrna was persecuted and put to death, but it survived and lived. Sardis had a reputation that it is alive, but it was spiritually dead. When a church dies, members begin to leave one at a time; tithing and offerings dwindle; operating expenses pile up and finances decline rapidly. Soon after, the church ceases to exist, as the light that the Lord intended to shine in the community is extinguished. Do you know any churches like that in your community? I am sure there are some.

This is a reminder to us that the Lord is not really impressed at all by a church's outward appearance, knowing that inside are people like you and I who have forgotten why they were in that church in the first place, and coming to church had become a routine they did on Sunday for one hour, and then went back to their daily routines where there was no room for God in their daily lives.

The members of the church in Sardis were physically alive but spiritually dead. If you look throughout the Bible, you will find this was a common problem in the Old Testament that was addressed by the prophets. For example, in Isaiah 29:13, the prophet Isaiah records this

84

of the people outwardly worshipping our Lord instead of worshipping Him in the temple. Isaiah 29:13: *"Therefore the Lord said: "Inasmuch as these people draw near with their mouths And honor Me with their lips, But have removed their hearts far from Me, And their fear toward Me is taught by the commandment of men".*

From God's perspective, everything on the outside of the church looked great, but there were serious problems on the inside. Remember the Lord is the One who examines the church with piercing flaming eyes, and He sees past its outward appearance through its innermost parts right into the heart of the church.

Jesus saw the same problem with the Pharisees in the New Testament when he addressed them in Matthew 15:1-9: *"Some Pharisees and teachers of religious law now arrived from Jerusalem to see Jesus. "Why do your disciples disobey our age-old traditions?" they demanded. "They ignore our tradition of ceremonial hand washing before they eat."*

Jesus replied, "And why do you, by your traditions, violate the direct commandments of God? For instance, God says, 'Honor your father and mother,' and 'Anyone who speaks evil of father or mother must be put to death.' But you say, 'You don't need to honor your parents by caring for their needs if you give the money to God instead.'

And so, by your own tradition, you nullify the direct commandment of God. You hypocrites! Isaiah was prophesying about you when he said, 'These people honor me with their lips, but their hearts are far away. Their worship is a farce, for they replace God's commands with their own man-made teachings".

Revelation 3:2

The second thing our Lord said was wrong with this church is they did not accomplish what they set out to do. The Christians in Sardis showed no effort to finish what they set out to do. In other words, all they did was talk about doing work for the Lord but nothing to show for it: No mission trips; no evangelism; no help offered to feed the poor and the needy and no effort to revive their ministry.

Revelation 3:3

Our Lord gives a corrective action plan to the dead church and resulting consequences if they do not implement this plan. He says first you must change and become watchful and alert, otherwise you are about to lose everything you have. Then you must strengthen the things that remain. The Lord is saying to the church in Sardis there is still a small group of people within the church who have remained faithful and are not spiritually dead, and you are to build them up and encourage them. Then the Lord tells them not only you need to be watchful and alert but remember what you heard and believed at first.

When a person invites Jesus Christ into his/her heart and accepts Him as his/her Savior, that person is born again, and he/she receives the Holy Spirit at that moment. The Holy Spirit indwells in the human heart. But when a Christian believer dies, his spirit is separated from his body. The apostle Paul makes it clear that believers go immediately into the Lord's presence when they die. He calls this being "absent from the body and at home with the Lord" in 2 Corinthians 5:8. In the same way, when the Holy Spirit leaves a church, the church dies.

At the end of vs. 3, the Lord gives the dead church His fourth warning. He says, "*Hold fast or hold to it firmly.*" Whenever you see the words "Hold Fast", "Hold Firmly" or "Hold Tight" in the Bible, it is always about the Bible doctrine. The Lord is saying to this church which he pronounced dead, if you want to have any hope of living again, not only must you be watchful, not only must you be strong in encouraging the remnant that is there, not only must you be victorious in allowing the spirit of God to have life in the church, you must create again within the church the enthusiasm which comes from teaching the word of God and Bible doctrine, and hold fast to that truth.

Then at the end of vs. 3 the Lord gives the dead church in Sardis His corrective plan of action: Repent and turn to me again. We should take note of that, as we need to take an in-depth look at our hearts and examine them just like our Lord did with the seven churches. If there is unconfessed sin in our hearts, we need to get down on our knees and ask forgiveness from our Lord.

Revelation 3:4

Jesus says "*Yet there are some in the church in Sardis who have not soiled their clothes with evil. They will walk with me in white, for they are worthy*". The Lord is saying there are some in Sardis who continue to live virtuous lives, but the majority has soiled their clothes with sin and evil. The only hope you have is to repent of your sin and turn away from your evil deeds and become once again what I intended you to become.

Revelation 3:5

At the end of this letter, the Lord gives three promises to those who are overcomers:

1. They will be clothed in white
2. Their names will never be erased from the Book of Life
3. They will be confessed before God the Father and His angels

Clothed in white has to do with the righteousness and purity of the saints. They are going to be clothed in their righteousness. They have not defiled themselves. When we get to heaven, we are going to be dressed in white clothes symbolic of our righteousness, just as Jesus Christ was shining bright when He appeared to His disciples at the Mount of Transfiguration known as Mount Tabor in Matthew 17:1-9, Mark 9:2-8 and Luke 9:28-36.

Jesus became radiant, spoke with Moses and Elijah, and was called "Son" by God the Father. It is one of the many miracles Jesus performed while here on earth. When we receive Jesus in our heart and the Holy Spirit indwells in us, we take on the righteousness of Christ, and when we get to heaven, we will be clothed in white just like the Old Testament Saints are dressed in white.

Our Lord continues by saying "*All who are victorious (or overcomers) I will never erase their names from the Book of Life*". The Book of Life is mentioned many times in the Bible as follows:

Exodus 32:32
Daniel 12:1
Luke 10:20
Philippians 4:3
Revelation 3:5; 13:8; 17:8; 20:12 and 20:15.

Some Christians have taken this passage out of context and said, see the Bible teaches that you can be a Christian and have your name taken out of the Book of Life. But that is not what our Lord is saying here. Dr. David Jeremiah wrote a thesis on this topic during his study at Dallas Theological Seminary. Here is his perspective on it.

"The Book of Life has the names of all members of the human race who would ever live from the time of Adam and Eve to the last person in human history. The reason it has the names of all members of the human race is because Jesus Christ died on the cross and paid for all the sins of the human race as we are told in John 3:16". When a believer accepts Jesus Christ as his/her Lord and Savior through faith, his/her name is permanently recorded in the Book of Life, and it will never be erased. That's why we often see the Bible refers to this book as the Lamb's Book of Life.

When an unbeliever dies and has not accepted Jesus Christ as his/her Lord and Savior through faith, his/her name is blotted out of the Book of Life as Jesus tells us in Revelation 17:8: "*The beast you saw (the antichrist) was once alive but isn't now. And yet he will soon come up out of the bottomless pit and go to eternal destruction.*

And the people who belong to this world, whose names were not written in the Book of Life before the world was made, will be amazed at the reappearance of this beast who had died". And again, in Revelation 20:15: *"And if anyone's name was not found written in the book of life, he was thrown into the lake of fire"*.

Therefore, when eternity begins, the only names left in the Book of Life are those who put their trust and faith in Jesus Christ as per <u>John 3:36 (NLT):</u> *"Whoever believes in the Son has eternal life, but whoever rejects the Son will not see life, for God's wrath remains on him."*

At the end of vs. 5 our Lord says, *"I will announce before my Father and his angels that they are mine"*. He also tells us in <u>Matthew 10:32-33</u>: *Whoever acknowledges me before men, I will also acknowledge him before my Father in heaven. But whoever disowns me before men, I will disown him before my Father in heaven"*.

There is something special in these three words that Jesus gives to the overcomers. Sacrifice and loss may be our experience here on earth, but abundant rewards are waiting for us in heaven. When we walk with the Lord and become overcomers despite the persecution we may experience on earth, and we take the high road, the Lord promises we will be clothed in white, our name will always be in the Book of Life, and Jesus will confess us to the Father and His angels.

Revelation 3:6

The message to the church in Sardis ends with the same message given to the church in Ephesus, a word of wisdom and encouragement from our Lord: *"Anyone who is willing to hear should listen to the Spirit and understand what the Spirit is saying to the churches"*. In other words, pay attention and listen up!

Church in Philadelphia

Revelation 3:7

As our Lord addresses the congregation in Philadelphia, Jesus is described as the One who is holy and true, the one who has the key of David, which is given to us in Revelation 1:18.

The city of Philadelphia is known in modern Turkey by the name Alaşehir. It is located about twenty-eight miles southeast of Sardis. It was named Attalus Philadelphus after the king of Pergamum who built the city between 220 B.C. and 138 B.C. The word "Attalus" means the loving brother. That is how Philadelphia got its name as "the city of brotherly love".

Philadelphia was a prosperous city. It was called the "Little Athens" in the sixth century A.D. because of the Greek influence on its culture and its festivals and temples (http://en.wikipedia.org, the free encyclopedia).

When our Lord writes to the angel of the church in Philadelphia, He establishes His holiness by designating Himself as *"Holy, True and the One who has the key of David. He opens doors, and no one can shut; he shuts doors, and no one can open"*.

When the Lord refers to Himself here as Holy, He is simply saying He and only He has the characteristic that only God himself possesses, and no man can ever possess that characteristic in the human flesh. He is a Holy God. He is calling the Christians in Philadelphia to a life of faith in Him. We are told in 1Peter 1:15-16: *"But now you must be holy in everything you do, just as God who chose you is holy. For the Scriptures say, "You must be holy because I am holy."*

Then our Lord adds to that the characteristic the One who is true. He is not talking about truth as opposed to that which is a lie, but

90

rather as truth as in the word of God. In other words, He is saying I am the only genuine true God, as opposed to many false gods like the coming antichrist and many false christs in our world today for example. When you understand who Jesus is and you understand His character, you can then understand how He is holy and true. In the same way, he wants us to be holy and He wants us to live our life in holiness so we can reflect His holiness.

The other characteristic of our Lord Jesus Christ mentioned is this: "*the One who has the key of David. He opens doors, and no one can shut them; he shuts doors, and no one can open them*". This scripture is in reference to the scripture in Isaiah 22:20-22: "*And then I will call my servant Eliakim son of Hilkiah to replace you. He will have your royal robes, your title, and your authority. And he will be a father to the people of Jerusalem and Judah. I will give him the key to the house of David -- the highest position in the royal court. He will open doors, and no one will be able to shut them; he will close doors, and no one will be able to open them*".

The Lord's servant Eliakim in this scripture had replaced Shebna, the palace administrator. He had the key to all the treasures of the king. When he opened the door, it was open, and when he closed the door it was closed. No one had access to the king's treasure other than Eliakim. Here in this passage, Jesus Christ is pictured in the same way. He is represented as greater than Eliakim. He has the key of King David and has the power to open and shut the door according to His sovereign will.

Revelation 3:8

Jesus tells the church in Philadelphia that He knows all the things they do, and He has opened a door for them that no man can shut. What does He mean by that? He means He has opened a door to witnessing and evangelism by spreading the Gospel. In 1 Corinthians 16:8-9 there is a passage where that same phrase is used by the Apostle Paul: "*In the meantime, I will be staying here at Ephesus until the*

Festival of Pentecost, for there is a wide-open door for a great work here, and many people are responding. But there are many who oppose me".

In Colossians 4:3-4 Paul asked the people in Colossae to pray for him while imprisoned. He says "*Don't forget to pray for us, too, that God will give us many opportunities to preach about his secret plan -- that Christ is also for you Gentiles. That is why I am here in chains. Pray that I will proclaim this message as clearly as I should*". Paul asked the Colossians to pray for him that there would be an opportunity for him to witness to the people to whom God had sent him. Let me ask you this question: Are you spreading the gospel in your community through the door that the Lord opened for you?

Our Lord continues by commending the Christian believers for obeying His word and did not deny Him when they had little strength and faced persecution. In other words, He wanted them to know they have kept His word and the power of the church is weak without the power of the Lord guiding it. From God's perspective, the church in Philadelphia was a great example of the period in church history when missionaries were being commissioned to spread the Gospel and evangelism was beginning to bloom.

Revelation 3:9

Our Lord mentions the same liars who say they are Jews but are not. These are the same Jews we saw in the church of Smyrna in Revelation 2:9, but here they infiltrated the church in Philadelphia. The Lord is saying I am not going to put up with those Jews anymore in this church, and I will take care of that problem. Before too long, they will come to you, bow down at your feet, and look up to you for direction and for guidance.

A great of example of those Jews is the Apostle Paul. He started out as a Jew by the name of Saul of Tarsus persecuting Christians and the church (Acts 9). He was out trying to kill them, to put them in chains and to drag them to prison. In fact, he was on a persecution mission on the road to Damascus when the Lord appeared to him and would not let him arrest the Christians anymore. The next thing we know this persecutor has become a worshipper and a champion for the cause of Jesus Christ, and he changed his name from Saul of Tarsus to Paul.

Revelation 3:10

Our Lord makes a great promise that has great prophetic ramification, which you should memorize, so you can answer from the Bible and defend the pre-tribulation rapture and the ensuing seven-year tribulation:

"Because you have obeyed my command to persevere, I will protect you from the great time of testing that will come upon the whole world to test those who belong to this world". In other words, what the Lord is saying to the church in Philadelphia, and it applies to us as well, "I will protect you from going through the judgments of the seven-year tribulation that will come upon this world in the last days by taking you to be with me at the rapture".

There are five views among Christian believers about the rapture:

The first view, pre-tribulation, or pre-millennialism is the church of Jesus Christ, which includes all the Christian believers on this earth, is going to be raptured before the seven-year tribulation on earth begins. In other words, the body of Christ will be suddenly taken out of this earth to be with the Lord before disasters come upon the earth.

The second view, mid-tribulation, is the Christian believers will go through three-and-a-half years of tribulation on earth and then they will be raptured.

The third view, post-tribulation, is the Christian believers will go through the seven-year tribulation, and after the tribulation is over, they will be raptured.

The fourth view, a-millennialism, rejects the fact that Jesus will set up his thousand-year reign on earth as described by the apostle John in Revelation 20, and rejects the fact that rapture and seven-year tribulation exist.

The fifth view, post-millennialism, teaches there is a literal thousand-year period known to God when Christ reigns by virtue of the spread of the gospel, but Christ does not usher in the thousand-year reign on earth. Post-millennialists believe Christ's second coming will occur at the end of the Millennial Kingdom.

I want to share with you what the Bible says about this. The Lord is addressing this letter to the church in Philadelphia, which represents the true church of the last days, and He says to the true believers in vs. 10 *"Because you have obeyed my command to persevere, I will protect you from the great time of testing that will come upon the whole world to test those who belong to this world"*.

The phrase "hour of testing (NLT & NASB) or hour of temptation (KJV) or hour of trial (NIV)" is in reference to the seven-year tribulation period that will come upon this earth. Here is a promise that the Lord gives to the church that He will deliver us from going through the tribulation.

Do you remember in the Old Testament in the book of Daniel the story of Shadrach, Meshach, and Abednego in Daniel 3:19? These young Jewish men were cast into the fiery furnace, and they were preserved through the flames of fire by a messenger of God who protected them from burning.

Some post-tribulation prophecy teachers use this same example to teach that the church is like Shadrach, Meshach, and Abednego, that

Christian believers will go through the flames of persecution during the seven-year tribulation, and God is going to keep us safe in the midst of it. But I want you to carefully note what the Bible says.

The Word of God in this verse does not say I will protect you "through" the great time of testing. It says I will protect you "from" the great time of testing. This means the body of Christ will be raptured before the seven-year tribulation here on earth, and we will not go through it.

The reason we believe so is first of all we are the bride of our Lord Jesus Christ, and he is preparing a meal to share with us at the marriage supper of the Lamb (Revelation 19:6-9). Why would our Lord put His bride, the church, through seven years of hell on earth before He accepts her as His bride?

There is another especially important Biblical reason why we believe so. During the seven-year tribulation, the Lord will focus on Daniel's 70th week when His judgments will come down on the nation of Israel and the Jewish people who denied Him as their Savior, and on the Arab nations who oppressed Israel. That is why I believe the church will be raptured before these events take place.

Some of you may not be quite convinced yet, so I would like to share with you several verses in the Bible where The Lord promises us, He will spare His followers from His judgment, and reaffirms His protection for us in times of trouble:

Genesis 19:15

"With the coming of dawn, the angels urged Lot, saying, "Hurry! Take your wife and your two daughters who are here, or you will be swept away when the city is punished".

Exodus 14:21-22

"Then Moses stretched out his hand over the sea, and all that night the LORD drove

the sea back with a strong east wind and turned it into dry land. The waters were divided, and the Israelites went through the sea on dry ground, with a wall of water on their right and on their left.

Malachi 3:17

"They will be my people," says the Lord of Heaven's Armies. "On the day when I act in judgment, they will be my own special treasure. I will spare them as a father spares an obedient child."

Psalm 91:14-16

"The Lord says, I will rescue those who love me. I will protect those who trust in my name. When they call on me, I will answer; I will be with them in trouble. I will rescue and honor them. I will reward them with a long life and give them my salvation."

Psalm 94:14

"The Lord will not reject his people; He will not abandon his special possession."

Daniel 12:1

"At that time Michael, the archangel who stands guard over your nation, will arise. Then there will be a time of anguish greater than any since nations first came into existence. But at that time every one of your people whose name is written in the book will be rescued."

Luke 21:36

"Keep alert at all times. And pray that you might be strong enough to escape these coming horrors and stand before the Son of Man."

John 3:36	*"And anyone who believes in God's Son has eternal life. Anyone who doesn't obey the Son will never experience eternal life but remains under God's angry judgment."*
Romans 5:9	*"And since we have been made right in God's sight by the blood of Christ, he will certainly save us from God's condemnation."*
Romans 8:1	*"So now there is no condemnation for those who belong to Christ Jesus."*
1Thessalonians 1:10	*"And they speak of how you are looking forward to the coming of God's Son from heaven—Jesus, whom God raised from the dead. He is the one who has rescued us from the terrors of the coming judgment."*
1Thessalonians 5:9	*"For God chose to save us through our Lord Jesus Christ, not to pour out his anger on us."*
Revelation 3:10	*"Because you have obeyed my command to persevere, I will protect you from the great time of testing that will come upon the whole world to test those who belong to this world."*

When we begin to study the seven-year tribulation in Revelation 4, you will see how gruesome and awful it is. Do you think the Lord would allow us to go into that kind of suffering without preparing us and helping us to understand what we are to expect? That is why He promised to bless us in Revelation 1, so we can take that blessing and share it with people who do not know the Lord as their Savior, tell them about the horrors of the tribulation, because if they do not accept Him as their Savior, they will go through the tribulation.

In Revelation 4 through 19, there is not one reference to the church. That is because the church is in heaven at the Judgment Seat of Christ being judged for the works done while here on earth, and while we are being judged by our Lord, the world is in turmoil about to be ruled by the antichrist. This is true and this is what the Bible teaches, and I believe it.

So, the Lord is saying to the church in Philadelphia, "I want to make a promise to you. The promise is this: Because you have obeyed my commands to persevere during a time of persecution, and you kept your trust and faith in me, I will come to take you to be with me at the rapture, and I will protect you from the hour of testing, which is the seven-year tribulation that will come upon this whole world after the rapture.

Revelation 3:11

The Lord promises the Christian believers in the church of Philadelphia that he is going to come quickly, and to hold on to what they have so that no one will take away their crown. Which crown is the Lord referring to here?

Do you remember the five crowns of the believers which I discussed in Revelation 1? Christians have differing gifts, abilities, and spiritual maturity. God does not expect us all to act the same way, but He does expect us to "hold on" to what we have, to persevere in using our resources to serve Him.

If the Lord blessed us financially, then we should use our finances to bless others and glorify Him and not glorify ourselves. If He blessed us with unique gifts, then we should use our gifts to bless others. If He blessed us with beautiful children and grandchildren, then we should teach them to glorify Him.

You may be just like the believers in Philadelphia, a new believer in Jesus Christ, and you feel that your faith and spiritual growth are not as strong as they should be. It is quite common for married couples to be at different levels in their spiritual growth. Do not be discouraged, continue to study the Bible, participate in small group Bible study, and use your gifts and abilities to help others in need, live for Christ and glorify His name. God will commend you and reward you for it.

Revelation 3:12

The Lord promises all the overcomers and victorious they will become pillars in His Temple; they will never leave it, and they will be sealed with the name of God the Father. What is our Lord's Temple and what is the name of God the Father?

We will see later in Revelation 11 the apostle John is given a measuring stick and was told by the angel of God to go measure the Temple of God and the altar and count the number of worshipers. This Temple is in reference to the Millennial Temple from which our Lord Jesus Christ will rule the world with His right-hand man King David.

The Bible gives us the many names of God the Father (Appendix A), God the Son Jesus Christ (Appendix B), and God the Holy Spirit (Appendix C). No one knows for sure which name God will seal His overcomers with, but I personally believe the name of God the Father "YHWH" is most likely the name the overcomers will receive.

Then our Lord promises all the overcomers and victorious, they will dwell in the Heavenly City, the New Jerusalem, which we will discuss in detail in Revelation 21. I do not know about you, but I have already made reservations for me and my family in the New Jerusalem, and if you have not already done so, you should make yours soon, as our time on this earth is short.

We will all have new citizenships, new heavenly bodies, new names, and a new common language in God's future Kingdom.

99

Zephaniah 3:9: *"Then I will purify the speech of all people, so that everyone can worship the Lord together"*. Everything will be new and secure with God reigning as King of kings and Lord of lords.

Revelation 3:13

As with previous letters, our Lord closes His message to the church in Philadelphia with a sense of urgency: *"Anyone who is willing to hear should listen to the Spirit and understand what the Spirit is saying to the churches"*. In other words, pay attention and listen up!

Church in Laodicea

So far, we have studied six out of the seven churches in Revelation: The churches in Ephesus, Smyrna, Pergamum, Thyatira, Sardis, and Philadelphia, and here is what we learned about them:

Church	Revelation	Positive Things	Negative Things	Action & Discipline
Ephesus	2:1-7	Hard work perseverance	Forsaken first love	Remember & repent
Smyrna	2:8-11	Suffered persecution & poverty	None	Do not fear; be faithful
Pergamum	2:12-17	True to faith	Compromise	Repent
Thyatira	2:18-19	Love, faith & service	Immorality	Repent
Sardis	3:1-6	Effective	Superficial	Wake up & repent
Philadelphia	3:7-13	Faithful	None	Hold On

Revelation 3:14

Now we come to the last of the seven churches in Asia Minor, the church in Laodicea. As our Lord addresses the congregation in Laodicea, Jesus describes Himself as the Faithful Witness who sacrificed his life for us on the cross and rose from the dead, which is also given to us in Revelation 1:5.

There is not one good thing about the church in Laodicea from our Lord's perspective, as He examines it with His piercing eyes, while penetrating right into the heart of its congregation. It is the only church out of the seven churches that God has nothing good to say about. In the other six churches, there was something positive said about them, but in this church, it is all negative.

The city of Laodicea was founded by Antiochus Epiphanes II who was the king of Syria back in the third century B.C. and mentioned in Daniel 11. He named this city after his wife Laodice. Today Laodicea is non-existent in Southeast Turkey. All that is left is ruins located about forty miles southeast of Philadelphia on the road to Colossae.

Laodicea was one of the triple cities that were close in connection: Colossae, Hierapolis, and Laodicea (http://en.wikipedia.org). Note these three cities were mentioned by Paul in Colossians 4:12-18 in the closing words of his letter to the church in Colossae.

Under Roman rule the city of Laodicea had become very wealthy. Its profitable business was the result of manufacturing of wool and cloth. Its economic self-sufficiency perhaps was the reason our Lord condemns it as neither cold nor hot but lukewarm.

The word lukewarm means indifferent. It is a church that believes it is self-sufficient apart from the Lord with no enthusiasm for Him, just like many mega churches in our nation today, and perhaps this is the reason our Lord condemns them as wretched and miserable in vs.17: *"You say, 'I am rich. I have everything I want. I don't need a thing!' And you don't realize that you are wretched and miserable and poor and blind and naked"*.

The message of our Lord to this church is the same message to us today: Beware of the danger of materialism, which gives us a false sense of security about self-sufficiency. In Matthew 6:24 the Lord says: *"No one can serve two masters. For you will hate one and love the other or be devoted to one and despise the other. You cannot serve both God and money"*. So, our Lord condemns this church for their love of money which has outgrown and displaced their love for Him.

Revelation 3:15-16

Jesus tells the congregation in Laodicea He knows all the things they do. When God looks at indifferent people in His church, people who do not care about other people and think they are self-sufficient with no need for Him, He gets sick to a point He will spit them out His mouth.

Revelation 3:17

The apostle John tells us the congregation of the church in Laodicea was rich, and they needed nothing. They had everything they wanted, but God did not approve of them, as we are told in Proverbs 18:11: *"The rich think of their wealth as an impregnable defense; they imagine it is a high wall of safety"*.

We should not lose perspective that each of the seven churches in Asia Minor represents a certain period in history from the first century church that Paul established in Ephesus to the last church that will be on earth before the rapture of the body of Christ. The church of Philadelphia represents the good church of the last days and the church of Laodicea represents the indifferent church of the last days.

Think about it as drinking a glass of warm salt water which we use to gargle with to sooth our sore throats. It has a horrible taste, but it works. If you ever drank warm mineral bottled water in a restaurant, you would know it does not taste good even when chilled, even though it has great digestive properties. I usually add a slice of lime to mine to give it some flavor when it is chilled.

The Lord is telling us here a lukewarm Christian is a comfortable, complacent Christian who is satisfied with the status quo. He does not want to change; he does not want to serve; he does not want to be involved in any church activities; he does not want to participate in any committee work; he does not want to volunteer to help with any ministry; he comes to church for one hour on Sunday every week, and the rest of the week he is involved in other worldly activities.

Do you know someone in your church that fits into this category? As believers in Jesus Christ, we have every reason to be on fire for the Lord. Romans 12:11 tells us: *"Never be lazy in your work but serve the Lord enthusiastically. Be glad for all God is planning for you. Be patient in trouble, and always be prayerful"*.

Revelation 3:18

Our Lord Jesus Christ gives His counsel to the church in Laodicea to help them see the truth. He gives them a three-part advice:

1. He advises them to buy gold from Him, gold that has been purified by fire. This is about eternal spiritual treasures that only He can provide. Jesus said to them I will let you buy some real gold, the spiritual gold that will enrich your life, the type of gold the churches in Smyrna and Philadelphia knew about.

2. He told them to purchase white garments from Him, which are symbolic of His righteousness. The Laodicean Christians thought and believed they were clothed in fine wool and garments, but from our Lord's perspective, they were naked.

To be naked in the Bible means to be defeated or

humiliated. This is what happened to Adam and Eve after they sinned in the Garden of Eden. What they needed was God's white garments of righteousness and grace. Revelation 19:8 tells us pure white linen represents the good deed of God's holy people, the saints.

3. Laodicea prided itself on its precious eye ointment that healed many eye problems (http://en.wikipedia.org, the free encyclopedia); Christ told them I have spiritual eye drops that will truly open your eyes so now you can get medicine from Me to heal your eyes so you could see the truth.

Christ is showing the Laodicean church that true value was not in material possessions but in a personal relationship with Him. Their possessions and achievements are worthless compared with the everlasting future in Christ's Kingdom.

Revelation 3:19

Just like the father disciplines his children when they stray and do something they are not supposed to do, our Lord disciplines the children that he loves and encourages them to be aware of that, be diligent and turn from their indifference so they will not make that same mistake again.

Revelation 3:20

Jesus offers a unique invitation to all of us. Here He is standing at the door of the last days church knocking on the door waiting on the congregation to let Him back in. It is important to note here that He does not force Himself on the church, but He is there waiting on them to open the door. The Lord is saying here would you find some room for me in your church? If the Laodicean church wanted to have Christ in their church, they must invite him back in. Jesus is standing outside the door knocking, and He will only come in if he is asked.

God is not asking you to clean up your life and get yourself ready so you can invite Him in. He wants to come in right now just as you are. When we try to clean ourselves up, we have a tendency to work from the outside in. When Jesus Christ comes to live within our hearts, He cleanses us from the inside out.

If you have not opened your heart to Jesus Christ, this is the day to do it. Just say this simple prayer: "Dear Jesus, I realize I am a sinner, and I am lost without you. I confess all my sins to you, and I ask for your forgiveness of my sins. I ask you to come into my heart and I make you my Lord and Savior. If you prayed this simple prayer with a sincere heart, you are now a born-again believer, the Holy Spirit indwells in you, and you are guaranteed eternal life in heaven.

Revelation 3:21

Our lord gives us an amazing promise in this verse. He promises to invite every one of us who is victorious and an overcomer to sit with Him on His throne in the same way He overcame sin and death and sat with God the Father on His throne. Let us summarize what we have learned so far about each church in Asia Minor:

Church	Revelation	Positive Things	Negative Things	Action & Discipline
Ephesus	2:1-7	Hard work perseverance	Forsaken first love	Remember & repent
Smyrna	2:8-11	Suffered persecution & poverty	None	Do not fear; be faithful
Pergamum	2:12-17	True to faith	Compromise	Repent
Thyatira	2:18-19	Love, faith & service	Immorality	Repent
Sardis	3:1-6	Effective	Superficial	Wake up & repent
Philadelphia	3:7-13	Faithful	None	Hold On
Laodicea	3:14-22	None	Lukewarm	Be earnest & repent

Revelation 3:22

As noted in the table, out of the seven churches, only the church in Smyrna and the church in Philadelphia hear from our Lord in a positive encouraging way without condemnation. The Lord commends them and encourages them, as both churches were faithful to Christ and faithful to His word, one for its diligent work despite persecution and poverty and the other for its missionary work.

The message to us from all these letters is this: Jesus Christ is standing in the midst of his churches, knowing everything that goes on within His churches, good or bad. He then gives them an opportunity to either repent, go back to do the good things they started doing at first, or He encourages them to continue to do the good things they are doing, and in the end, He promises them great rewards if they do what they are told.

As with the previous letters, the Lord closes with a message of urgency: *"Anyone who is willing to hear should listen to the Spirit and understand what the Spirit is saying to the churches"*. In other words, pay attention and listen up!

Chapter Four
The Raptured Church - Worship in Heaven

In the first three chapters of Revelation our attention was focused on the seven churches here on the earth. When chapter three ends, and we turn to chapter four, immediately we recognize that something drastic has happened: Our attention is now focused on the throne of God in Heaven. We must take note of the changes that have taken place.

First, there is no longer any mention of the church beginning with Chapter four. Why is that? The answer is the church age has ended, and the church, which is the body of Christ, was raptured and now it is in heaven with our Lord Jesus Christ. The Holy Spirit has left this earth and He is present as a seven-fold spirit in front of the throne of God in heaven (Revelation 4:5).

The rapture of the church is described by the Apostle Paul in 1 Thessalonians 4:15-17:

"I can tell you this directly from the Lord: We who are still living when the Lord returns will not rise to meet him ahead of those who are in their graves. For the Lord himself will come down from heaven with a commanding shout, with the call of the archangel, and with the trumpet call of God. First, all the Christians who have died will rise from their graves. Then, together with them, we who are still alive and remain on the earth will be caught up in the clouds to meet the Lord in the air and remain with him forever".

When we studied Revelation 1:4 we learned of the seven spirits of God which are given to us in Isaiah 11:2 (NLT) *"And the Spirit of the LORD will rest on him -- the Spirit of wisdom and understanding, the Spirit of counsel and might, the Spirit of knowledge and the fear of the LORD"*. I pointed out to you the seven spirits of God are in

107

reference to the Holy Spirit in His perfect work symbolized by the number seven, a symbol of our Lord's perfection. If you recall from the first chapter of Revelation, there are three sections outlined to the Apostle John:

-The things he has seen, which is the vision of the glorified Christ.
-The things which are happening now, that is the church age in which we live in represented by the seven churches in Asia Minor, which we have just finished studying.
-The things yet to come after the church age.

We have completed the first two sections. From here on out, we will focus on the last section which is larger than the first two put together.

In Revelation 1:19 the apostle John is instructed by our Lord to write the things which are yet to come. Here in Revelation 4:1 John takes his instructions and starts writing about the future. He is going to describe the things that will happen after the church age has come and gone. The church age ended with the church of Laodicea in the previous chapter.

As you read the Book of Revelation, please note there is not one single mention of the church anywhere between Revelation 4 and Revelation 19. Why is that? Because the church is no longer on this earth; it is in heaven with the Triune God, God the Father, God the Son and God the Holy Spirit, and while the church is in heaven, the seven-year tribulation period has already begun on this earth.

Something else has happened that signals a drastic change. The Holy Spirit has been transferred from earth to heaven. In Revelation 2 and 3, the Holy Spirit is said to be amid his churches (Sevenfold Spirit) on earth. In Revelation 4:5 we are told the sevenfold Holy Spirit is in heaven. He is not on the earth anymore. He was taken to heaven with the body of Christ. He is the part of the Godhead who indwells the believers at the moment of their salvation, and now the believers are in heaven.

Revelation 4:1

In the book of Revelation the door to heaven opens twice. The first time is in Revelation 4:1 and the second time in Revelation 19:11 when Jesus Christ gets ready to lead his heavenly armies at the battle of Armageddon. The door in heaven will open again to receive us when we are raptured, and we will be there with the Lord for seven years going through the Judgment Seat of Christ and participating in the marriage supper of the Lamb while the seven-year tribulation takes place here on earth.

At the end of the seven-year tribulation in Revelation 19, heaven opens again, and we come back to earth with our Lord and his angels to witness His awesome power and miracles at the battle of Armageddon. Afterwards the earth will be purified by fire and transformed, and we will reign and rule with Jesus Christ on this earth for a thousand years.

When the door of heaven opens, the first thing the Apostle John tells us he heard the voice of God like a trumpet sound, and the voice said to him "come up here" to show him what must happen after the church age.

Revelation 4:2

The apostle John was taken from his earthly body to heaven in the spirit to see what our Lord wanted to show him. This is the same expression John used in Revelation 1 when he said I was caught up in the spirit. "When in the spirit" literally means he was transformed in shape and structure to another dimension. He is no longer in his earthly body, now he is in the spirit.

In 1 Corinthians 15:51-52 Paul said at the rapture we will all be changed in the twinkling of an eye: *"But let me tell you a wonderful secret God has revealed to us. Not all of us will die, but we will all be transformed. It will happen in a moment, in the blinking of an eye, when the last trumpet is blown. For when the trumpet sounds, the Christians who have died will be raised with transformed bodies"*. So, John in Revelation 4:2 gives us a preview of how the Rapture of the church will take place.

We should note here the Apostle John had a special relationship with our Lord Jesus Christ. The Bible tells us in John 13:1 Jesus loved his disciples unto the end, but he loved John in a special way just like Jacob loved his son Joseph in a special way. The Bible refers to John as the disciple whom Jesus loved in John 13:23 and 19:26. In fact, the name John means the beloved one.

Now let us look at a passage in John 21:20-24 that students of the Bible disagree on its meaning regarding what Jesus said about the apostle John: *"Peter turned around and saw the disciple Jesus loved following them -- the one who had leaned over to Jesus during supper and asked, "Lord, who among us will betray you?"*

Peter asked Jesus, "What about him, Lord?" Jesus replied, "If I want him to remain alive until I return, what is that to you? You follow me." So, the rumor spread among the community of believers that that disciple would not die. But that isn't what Jesus said at all. He only said, "If I want him to remain alive until I return, what is that to you?" This is that disciple who saw these events and recorded them here. And we all know that his account of these things is accurate.

Some people interpret this passage in the scripture that John the apostle is told that he is going to remain alive until the second coming of Christ. This could only be a true statement in a sense that John is alive in Revelation 1 when God caught him up in the Spirit and sent him through future time and showed him what must happen during the seven-year tribulation and at the second coming of Christ, because we know John did die, but through his heavenly vision, he saw the Lord's second coming before he died.

What I believe Jesus told Peter, what is it to you if I want John to remain alive until I return? I want to keep him alive until I reveal to him the events that must happen before my second coming. So, He kept him alive exiled on the Isle of Patmos until he was given a preview of the second coming of Christ, and he wrote Revelation to tell us about it.

Revelation 4:3

The apostle John sees our Lord God the Father sitting on His glorious throne in heaven, which is indescribable in human terms for its magnificent colors, beauty, and majesty. In fact, John does not readily identify our Lord as God the Father sitting on His throne; instead, he says "I saw a throne in heaven and someone sitting on it as brilliant as jasper and carnelian gemstones (sardine or sardius, KJV)". Why doesn't John tell us right away he saw God the Father sitting on His throne? The answer is because the sight in front of him was too wonderful and too overwhelming to describe beyond his imagination and understanding.

The carnelian and jasper stones that John saw on God's Throne in heaven were also chosen by God as two of the precious stones in the breastplate of Moses' brother Aaron the high Jewish priest, as well as in the foundation of the Heavenly City, the New Jerusalem.

Exodus 28:15-21: *"Then, with the most careful workmanship, make a chest piece that will be used to determine God's will. Use the same materials as you did for the ephod: fine linen cloth embroidered with gold thread and blue, purple, and scarlet yarn. This chest piece will be made of two folds of cloth, forming a pouch nine inches square. Four rows of gemstones will be attached to it.*

The first row will contain a red carnelian, a chrysolite, and an emerald. The second row will contain a turquoise, a sapphire, and a

111

white moonstone. The third row will contain a jacinth, an agate, and an amethyst. The fourth row will contain a beryl, an onyx, and a jasper. All these stones will be set in gold".

Revelation 21:10-20: *"The wall of the city was built on foundation stones inlaid with twelve gems: the first was jasper, the second sapphire, the third agate, the fourth emerald, the fifth onyx, the sixth carnelian, the seventh chrysolite, the eighth beryl, the ninth topaz, the tenth chrysoprase, the eleventh jacinth, the twelfth amethyst".*
To summarize, we are going to be in heaven with our Lord Jesus Christ while the seven-year tribulation takes place here on earth. God opened the door for us through his Apostle John so we can get a glimpse of His throne in heaven to see what awaits us believers in Christ when we leave this earth. What a blessing that is!

Remember John had that vision while he was exiled on the Isle of Patmos, and he is trying to convey to us as much as he remembers in symbols without a lot of details as he was overwhelmed with what he saw. To him, what he saw was beyond description. The description of God is possible to John only by comparison to precious stones that are associated with the Heavenly City, the New Jerusalem. Revelation 21:11 says it this way: *"It shone with the glory of God and sparkled like a precious stone—like jasper as clear as crystal".*

Let us now look at what surrounds the throne of God in heaven. Notice what it says in the last part of vs. 3. *"And the glow of an emerald circled his throne like a rainbow."* This is not the rainbow we are used to seeing from an earthly view with multiple colors in a half circle. This is a full circle emerald, green rainbow surrounding the throne of God.

What did the Lord say when he sent the rainbow in the Old Testament after the flood? He said in Genesis 9:11-15 *"I solemnly promise never to send another flood to kill all living creatures and destroy the earth." And God said, "I am giving you a sign as evidence of my eternal covenant with you and all living creatures. I have placed*

112

my rainbow in the clouds. It is the sign of my permanent promise to you and to all the earth. When I send clouds over the earth, the rainbow will be seen in the clouds, and I will remember my covenant with you and with everything that lives. Never again will there be a flood that will destroy all life".

So why is the rainbow circling the great Judge of the universe in this verse? Because it is a reminder to us that our Lord is getting ready to judge this world.

Revelation 4:4

The apostle John now sees twenty-four thrones and twenty-four elders sitting on them surrounding the throne of God. Who are these twenty-four elders?

There has been much disagreement among Bible prophecy teachers on who these twenty- four elders are. Some say twelve of them are the disciples of Jesus including Matthias who replaced Judas Iscariot. The other twelve are Old Testament prophets including Daniel, Isaiah, Jeremiah, and Ezekiel. Others have said twelve of them are the sons of Jacob who formed the twelve tribes of Israel. Let us examine what the scripture says.

In <u>Matthew 19:27-28</u> Peter asked Jesus: *"We've given up everything to follow you. What will we get out of it?* "*Jesus said to them, "I tell you the truth, at the renewal of all things, when the Son of Man sits on his glorious throne, you who have followed me will also sit on twelve thrones, judging the twelve tribes of Israel*". When I first read this passage of the scripture, I thought surely the twelve disciples are half of the twenty-four elders, and the other twelve are the sons of Jacob who formed the twelve tribes of Israel.

But there is a key passage in this scripture, "you who have followed me" tells us who they are. I believe those who followed Jesus

113

include the disciples, the apostles and all the believers who put their trust and faith in Jesus Christ.

So, the twenty-four elders seated around the throne of God represent the bride of Christ, the church in heaven, who earned their Victor's Crown at the Judgment Seat of Christ which I discussed in Revelation 1.

Now let us look at the clothes the twenty-four elders are wearing. The second part of vs. 4 says "*they were all clothed in white and had gold crowns on their heads*". Revelation 19:7-8 tells us the bride of Christ, the church, is permitted to wear the finest white linen at the marriage supper of the Lamb.

So, the twenty-four elders in heaven in this verse are rewarded with gold crowns symbolizing their righteousness. Remember the Apostle John is looking into the future and not the present. He is being catapulted into a fourth dimension by our Lord to get a glimpse of future events yet to come. Do not lose perspective of that throughout this chapter and in the chapters to follow.

Revelation 4:5

Now notice what happens next: "*From the throne came flashes of lightning and the rumble of thunder. And in front of the throne were seven lampstands with burning flames.*" This is an awesome picture of the throne of God, but what does it mean?

The answer is in Hebrews 4:16: "*So let us come boldly to the throne of our gracious God. There we will receive his mercy, and we will find grace to help us when we need it*" The writer of the book of Hebrews tells us we no longer have to come to the throne of thunder and lightning just like the Israelites used to do when they were wandering in the desert for forty years. We see a great illustration of it when the Ten Commandments were given to Moses on Mount Sinai in Exodus 20:18-20.

114

We came to the end of the Law of Moses with the first coming of Jesus Christ Who fulfilled the Law and instituted the age of grace through the Apostle Paul. We no longer must submit to thunder and lightning and the blast of the ram's horn. We now have access to the throne of grace through Jesus Christ.

But here in John's vision, suddenly, the day of grace is over. The church is raptured and is in heaven; the Holy Spirit has departed from the earth to be in heaven. Our Lord God is about to judge the people on earth left behind after the rapture of the church. And now we are about to see God's judgment the way it was in the Old Testament when lightning flashed, and thunder rolled.

You will find that mentioned over and over in the following passages:

-Revelation 8:5, *"Then the angel filled the incense burner with fire from the altar and threw it down upon the earth; and thunder crashed, lightning flashed, and there was a terrible earthquake"*.
-Revelation 10:3, *"And he gave a great shout, like the roar of a lion. And when he shouted, the seven thunders answered"*.
-Revelation 11:19, *"Then, in heaven, the Temple of God was opened, and the Ark of his covenant could be seen inside the Temple. Lightning flashed, thunder crashed and roared; there was a great hailstorm, and the world was shaken by a mighty earthquake"*.
-Revelation 16:18, *"Then the thunder crashed and rolled, and lightning flashed. And there was an earthquake greater than ever before in human history"*.

What are the voices of thunder and lightning that emanate from the Throne of God in heaven? What the Apostle John saw through the open door was the Throne of the Triune God circled by a rainbow, and out of the Throne were these awesome sounds and sights. They were reminders to John that God was about to judge the nations of the world that rejected His Son Jesus Christ as their Lord and Savior. Those who have accepted His Son are in heaven with Him enjoying their rewards as the Lord promised them.

In the second part of vs. 5 spread out before the Throne of God are seven lampstands with burning flames representing the seven-fold Spirit of God. The prophet Isaiah describes the Holy Spirit in seven different ways in Isaiah 11:2 (NLT):

1. The Spirit of the Lord
2. The spirit of wisdom
3. The spirit of understanding
4. The spirit of counsel
5. The spirit of might
6. The spirit of knowledge
7. The spirit of fear (reverence)

The seven-fold Spirit does not imply there are seven different Holy Spirits, it means there is one Holy Spirit with a seven-fold manifested ministry, just as there is one Holy Spirit with a nine-fold manifested fruit described by the Apostle Paul in Galatians 5:22-23. So, we know now the Holy Spirit has left the earth while the tribulation is taking place on earth, and He is in heaven in front of the throne of God fulfilling Isaiah's prophecy.

Revelation 4:6

The sea of glass in front of the Throne of God is a reference to the streets of gold of the heavenly city, the New Jerusalem. Revelation 21:18: *"The wall was made of jasper, and the city was pure gold, as clear as glass"*. This was also foretold in the Old Testament in Exodus 24:9-10: *"Then Moses, Aaron, Nadab, Abihu, and seventy of the leaders of Israel went up the mountain. There they saw the God of Israel. Under his feet there seemed to be a pavement of brilliant sapphire, as clear as the heavens"*. And Ezekiel 1:22: *"There was a surface spread out above them like the sky. It sparkled like crystal"*.

116

Revelation 4:6-7

The apostle John then sees four living creatures standing in the midst of the throne of God, each covered with eyes, front and back. The first had the form of a lion, the second looked like an ox, the third had a human face, and the fourth had the form of an eagle. Who are these four living creatures?

If you study the Bible, you will find answers to all your questions in life. Let us go back to Ezekiel 1 in the Old Testament. Ezekiel tells us who these four living creatures are. He had a similar vision of heaven to the one John had about these four creatures between 593 and 565 B.C. during the Babylonian captivity of the Jews.

Ezekiel 1:5-9: *"From the center of the cloud came four living beings that looked human, except that each had four faces and four wings. Their legs were straight, and their feet had hooves like those of a calf and shone like burnished bronze. Under each of their four wings I could see human hands. So, each of the four beings had four faces and four wings. The wings of each living being touched the wings of the beings beside it. Each one moved straight forward in any direction without turning around"*.

The description of the four living creatures is somewhat different from the one John sees in Revelation 4, but we are looking at the same picture from two different periods of time by a prophet and an apostle, but they both saw the same thing and described it in slightly different ways, as they both were overwhelmed by what they saw.

In Ezekiel 1:10-14, Ezekiel tells us these four living creatures are cherubim angels: *"Each of the four cherubim had four faces -- the first was the face of an ox, the second was a human face, the third was the face of a lion, and the fourth was the face of an eagle.* These are the same four living creatures that John sees in Revelation 4 standing in the midst of God's Throne. My Bible commentary tells me the four faces represent God's attributes and perfect nature:

117

-The lion represents sovereignty and strength, as Jesus is referred to as the lion of the tribe of Judah in Genesis 49:9 and Revelation 5:5.
-The human face represents God's creation of man in His own image and human intelligence.
-The ox represents God's creation of animals with diligent service and endurance.
-The eagle represents God's creation of majestic birds and His majesty.

These cherubims are standing in the midst of the throne of God as angelic protection for God Himself just as God sent his angels to guard the entrance to the Garden of Eden when Adam and Eve were expelled from there. To summarize, the apostle John sees the four angelic beings standing in the midst of the throne of God, taking on four different faces: Face of a lion, face of an ox, human face, and a face of an eagle.

Revelation 4:8

The apostle John goes on to describe these cherubim angels in detail: "Each of these living beings had six wings, and their wings were covered all over with eyes, inside and out. Day after day and night after night they keep on saying, *"Holy, holy, holy is the Lord God, the Almighty, the one who always was, who is, and who is still to come"*.

The prophet Isaiah had a similar vision to Ezekiel's and John's in Isaiah 6:1-4: *"It was in the year King Uzziah died that I saw the Lord. He was sitting on a lofty throne, and the train of his robe filled the Temple. Attending him were mighty seraphim, each having six wings. With two wings they covered their faces, with two they covered their feet, and with two they flew. They were calling out to each other, "Holy, holy, holy is the Lord of Heaven's Armies! The whole earth is filled with his glory!" Their voices shook the Temple to its foundations, and the entire building was filled with smoke"*.

As we draw closer to our Lord Jesus Christ, His Holy Spirit reveals things to us in the scripture that we did not know before. Here is a great example of that. We are privileged to see here how the Bible comes together in the Old and New Testaments, from the writings of the prophets to the writings of the apostles. What is more amazing is the similar praise of our Lord that we see in <u>Isaiah 6:4</u>: "*Holy, holy, holy is the Lord God, the Almighty, the one who always was, who is, and who is still to come*". And <u>Revelation 4:8</u>: "*Holy, holy, holy is the Lord of Heaven's Armies! The whole earth is filled with his glory!*"

<u>Revelation 4:9-11</u>

Next the apostle John sees the twenty-four elders fall on their knees and begin worshipping our Lord Who is sitting on His Throne in a manner showing they are not worthy of these crowns that they earned, because of what they did for Him while they were here on earth.

In a similar manner, we who have earned our crowns will fall on our knees before our Lord and we begin to worship Him. We will thank the Lord who redeemed us by removing the crowns off our head and putting them at the feet of Jesus. We will say Lord I do not deserve this crown. I give it to you as an act of my worship to you for all you have done for me on the cross.

I do not know where you are with your personal walk with Jesus Christ, but I pray that someday you will wear one of these crowns and will sit around His throne and worship Him. Time is getting short before our Lord decides to come for His church, but you still have time to earn one of these crowns by putting your trust and faith in Him.

Chapter Five
The Lamb Opens the Scroll

This chapter focuses on two scenes in heaven: The first scene is about our Lord Jesus Christ in His glory no longer depicted as the Lamb that was slain, but as the Lion of the tribe of Judah, the Heir to David's throne. The second scene is the unfolding of a sealed scroll, which is in the right hand of the One Who Sits upon the Throne. We know that the One sitting upon the Throne is our God the Father.

The scroll here is described as one which has writing on the inside and on the outside, and it is sealed with seven seals, which is God's favorite number indicating completion. The fact that the scroll was written upon the front and on the back is an indication that the scroll is full and that nothing more could be added to it. In other words, God's plan to bring judgment on the earth is already written and it is about to be executed.

Revelation 5:1

The fifth chapter of Revelation begins with the word "And" which is a continuation of the glimpse into heaven by the Apostle John, which began in the fourth chapter. If you recall, Daniel was also given a glimpse of the same vision in Daniel 12:5-13, but he was told by our Lord to keep this vision secret and sealed until the time of the end, because the time was not right to reveal God's plan to the Israelites.

The prophets Ezekiel and Isaiah, and the apostles John and Paul, I believe, saw that same vision at different times, and each one of them described it from a slightly different perspective, except for Paul who was caught up to the third heaven, which he describes as Paradise, and hearing inexpressible words which he was not permitted to speak or boast about it (Acts 9:1-19 and 2 Corinthians 12:1-10).

121

But God gave the Apostle John the responsibility to write about it in John 21:20-23, and John was the disciple that Jesus loved as we learned in the previous chapter: *"Peter turned around and saw behind them the disciple Jesus loved - the one who had leaned over to Jesus during supper and asked, "Lord, who will betray you?"*

Peter asked Jesus, "What about him, Lord?" Jesus replied, "If I want him to remain alive until I return, what is that to you? As for you, follow me." So, the rumor spread among the community of believers that this disciple would not die. But that is not what Jesus said at all. He only said, "If I want him to remain alive until I return, what is that to you?"

The scroll our Lord is holding in his hands is all about Him re-gaining control of this earth which belongs to Him. Revelation 11:15 says this: *Then the seventh angel blew his trumpet, and there were loud voices shouting in heaven: "The whole world has now become the Kingdom of our Lord and of his Christ, and he will reign forever and ever"*.

Does God have control of the world today? The answer is yes, but his enemy and our enemy called Satan roams on this earth like a roaring lion seeking whom he may devour (1 Peter 5:8).

The Bible says Satan is the prince of the power of the air (Ephesians 2:1-3), and 2 Corinthians 4:4 tells us he is the god of this evil world. So, Satan is roaming the earth right now, but our Lord restrains him from going rampant through the presence of the Holy Spirit in the believers.

But once we are raptured to be with our Lord, the Holy Spirit will be lifted from the earth to be on the Throne of God the Father in heaven, and Satan will be no longer be restrained. He will be in total control of this world during the seven-year tribulation. But in the end, God is going to rule the world, and it will be His forever and ever.

Revelation 5:2-3

The apostle John sees a strong angel shouting with a loud voice: "Who is worthy to break the seals on this scroll and open it?" But no one in heaven or on earth or under the earth was able to open the scroll and read it. It is apparent from this passage of scripture that the strong angel is preparing us for the special moment God the Father is about to give the responsibility of opening the sealed scroll to His Son Jesus Christ, the Lion of the Tribe of Judah.

Revelation 5:4-5

In this passage, the apostle John, while focusing on the two scenes in heaven, becomes emotional and begins to weep because he could not find anyone worthy to open the scroll and read it. But suddenly, one of the twenty-four elders says to him, "*Stop weeping! Look, the Lion of the tribe of Judah, the heir to David's throne, has won the victory. He is worthy to open the scroll and its seven seals*".

Revelation 5:6

Here we are told Jesus Christ, God the Son, is no longer sitting at the right hand of God the Father, but He is standing between the throne of God and the four living beings just like He did when he was ready to receive the apostle Stephen when he was stoned to death in Acts 7:56, but now He is described in terms we have not heard before: He is depicted as a lamb that was slain, but He has seven horns and seven eyes. What do the seven horns and seven eyes represent?

First, the number seven is God's favorite number, and it represents completion. The Bible tells us here the seven horns and seven eyes are the seven-fold spirit of God that is sent out into every part of the earth. They also symbolize the complete control and power of the Lord, because in the Old Testament the horns were symbols of power (1 Kings 22:11and Zechariah 1:18).

In Zechariah 4:10 we are told the seven eyes represent the eyes of the Lord that search all around the world: "*Do not despise these small beginnings, for the Lord rejoices to see the work begin, to see the plumb line in Zerubbabel's hand*". "*The seven lamps represent the eyes of the Lord that search all around the world*".

Revelation 5:7

In these verses we see a picture of worship in heaven. The One who is worthy to open the scroll and unfold its truth is our Lord Jesus Christ. There are three names given to Him in this scripture. Let us look at them one at a time.

1. One of the twenty-four elders said in vs. 5 "*He is the Lion of the tribe of Judah*". This title takes us back in our Bibles to Genesis 49. In this chapter of the life of Joseph, Jacob blessed his twelve sons. The blessings were specific to each one of the twelve sons before he died.

    The blessing for Judah was in Genesis 49:8-9: "*Judah, your brothers will praise you. You will defeat your enemies. All your relatives will bow before you. Judah is a young lion that has finished eating its prey. Like a lion he crouches and lies down; like a lioness -- who will dare to rouse him?*"

    What Jacob prophesied to Judah, which he may not even have understood himself at that time, was out of the tribe of Judah will come the Messiah who is our Lord Jesus Christ. This is confirmed in Hebrews 7:14 and Isaiah 11:1.

2. Notice the second name. *He is the root of David or the heir to David's throne.* As far as Jesus' humanity was concerned, Jesus had his roots in King David. He came from the tribe of Judah through the descendants of David (Matthew chapter 1). King David was from the tribe of Judah, and one of the common titles for Jesus when He was on this earth is the Son of

David. The other two are the Son of God and the Son of Man.

In <u>Matthew 22:41-46</u>, when the religious leaders questioned Jesus who He is, Jesus asked them a question: *"What do you think about the Messiah? Whose son is he?"* They replied, "He is the son of David." Jesus responded, *"Then why does David, speaking under the inspiration of the Holy Spirit, call him Lord? For David said, 'The LORD said to my Lord, Sit in honor at my right hand until I humble your enemies beneath your feet.' Since David called him Lord, how can he be his son at the same time?* "No one could answer him. And after that, no one dared to ask him any more questions.

The Pharisees could not figure out how David could both be related to Jesus and to the one who came before Jesus. Do you remember what Jesus said in <u>John 8:56-58</u>? *"Your father Abraham rejoiced to see My day, and he saw it and was glad". So, the Jews said to Him, "You are not yet fifty years old, and have You seen Abraham?" Jesus said to them, "Truly, truly, I say to you, before Abraham was born, I am."*

In this passage Jesus was quoting from <u>Exodus 3:13-15:</u> *"Then Moses said to God, "Behold, I am going to the sons of Israel, and I will say to them, 'The God of your fathers has sent me to you.' Now they may say to me, 'What is His name?' What shall I say to them?" God said to Moses, "I AM WHO I AM ".* So, Jesus was in His humanity from the descendants of David and in His deity existed before David. He is the root of David and the heir to David's throne.

3. The third name of the One Who is about to unfold the scroll is the Lamb who was slain. In <u>Genesis 22:7</u>, do you remember the story when Abraham's faith was being tested on Mount Moriah, when Abraham was about to sacrifice his son Isaac, and Isaac asked him *"We have the fire and the wood but where is the lamb"*? And in <u>John 1:29</u> John the Baptist saw Jesus coming

toward him and said, *"Behold the Lamb of God who takes away the sin of the world"*.

The Lamb that was slain is now standing in the midst of the throne of God. It is a picture of the resurrected Jesus Christ in heaven. He was slain on the cross and died for our sins, but now He is alive, and He is standing in the midst of the Throne of God the father!

In heaven, our Lord is seen as seated at the right hand of God the Father, which signifies his work of redemption is all done. But when you see the Lord pictured as a Lamb standing, be ready because judgment is about to take place. He is ready to move out of the glory of heaven down upon this earth where judgment is about to break out while He reclaims the earth that belongs to Him.

Notice the Lamb is not only standing after He was slain, but He is now strong and powerful as depicted by the seven horns and seven eyes, which is a picture of strength. When we read about horns in the Bible, it always has to do with strength. We can find illustrations in the following passages of scripture:

1 Kings 22:11: *"One of them, Zedekiah son of Kenaanah, made some iron horns and proclaimed, "This is what the LORD says: With these horns you will gore the Arameans to death!"*

Zechariah 1:18-21: *"Then I looked up and saw four animal horns. "What are these?" I asked the angel who was talking with me. He replied, "These horns represent the world powers that scattered Judah, Israel, and Jerusalem." Then the LORD showed me four blacksmiths. "What are these men coming to do?" I asked. The angel replied, "The blacksmiths have come to terrify the four horns that scattered and humbled Judah. They will throw them down and destroy them."*

In Zechariah 4:2-10 we are told the seven lampstands represent the eyes of the Lord that search all around the world. Here we are told the seven horns and seven eyes represent the Holy Spirit of God sent out into every part of the earth.

At the end of vs. 7, John sees our Lord and Savior Jesus Christ stepping forward and He took the scroll from the right hand of God the Father.

Revelation 5:8-10

We now come to the part of this chapter where we see true worship in heaven. The next thing John sees are the four living beings and the twenty-four elders falling before our Lord Jesus Christ, each one had a harp, and they held gold bowls filled with incense, which are the prayers of God's people (the saints).

This brings up the question: What is the prayer of the saints and what are the gold bowls filled with incense?

I believe it is the Lord's Prayer given to us in Matthew 6:9-13. Our Lord taught His disciples to pray like this: "Our Father in heaven, hallowed be Thy name, Thy Kingdom come, Thy will be done on earth as it is in heaven". This prayer is about the Millennium Kingdom of our Lord Jesus Christ when He will reign on this earth for a thousand years from His throne in Jerusalem.

This prayer will ultimately be fulfilled when the Lord takes control of this earth. He is going to answer the prayer that He taught His disciples. His Kingdom will come; His "will" will be done on earth as it is in heaven. Not until that time will this prayer be fully answered. The gold bowls filled with incense are symbolic of the prayers of the saints in heaven.

Next John sees the four living beings and the twenty-four elders in heaven. They begin to praise the Lord by singing a new song with these words: "*You are worthy to take the scroll and break its seals and open it. For you were slaughtered, and your blood has ransomed people for God from every tribe, language, people and nation. And you have caused them to become a Kingdom of priests for our God. And they will reign on the earth*".

This song of praise foretells about what God has in store for the believers who put their trust and faith in Him: They will reign with Him on this renovated earth during the Millennium Kingdom. This is confirmed by our Lord when he promised His disciples, they will judge the twelve tribes of Israel in Matthew 19:28: "*Jesus replied, "I assure you that when the world is made new and the Son of Man sits upon his glorious throne, you who have been my followers will also sit on twelve thrones, judging the twelve tribes of Israel*".

Now let's recap the picture the apostle John captured of heaven in chapters 4 and 5. God the Father sits on His Throne; behind His Throne is a rainbow; around the Throne are twenty four elders; on each side of the Throne are the four cherubim angels; in God's right hand is a seven-sealed scroll; the voice of the strong angel says "*who is worthy to open the scroll?*" one of the elders says, there is the One, the Lion of the tribe of Judah is worthy to open the scroll; As Jesus comes, all heaven breaks forth into praise and worship as He gets ready to unfold the scroll and send judgments on this earth.

Revelation 5:11-12

The apostle John looks again, and he sees new participants in praise and worship. Millions of angels!! I want to point out here in the Bible we are not told how many angels are in heaven, but based on this scripture, they are beyond our ability to count. The scripture tells us there are multitudes of angels standing around the throne. As the elders begin to sing, the angels join them in worship as our Lord Jesus Christ begins to unfold the scroll.

Revelation 5:13

Here we see fulfillment of the scripture in Philippians 2:9-11: *"Because of this, God raised him up to the heights of heaven and gave him a name that is above every other name, so that at the name of Jesus every knee will bow, in heaven and on earth and under the earth, and every tongue will confess that Jesus Christ is Lord, to the glory of God the Father".*

What this scripture is telling us, after everything is said and done, and our Lord Jesus Christ rules from Mount Zion in Jerusalem, every creature in heaven, on earth, under the earth and in the sea will bow down to Him and will confess He is King of kings and Lord of lords. This will be followed by an angelic chorus *"Blessing and honor and glory and power belong to the one sitting on the throne and to the Lamb forever and ever."* I do not know about you, but I cannot wait to join the angels in praising our Lord!

In closing, I want to point out something important about praise in heaven. Dr. David Jeremiah in his CD series Escape the Coming Night explains it this way: 'From the beginning of worship in heaven, there is going to be a growth in the praise of our Lord, just like we experience the spiritual growth of the believer while we are here on this earth:

Revelation 1:6	Two-fold praise	Glory and power
Revelation 4:11	Three-fold praise	Glory, honor, and power
Revelation 5:13	Four-fold praise	blessing, honor, glory, and power
Revelation 7:12	Seven-fold praise	blessing, thanksgiving, glory, wisdom, honor, power and might

Our journey in heaven will culminate in seven praises, which is God's favorite number indicating completion".

Revelation 5:14

In this last verse, the four living beings said, "Amen!" and they fell and worshiped our Lord Jesus Christ.

Chapter Six
The Lamb Breaks the First Six Seals

In this chapter, we see the openings of the seven seals mentioned in the previous chapter. As the seals are opened, the scroll reveals the judgments of God that will come upon this earth, which fulfills the prophecy in Daniel 12 and foretold by Jesus Christ in the Olivet Discourse in Matthew 24:15, when Jesus warned his disciples what would happen in the last days.

In Revelation 4 and 5, I discussed the scenes in heaven. Beginning with Revelation 6 and all the way through Revelation 19, I will discuss the things that will happen soon.

In the previous chapter, we saw our Lord depicted as the worthy Lamb Who was slain and as the Lion of the tribe of Judah approaching the throne of God. He took the scroll which has seven seals, and now He is about to open the seals one by one which will usher in seven years of tribulation upon this earth.

Revelation 6:1

As the first four seals are opened, we see the four cherubim angels in front of the throne of God carrying out His orders to inflict judgment on earth using the symbols of four horsemen of the apocalypse riding on four horses each having a different color: A white horse, a red horse, a black horse, and a pale green horse. The word "apocalypse" means a major event involving destruction on a catastrophic scale (www.google.com). I want to mention a couple of things to help us understand this passage.

The Bible is an amazing book. The more you read it the more you understand how the Old and the New Testaments complement each other, and the closer you draw to God, the closer He draws to you (James 4:8). He helps you understand the scripture through the power and wisdom of His Holy Spirit in a way you have never experienced before. The key to have this understanding is to read the Bible every day.

In Matthew 24:3 Jesus' disciples asked Him this question: "Will there be any sign ahead of time to signal your return and the end of the world?" Jesus replied in Matthew 24:4-8 *"Don't let anyone mislead you. For many will come in my name, saying, 'I am the Messiah.' They will lead many astray. And wars will break out near and far, but don't panic. Yes, these things must come, but the end won't follow immediately. The nations and kingdoms will proclaim war against each other, and there will be famines and earthquakes in many parts of the world. But all this will be only the beginning of the horrors to come"*.

Here is what Jesus said will happen in the last days:

1. False messiahs and false teachers will arise and will lead many astray
2. Wars will break out near and far
3. There will be famines, diseases, and earthquakes in many parts of the world
4. All this will be the beginning of the horrors to come

If you have been watching the evening news in the past ten years, all these events are converging at a rapid pace in our world today with increased frequencies, and the four horsemen of the apocalypse simply imply get ready for disaster to intensify after the rapture of the church.

Revelation 6:2

When the first seal is open, the four horsemen of the apocalypse are revealed on the scroll. The rider on the white horse is a picture of a conquering king holding a bow without arrows, which indicates he is coming on the scene peacefully. He is symbol of the antichrist. He will come on the scene at the beginning of the seven-year tribulation, and he will make a peace covenant with Israel, which gives the Jewish people a false sense of security.

The rider on the white horse is depicted as counterfeit of our Lord Jesus Christ roaming across the earth. 1 Peter 5:8 tells us: *"Be careful! Watch out for attacks from the Devil, your great enemy. He prowls around like a roaring lion, looking for some victim to devour"*. The antichrist is Satan's agent who will carry out his commands during the seven-year tribulation.

Many people at first assume the rider on the white horse must be our Lord Jesus Christ. Over in Revelation 19:11, we read: *"Then I saw heaven opened, and a white horse was standing there. And the one sitting on the horse was named Faithful and True. For He judges fairly and then goes to war"*. In this verse, the rider on the white horse is our Lord Jesus Christ depicted at His second coming.

If Jesus is depicted on a white horse in Revelation 19:11 and we see a rider on a white horse in this verse with no identity, we may be tempted to conclude the riders must be one in the same, but that is not true.

In Revelation 19:11, we are told from the mouth of Jesus Christ came a sharp sword, and He wore many crowns, symbolic of King of kings. What does the sharp sword represent based on what we have learned so far? It represents the Word of God. In this verse, the weapon is not a sword; it is a bow, but something is missing from it: Arrows. There are no arrows with this bow. He also wore one crown, symbolic of a crown an earthly king would wear when he goes to battle.

Here the appearance of a white horse signifies the beginning of the time of judgment upon the earth. In Revelation 19, the appearance of a white horse signifies the end of the time of judgment. Our Lord Jesus Christ ends the seven-year tribulation by His second coming.

So, if this is not Christ in this verse, who could it be? It is a false christ or the antichrist. He is riding into the world as a conqueror. The fact that his bow has no arrows indicates he will take control of the world peacefully at the beginning of the seven-year tribulation.

Daniel says in Daniel 9:27: "*He will make a treaty with the people (of Israel) for a period of one set of seven, but after half this time, he will put an end to the sacrifices and offerings. Then as a climax to all his terrible deeds, he will set up a sacrilegious object that causes desecration, until the end that has been decreed is poured out on this defiler.*"

Here is what is going to happen. When the antichrist comes on the scene at the beginning of the seven-year tribulation, he will be the answer to everything people have been longing for. He will make a peace covenant with Israel. Everyone will think the world's economic and military problems are solved now that peace is established in the Middle East, which no U.S. president or United Nations have been able to accomplish throughout history.

But after three-and-a half years, he will break the covenant with Israel, and the second half of the tribulation period begins. The antichrist will win many battles and will gain victory for a short time, but do not be confused by the similarity of the white horses in Revelation 6:2 and Revelation 19:11, because it has always been the purpose of Satan to counterfeit the work of Jesus Christ.

Let me remind here the antichrist could very well be alive and well in our world today. He is not going to appear at the beginning of the tribulation as a new-born baby. The Bible tells us in Revelation 11:7 his journey originates from the abyss, which means he is a demonic spirit that will indwell in a human body. He will be an adult in a position of leadership who lived on this earth several years before his appearance.

Revelation 6:3-4

Notice next as the second seal is opened, a red horse appears, and its rider is given a mighty sword and the authority to remove peace from earth. The red horse personifies war and resulting bloodshed. Our Lord Jesus Christ spoke about this in Matthew 24:6-8 when he said: *"And wars will break out near and far, but don't panic. Yes, these things must come, but the end won't follow immediately. The nations and kingdoms will proclaim war against each other, and there will be famines and earthquakes in many parts of the world. But all this will be only the beginning of the horrors to come"*.

Since the day Cain killed his brother Abel, the world has seen many wars. The Israelites endured many horrors and battles since their exodus from Egypt until Joshua led them to the Promised Land by conquering their pagan enemy tribes who occupied this land and fulfilled the promise our Lord gave to their ancestors, Abraham, Isaac, and Jacob.

The twentieth century is considered the most violent because of the many wars fought in that era. Twice in one generation, the world was plunged into major world wars. WWI involved twenty-seven nations and cost the lives of ten million men. It left twenty million men wounded, and it was to be the war that would end all wars.

But within a short span of twenty years, WWII erupted. The nations were all engaged in war again; a war that would be longer, costlier, and deadlier than the first war. History tells us WWII claimed thirty-two million people killed on the battle fields; fifteen to twenty million people were killed in bombing raids on civilian populations; twenty-five million people died in concentration camps and over thirty million people wounded.

War and tensions continue to escalate in our world today, especially in the Middle East and Far East, as evident by the Arab Spring, the rise and diffusion of ISIS, the revolts against current regimes in Syria, Libya and Egypt, and the continued threats by North Korea and Iran.

The rider on the red horse holding a mighty sword represents not only nations revolting against nations, but men fighting against men. It is a time of murder and assassination, bloodshed, and rebellion. The second three-and-a- half years of tribulation is a time when war breaks out all over the nations of the earth, and we are now seeing the foreshadowing of that in our world today.

As we see the escalation of these events according to the scripture, we certainly realize that the Day of the Lord is nearer than most people think, and Jesus Christ is coming for His church soon. We all hear every day from our government representatives and world leaders that the world needs to come together in alliances.

We see great examples of that in the European Union, NATO, the G8, G10 and G20 nations. Their common message is we need to be united, and we need someone to solve our economic crises and dependence on foreign oil. That is the context in which the antichrist will appear, and he will have all the answers to the world problems; the sad thing is millions of men and women will follow him as he delivers false promises, as they have become more and more dependent of the government to rescue them.

Revelation 6:5-6

When the third seal is opened, we see the black horse and its rider holding a pair of scales in his hand. The black horse in the Bible is often associated with famine because of war and diseases.

Famine, disease, and war go together. When war breaks out, shortages of food and commodities always drive-up prices and force the government to ration what is available. We saw that in the seventies when the so-called energy crises took place in 1974 and again in 1979 when price of gasoline doubled or tripled at the pump and long lines were common at the gas stations. We saw that right after 9/11. Our parents and grandparents went through similar experiences during WWI and WWII.

When our Lord speaks of a denarius in vs. 6, He is referring to the standard daily wage for a laborer in ancient Rome. The scripture is saying a measure of wheat costs a denarius. A measure of wheat is about two pints or one quart of wheat. This is the minimum amount necessary to sustain one person for one day.

What the scripture says, to get enough wheat to stay alive, you had to give up a whole day's wage. You could get a little more barley because it is a cheaper grain. But during the seven-year tribulation, when the antichrist rules, war and famine will spread throughout the globe, and many people will die of hunger, because there will not be enough food to go around. So, a person would have to work all day to get enough food to feed his/her family.

Now notice, the wealthy will continue to enjoy oil and wine. Oil and wine are the substances for wealthy people. Apparently at the beginning of the tribulation, only poor people will be affected by the famine. The wealthy people will not be as impacted by it. They will still have their oil and their wine. During the times of the Great Depression that the U.S. experienced between 1929-1938, the wealthy were able to survive famine. The lower and middle-class people were the ones who suffered the most.

The scripture tells us later in Revelation 13:16-17 the false prophet will take the hunger of the world and use it to manipulate the masses. He will require everyone - small and great, rich, and poor, free and slave - to be given a mark on the right hand or on the forehead. And no one could buy or sell anything without that mark.

Revelation 6:7-8

As the fourth seal is opened, the Apostle John now sees two

137

symbolic persons instead of one. The other three horses each have one rider. Now John sees a pale green horse with its rider and a companion walking behind him. He sees death riding the pale green horse and the grave following him.

The phrase death and Hades (or Grave) appears three times in Revelation. In Revelation 1:18 we are told Christ has the keys to death and Hades. In Revelation 20:13 we are told death and the grave gave up the dead in them. In Revelation 20:14 we are told someday death and Hades will be cast into the lake of fire. This lake of fire is the second death. The rider on the pale green horse and the companion Hades who walks behind him have a coming appointment with destiny. They may reign for a while during the seven-year tribulation, but one day the Bible says death and Hades will be cast into the Lake of Fire.

To summarize then, after the antichrist rises to power, comes war. After war comes famine and diseases. After famine and disease comes death, death of the body and death of the soul. Please note the rider on a pale green horse and his companion are armed with weapons of the sword, hunger, pestilence, and wild animals or beasts.

The Prophet Ezekiel gives us a glimpse about the fearsome punishments that will fall upon Jerusalem in the last days in Ezekiel 14:21: *"Now this is what the Sovereign Lord says: How terrible it will be when all four of these dreadful punishments fall upon Jerusalem— war, famine, wild animals, and disease—destroying all her people and animals"*.

Our Lord Jesus Christ warned his disciples in Matthew 24:4-8 about these terrible judgments. He said *"Don't let anyone mislead you. For many will come in my name, saying, 'I am the Messiah.' They will lead many astray. And wars will break out near and far, but don't panic. Yes, these things must come, but the end won't follow immediately. The nations and kingdoms will proclaim war against each other, and there will be famines and earthquakes in many parts of the world. But all this will be only the beginning of the horrors to come".*

When you read the scripture and learn what our Lord has in store for the globe, you will see one of the things that will happen in the early part of the tribulation is the world is going to be infected with pestilence that will take one fourth of the entire world population as we are told in vs.8. When you hear the word pestilence, you immediately think of epidemic and pandemic, a global spreading of disease. Here is a recap of the many pestilences that have already occurred in our world (http://en.wikipedia.org, the free encyclopedia):

- **1300s Black Death.** Disease spread by fleas that were carried by rats and other rodents throughout Europe because towns were overcrowded and unsanitary at the time, there was little to prevent the disease from spreading. It was responsible for the deaths of one quarter of the population of Europe. The disease is believed to have started in China earlier in the century and the Chinese are thought to have used infected bodies to contaminate their enemies. This helped the disease to spread as did ships that are thought to have carried the disease to Europe and the Mediterranean.
- **1918-1919   Spanish Flu.** The Spanish Flu Pandemic Influenza is hailed as being possibly the worst influenza pandemic to date. It killed more people in a single year than the Black Death caused in Europe over 4 years: 50 million people worldwide; 500,000 in the U.S. The source of Spanish Flu was not widely known, but its effects were swift and often fatal. Shipping and trade helped spread the disease which occurred during the last year of World War I (1918)
- **1957   Asian Flu.** Early in 1957 an Asian Influenza virus was discovered and because of technological advances, the world was able to quickly respond to this threat, and the impact was much less severe than it might otherwise have been
- **1968-1972   Hong Kong Flu.** Another Pandemic Flu to originate in Asia. The Hong Kong flu was responsible for a

significant number of deaths. However, the flu was often treatable and controllable with antibiotics

- **1980   AIDS. (Acquired Immune Deficiency Syndrome).** The world first became aware of AIDS in the early 1980s. Growing numbers of gay men in New York and California developed rare types of pneumonia and cancer, and a wasting disease was spreading in Uganda. Doctors reported AIDS symptoms under different names, including "gay-related immune deficiency" and "slim," but by 1985, they reported them all over the world. (www.aidshealth.org/learn-about-it)
- **2003   SARS. (Severe Acute Respiratory Syndrome).** Originated in China but Hong Kong which came under siege from the SARS virus. It spread to other countries through international travel. In all, SARS caused more than 800 deaths, but there have been no reported cases in recent times
- **2006   Avian Flu (H5N1).** Disease transmitted from birds, to poultry, to humans. Vaccine not available at that time and would be impossible to ward off. Several instances reported to the WHO. Symptoms include continuous runny nose, sore throat, lungs attacked, extreme pneumonia & cough and breathing difficulty
- **2009   H1N1 Virus (Swine Flu).** The first cases of human infection with H1N1 influenza virus were detected in April 2009 in San Diego and Imperial County, California and in Guadalupe County, Texas. The virus spread rapidly in the United States at this time and has been detected internationally as well. Symptoms of novel H1N1 flu in people are similar to those associated with seasonal flu: Fever, cough sore throat, runny or stuffy nose, body aches, headache, chills, fatigue, vomiting and diarrhea. Vaccines somewhat effective.
- **2014   Ebola Virus.** In 2014 over 1200 cases of deadly Ebola virus were reported in western African countries of Sierra Leone, Liberia, and Guinea with over 650 deaths. Symptoms after contracting the virus include fever, throat and muscle pains, headaches, nausea, vomiting and decreased functioning of the liver and kidneys.

- **2014 Enterovirus D68**. Cases of this virus that attacks the respiratory system were first reported in reported in California in 1962. In 2014, the number of people reported with this virus was much greater than that reported in previous years.
- **2014 Measles**. The U. S. experienced a record number of measles cases during 2014, with 644 cases from 27 states recorded by the CDC. This is the greatest number of cases since 2000.
- **2015 Measles**. The U.S. experienced 147 cases, in several states linked to an amusement park in California. The outbreak started from a traveler who became infected overseas with measles, then visited the amusement park. Analysis by CDC scientists showed that the measles virus type in this outbreak was identical to the virus type that caused the large measles outbreak in the Philippines in 2014.
- **2017 Measles**. A 75-case outbreak was reported in Minnesota in a Somali-American community with poor vaccination record.
- **2018 Measles**. The U.S. experienced 17 outbreaks in New York State, New York City, and New Jersey. Cases in those states occurred primarily among unvaccinated people in Orthodox Jewish communities. These outbreaks were associated with travelers who brought measles back from Israel, where a large outbreak was occurring. Eighty-two people brought measles to the U.S. from other countries in 2018. This is the greatest number of imported cases since measles was eliminated from the U.S. in 2000.
- **2019 Measles**. From January 1 to April 26, 2019, 704 individual cases of measles have been confirmed in 22 states. This is an increase of 78 cases from the previous week. This is the greatest number of cases reported in the U.S. since 1994 and since measles was declared eliminated in 2000.

Not only death, famine, and pestilence, but in the end times there will be the beasts. What does that mean? Whenever there is famine and plague, there is always disease followed by death and wild animals and birds feasting on the dead bodies. The rider on the fourth horse will reap a terrible harvest from this earth because he will have the sword, famine, pestilence, and death followed by the beasts. He will kill one fourth of the entire world population.

- **2020 Corona Virus**: Known as COVID-19, this disease has spread to every continent and cases continue to rise. As of October 2021, the number of reported cases worldwide is 246 million; the number of people recovered is 223 million; and the number of reported deaths is 4.9 million (www.worldometers.info).
- 2021-2022: The following variants of the Corona virus spread all over the world: Delta, Delta Plus, Gamma, Omicron, and Monkeypox.
- 2022: Poliovirus was detected in wastewater samples from Rockland County, Orange County, Sullivan County, New York City and Nassau County. New York Governor Kathy Hochul issued an Executive Order declaring a State Disaster Emergency, increasing the availability of resources to protect New Yorkers against this paralytic disease.
- A triple pandemic consisting of Covid-19, Flu and RSV spread across the U.S. putting many children and adults at risk of infection.

We will see later in Revelation 8, another one third of the world population will be killed when our Lord Jesus Christ breaks the seventh seal, and the angels blow their trumpets carrying on God's judgments on earth.

142

I want to take a couple minutes here to remind you of the Lord's promises to us. In <u>Revelation 3:10</u> He said: *"Because you have obeyed my command to persevere, I will protect you from the great time of testing that will come upon the whole world to test those who belong to this world"*.

In <u>Romans 8:1</u> the apostle Paul said: *Therefore, there is no condemnation for those who are in Jesus Christ"*. What does this scripture mean to us? It means the rapture of the church is much closer than what most people believe. My first response is praise to God for his promise, love, and protection for us. He is going to take us to be with Him before all of that happens, and we will be with Him forever. We will not go through the seven-year tribulation or experience the wrath of God.

I want to ask you this question: Where are you today with your personal relationship with Jesus Christ? Is your life influenced by what the world wants you to believe, or do you live your life for Him? Have you changed your priorities in life to serve the Lord in every way you can since you were saved, or have you continued to live your life as before?

When you hear about wars and rumors of wars, famines, diseases, earthquakes, hurricanes, tornadoes, and disasters, does it alarm you or create fear inside of you? You should not be afraid if you put your faith and trust in Jesus Christ. That is what the Word of God says is going to happen in the last days, the days in which we are living now. If you do not have a personal relationship with Jesus Christ, I encourage you to turn to Him so you will not be left behind and experience the wrath of God.

Revelation 6:9-11

As the Lamb breaks the fifth seal, the apostle John reveals to us the souls of all who had been martyred for their testimony about the Word of God and for being faithful in their witness. They called loudly to the Lord and said, "O Sovereign Lord, holy and true, how long will it be before you judge the people who belong to this world for what they have done to us"? When will you avenge our blood against those people?

We see here the persecution is almost over, because God gives the martyrs white robes symbolic of their righteousness and tells them to rest a little while longer until their brothers and sisters have been martyred. This brings up the question: Who are these martyrs, where did they come from and in what setting were, they slain?

We read about them in this verse, and we learn their souls are under the altar in heaven. How did they lose their lives, and where did they come from? First, we must remember the church of Jesus Christ has already been raptured as we studied in Revelation 4, and it is in heaven. It includes all the Gentile Christian believers and converted Messianic Jews.

Since the martyrs asked for judgment on those who dwell on earth in vs.10, it is obvious that their murderers are still alive on the earth during the seven-year tribulation. This would strongly suggest that these martyrs are saints who have been martyred for their faith during the tribulation. Most likely they are casualties of the fourth seal judgment which we have already looked at.

It is important that we understand when the church is taken out of this world at the rapture, God is going to focus his focus His attention on the nation of Israel, and He will deal with the Jews for the last time. We all know from studying the Bible, how many times our Lord dealt with the Israelites during times of prosperity and during times of famine, idolatry, and disobedience.

Many Jews will turn to God during the seven-year tribulation as a result of the evangelism of the two witnesses on the streets of Jerusalem (Revelation 11), and the evangelism of the 144,000 Jews from the twelve tribes of Israel, as we shall see in Revelation 7.

144

Writing to the Romans, the Apostle Paul said it this way in <u>Romans 11:25-32</u>: *"Blindness (KJV)) or hard hearts (NLT) in part has happened to Israel..."* Paul told the Romans that for a period the Jews will have partial blindness, but in the end, many from the Jewish faith will come to Christ. <u>Romans 11:25-26</u>: *"I do not want you to be ignorant of this mystery, brothers and sisters, so that you may not be conceited: Israel has experienced a hardening in part until the full number of the Gentiles has come in, and in this way all Israel will be saved. As it is written: "The deliverer will come from Zion; He will turn godlessness away from Jacob"*.

When the time of the Gentiles has come to leave this earth at the rapture, God will then turn his focus on the Jewish people, and he will deal with them for denying Him at the cross, just like He dealt with their disobedience, rebellion, and idolatry many times in the Old Testament. The prophet Jeremiah spoke of this time of terror for the Jewish people in <u>Jeremiah 30:7</u> as the time of Jacob's trouble.

The prophet Zechariah also spoke of this time of tribulation in <u>Zechariah 13:8-9</u> as the time when two thirds of the Jewish population will be cut off and die, and a third will be left in the land of Israel. This parallels what our Lord Jesus Christ said in <u>Matthew 24:9-14</u> in the Olivet Discourse. But in the end, Israel as a nation will be saved, because God made a promise to Abraham, Isaac, and Jacob that He will keep.

Back in March 2011, my wife and I had the opportunity to go on a guided tour of the Holy Land for ten days with a group from our church in Ponca City. This trip changed my life forever. I recall we all stood on top of Mount Megiddo with our pastor overlooking the Valley of Jezreel visualizing what it would be like during the battle of Armageddon when that valley will be covered with blood up to the horse's bridle as we are told in <u>Revelation 14:19-20</u>. What an awesome site that was!!

145

So, the reason many people will be martyred during the tribulation is simply this: They have come to know Christ as their Savior, and now they are under pressure from the false prophet to put the mark of the antichrist 666 on their foreheads. When they refuse the mark of the beast and acknowledge their faith in Jesus Christ, they will be martyred.

The Bible in the Old Testament gives many examples of how the Israelites were martyred for their faith. Let us look at some of them.

In Exodus 1, Pharaoh devised a plan after the Israelites were multiplying and becoming a threat to him. He ordered the Hebrew midwives to kill all the Hebrew male children born to Hebrew women, but they refused to do because they feared God. Then Pharaoh gave another order to drown all the newborn Israelite boys in the Nile River.

In Esther 3:1-6, under the Persian Empire rule, Satan inspired Haman, King Xerxes' right-hand man, to devise a wicked scheme to annihilate every Jew in the Persian Empire after Mordecai refused to bow down to him.

In Daniel 11:29-31, we are told about a Greek General by the name of Antiochus IV Epiphanes who ruled part of the Middle East between 168 and 167 B.C. after the collapse of the Greek Empire and after the death of Alexander the Great. He became one of Israel's unrelenting, evil enemy and ruler, whom most theologians refer to as the predecessor to the antichrist. He defiled the Jewish Holy Temple by sacrificing pigs on the altar.

In Matthew 2:16-18 we read about King Herod. When he learned about the birth of Jesus Christ, he tried to kill all the boys in and around Bethlehem who were two-years old and under.

In Acts 6:8 the Prophet Stephen was stoned to death because of his testimony about Jesus Christ and his insistence that the Jewish religious leaders murdered Jesus. But before his death he had a vision

146

of the throne of God where Jesus was standing ready to receive him in heaven.

In <u>Acts 12:1-2</u>, we read of James, the brother of apostle John, who was killed with a sword by King Herod Agrippa.

Adolph Hitler during World War II between 1938 and 1945 was determined to destroy all the Jews on the European Continent. He was filled with Satan's fury. Those who knew him well reported on the night before his major campaigns, Hitler would often consult with the spirit world, mediums, sorcerers, and fortune tellers. So great was the persecution of the Jews that the Jewish population of the world was almost extinguished, reduced by six million in genocide, keeping perspective that number is about 90% of the number of Jews living in Israel today.

The world Jewish population is now about 14 million, and about one third of them are living in the United States (http://en.wikipedia.org).

Since Israel became a nation in 1948, the Jews miraculously endured many wars in an attempt to annihilate them by their Arab neighbors. The apostle John tells us the persecution is not over yet. There is still more to come. The Jews who have suffered so tragically in the lifetime of that nation will yet suffer even more during the seven-year tribulation.

<u>Revelation 6:12</u>

As the Lamb breaks the sixth seal, the scripture tells us there will be a great earthquake the world has never seen before. God literally takes hold of this world and shakes it for all of its worth. I want to point out earthquakes are increasing in frequency and intensity in our world today. Most of us are familiar with the Richter scale. It assigns a single number to quantify the amount of seismic energy released by an earthquake.

The Richter scale is based on a logarithmic scale and it is exponential. In other words, a 7.5 magnitude earthquake is 10 times bigger than a 6.5 magnitude earthquake, and an 8.5 magnitude is 100 times bigger than a 7.5 earthquake. It is overwhelming to think of an 8.9 magnitude earthquake, but one hit recently off the coast of Japan which triggered the worst tsunami in the history of this country. If such a quake would hit the U.S. west coast, it would have a devastating effect on the western states from California to Washington.

When we read in the Bible of a global earthquake, it is beyond our human understanding to comprehend how it can happen. Given the direct intervention of God who is in control of this world, if He wanted to send an earthquake, He could send it any place he wanted it and at whatever level He determined. We have already seen the hand of God in the most recent devastations left behind by strong earthquakes all over the world.

Revelation 6:13-14

After the earthquake the scripture reveals devastation of the entire earth like never seen before. The sun becomes dark, the moon becomes red as blood, heaven is rolled back as a scroll, the mountains and the islands of the sea are tossed around like toys. If that is not enough to shake the entire world, there will be falling of the stars like figs falling from the trees (vs. 13).

Revelation 6:15-16

Kings, presidents, governors, prime ministers, generals, CEOs of major corporations and wealthy people who do not know the Lord as their Savior will cry out in terror and seek shelter in caves and mountains thinking they can escape God's judgment.

The scripture puts it this way: *"Then the kings of the earth, the rulers, the generals, the wealthy, the people with great power, and every slave and every free person-all hid themselves in the caves and*

148

among the rocks of the mountains. And they cried to the mountains and the rocks, "Fall on us and hide us from the face of the one who sits on the throne and from the wrath of the Lamb. For the great day of their wrath has come, and who is able to survive?""

With the opening of this sixth seal, we have now covered the first half of the seven-year tribulation, and we are approaching the second half. The first three-and-a- half years are commonly referred to as the tribulation period. The last three-and- a- half years are referred to as the great tribulation, which culminates with the battle of Armageddon and the return of our Lord Jesus Christ with His saints to claim the earth as His own.

So, the first six seals represent the first half of the tribulation period, and the seventh seal represents the last half of the tribulation period and God's all-out fury on this world since the great flood in Genesis 6.

The Old Testament prophets prophesied about the events described in vs.12-16. Let us look at examples.
Joel 3:14-16: *"Thousands upon thousands are waiting in the valley of decision. It is there that the day of the LORD will soon arrive. The sun and moon will grow dark, and the stars will no longer shine. The LORD's voice will roar from Zion and thunder from Jerusalem, and the earth and heavens will begin to shake."*

Amos 8:8-10: *"The earth will tremble for your deeds, and everyone will mourn. The land will rise up like the Nile River at flood time, toss about, and sink again. At that time," says the Sovereign LORD, "I will make the sun go down at noon and darken the earth while it is still day. I will turn your celebrations into times of mourning, and your songs of joy will be turned to weeping."*

Haggai 2:6-7: *"For this is what the LORD Almighty says: In just a little while I will again shake the heavens and the earth. I will shake the oceans and the dry land, too. I will shake all the nations, and the*

149

treasures of all the nations will come to this Temple. I will fill this place with glory, says the LORD Almighty."
In the New Testament, Jesus Christ prophesied about the events described in <u>vs.12-17</u>. Let us look at you some of them.

<u>Mark 13:8</u>: *"And there will be earthquakes in many parts of the world, and famines. But all this will be only the beginning of the horrors to come".*

<u>Luke 21:10-11</u>:*" There will be great earthquakes, and there will be famines and epidemics in many lands, and there will be terrifying things and great miraculous signs in the heavens."*

When Moses and Aaron went before Pharaoh asking him to release the Jewish people from bondage, he refused, and the plague of darkness fell upon Egypt as God's judgment (<u>Exodus 10:21</u>). There was darkness that covered the entire area.

When the Lord revealed Himself to Moses and the Israelites on Mount Sinai, there was a powerful thunder and lightning storm, and a dense cloud came upon the mountain (<u>Exodus 19:16</u>).

When Jesus Christ died on the cross, the whole earth became dark between noon and three o'clock (<u>Matthew 27:45</u>).

When darkness comes upon the earth during the great tribulation, the unbelievers will panic and wonder what is happening all around them. Just think for a moment. When darkness sets on this earth, the moon turns red as blood, businesses and entertainment will cease. Crime and looting will become widespread, and depression will settle over the earth.

Revelation 6:17

<u>Revelation 6</u> ends with a warning to the kings of the earth, the rulers, the generals, the wealthy, the powerful, and every slave and free

person who is left behind after the rapture of the church: *"For the great day of their wrath has come, and who is able to survive?"*

Chapter Seven
God's People Will Be Preserved

In Revelation 6 we discussed the disasters that will come upon this earth when our Lord Jesus Christ opens the sixth seal. We saw a great earthquake. The sun became dark, the moon became red as blood, and the stars fell from the sky to the earth like green figs falling from trees shaken by mighty winds. The sky was rolled up like a scroll and taken away, and all the mountains and islands disappeared.

When we read these passages in the scripture, we learn they can mean only one thing: Major heavenly and earthly transformations have taken place, but the Lord kept His promise of the rainbow in the covenant He made with Noah in Genesis 9:11-13 that he will not destroy the earth by flood again: *"Yes, I am confirming my covenant with you. Never again will floodwaters kill all living creatures; never again will a flood destroy the earth. Then God said, "I am giving you a sign of my covenant with you and with all living creatures, for all generations to come. 13 I have placed my rainbow in the clouds"*.

Revelation 7 is referred to as an interlude between God's judgments, and it begins with the greatest revival that will take place upon the earth during the great tribulation. It is a revival that is focused on the nation of Israel. When we study Revelation, we discover there is a pause after each of the seven judgments that are mentioned in the scripture as shown below:

	Pauses in the Judgments	
Six Seal Judgments in Revelation 6	Pause	Seventh Seal Judgment
Six Trumpet Judgments in Revelation 8-9	Pause	Seventh Trumpet Judgment
Six Bowl Judgments in Revelation 15	Pause	Seventh Bowl Judgment

These pauses are evidence of God's grace in between times of judgment. A time for healing and a time for people to turn to Him, just like after all the recent disasters that the world and the U.S. have recently experienced.

Revelation 7:1

The apostle John sees four angels standing at the four corners of the earth holding the winds from blowing across the earth in all four directions. We all know now the earth is spherical without corners, but here we see another symbol in the scripture. The four corners represent four directions: North, South, East and West.

If you are a student of the Bible, you would recall the winds in the scripture are not only symbolic of God's awesome display of power and miracles but also a display of His judgments. The one we are most familiar with is the parting of the Red Sea in Exodus 14. God opened a path through the waters of the Red Sea by sending a strong east wind, which blew all night, turning the seabed into dry land to allow the Israelites safe passage and escape from Pharaoh's army and chariots.

Another example is the plague of locusts in Exodus 10:13. Moses raised his staff, and the Lord sent an east wind to blow all day and through the night bringing a plague of locusts on Egypt.

154

Revelation 7:2-3

As the four angels hold the winds from blowing, suddenly, we see they are joined by a fifth angel. This fifth angel comes from the East and instructs the four angels not to harm the earth, the sea, or the trees until the servants of God are sealed in their foreheads. What the Apostle John is saying here, until the 144,000 servants are chosen, saved and sealed, these winds are not allowed to blow.

Can you imagine what would happen on earth when winds blow from every direction? Here in the U.S. and especially in Oklahoma, we are used to winds blowing from northwest to southeasterly direction, or from west to easterly/northeasterly direction. We recently experienced that in Joplin, MO, Piedmont, OK and Springfield, MA. Here in Oklahoma, we are accustomed to seeing tornadoes blowing in multiple directions causing tremendous destruction in their paths.

The second verse says the fifth angel is carrying the seal of the living God. Here in this scripture, we are not given any information about this seal. We are not told what it is, but it is simply there to protect the servants of God from the judgments of God that will come upon the earth. However, Revelation 14:1-2 tell us this seal is the name of God the Father "YHWH" (Appendix A).

My Bible commentary tells me just as a seal is put on a document or on a scroll to certify its content and protect it, God places His own seal on His followers, identifying them as His own and guaranteeing His protection over their souls. Our Lord promised He would do that in Revelation 3:10, Romans 8:1 and John 3:36.

Another reason God's servants are marked with His seal is to distinguish them from the followers of the antichrist who will receive his mark 666 (Revelation 13:18). But I want you to note this is not the first time God has sealed some of His people from judgment. For example, when God sent the flood to the earth, He sealed Noah and his family from the rest of the human race, and they were protected from

155

the flood. In Genesis 12, God sealed many people in Israel including the first newborns in a Jewish family who were faithful and applied the blood of the lamb on the doorposts of their Egyptian homes.

When God told Abraham He would spare Sodom and Gomorrah if he could only find ten righteous men or women in the city (Genesis 18), He was talking about sealing the entire city from judgment, but instead He sealed Lot and his family until Lot's wife disobeyed God's command, looked back, and turned into a pillar of salt.

When God destroyed Jericho, He sealed Rahab and her household by means of a scarlet cord in her window (Joshua 2:18, 21).

In 1Kings 19:18 Our Lord marked seven thousand Jewish people with His seal who had never bowed down to pagan god Baal or kissed him.

So, the sealing of God's servants means He set them apart for protection. During the great tribulation, Satan will have his sealed followers and we are told here God will have His sealed followers.

Revelation 7:4-8

The scripture tells us before the seventh seal is opened, there will be a time when 144,000 remnants of the Jewish people from the twelve tribes of Israel, will be saved and marked with the seal of God. Who are these 144,000 Jews mentioned in vs.4? They are from the twelve tribes of Israel with a couple exceptions: The tribes of Ephraim & Dan are excluded primarily because they were known for their rebellion and idolatry, traits unacceptable for God's followers (Genesis 49:17 and Judges 12).

The tribe of Levi is mentioned here was not allotted part of the promised land by Jacob, because the Levites were to be supported and provided for by the other eleven tribes as they take care of the Temple and their priestly duties (Numbers 3:40-41).

156

Dan is first mentioned in Genesis 30. He was the son of Bilhah, Rachel's handmaid. In Genesis 49:17 Jacob referred to him as a serpent or a snake because he knew Dan would become an idolater. In 1 Kings 12:28-33, after King Jeroboam had established the northern Kingdom of Israel, he built shrines from Bethel to the south to Dan in the north as alternative pilgrimage destinations to Jerusalem. At each of these high places, he built two golden calves, declaring: *"It is too much trouble for you to worship in Jerusalem. O Israel, these are the gods who brought you out of Egypt"*. This became a great sin in the eyes of God for all the Israelites who worshipped them.

Ephraim is also omitted from the twelve tribes mentioned in vs. 5-8. Remember both of Joseph's sons Manasseh and Ephraim? Manasseh is listed here but Ephraim is replaced by his father Joseph. Why is that? The Prophet Hosea wrote about this in Hosea 5:9-11: *"Ephraim will be laid waste on the day of reckoning. Among the tribes of Israel I proclaim what is certain. Judah's leaders are like those who move boundary stones. I will pour out my wrath on them like a flood of water. Ephraim is oppressed, trampled in judgment, intent on pursuing idols. Ephraim will be laid waste on the day of reckoning. Among the tribes of Israel I proclaim what is certain"*.

According to this passage of scripture, in the last days the sons of Jacob will be re-gathered and represented in this worldwide evangelism.

Revelation 7:9-10

The second vision that John sees is a scene in heaven, which reveals a great multitude of people from every tribe, nation and language on the earth standing before the throne of God in heaven and before our Lord Jesus Christ. When you read in the Bible "from every nation and tribe", it simply means these are Gentile people from all over the world and not from the Jewish nation Israel. They are in heaven, they are removed from the tribulation, and they are rewarded with white robes and holding in their hands palm branches in front of the Throne of God before the Lamb Jesus Christ.

I want to point out God's message is always to the Jews first, then to the Gentiles. You may ask how you know that. The answer is given to us by the Apostle Paul in <u>Romans 1:16</u>: *"For I am not ashamed of the gospel, because it is the power of God that brings salvation to everyone who believes: first to the Jew, then to the Gentile".*

The Apostle John sees a great Gentile multitude standing before the throne of God which no man could count, from every nation, race, and nationality. Their white robes indicate that they have put their trust in the Lord and are clothed in the righteousness of Christ. The waving of the palms in their hands signifies victory. They have overcome the world, the flesh, and the devil.

Do you recall when you read about palm branches in the Bible? It was on Palm Sunday during the triumphal entry of Jesus into the streets of Jerusalem riding on a donkey (<u>Matthew 21:1-9</u>). The Palms were also a part of the celebration of a Jewish feast called the Feast of Tabernacles (<u>Nehemiah 8:15-17</u>), when the Jews were released from the Babylonian captivity.

<u>Revelation 7:11-12</u>

Here we see the growth in praise and worship of our Lord Jesus Christ in heaven. If you recall in <u>Revelation 5</u>, we discussed the praise and worship of our Lord in heaven. Now in this chapter, we see a seven-fold praise as follows:

<u>Revelation 1:6</u>	Two-fold praise	Glory and power
<u>Revelation 4:11</u>	Three-fold praise	Glory, honor, and power
<u>Revelation 5:13</u>	Four-fold praise	Blessing, honor, glory, and power
<u>Revelation 7:12</u>	Seven-fold praise	Blessing, glory, wisdom, thanksgiving, honor, power and strength

Revelation 7:13-14

Next one of the twenty-four elders asks the apostle John: "Who are these who are clothed in white? Where did they come from?" The apostle John did not recognize any of them, and here is what the elder said to him in vs. 14: "These are the ones coming out of the great tribulation. They have washed their robes in the blood of the Lamb and made them white".

It is difficult for some people to imagine how blood could make any clothes white. But the blood of Jesus Christ is the world's greatest purifier because it removes the stain of sin. White clothes or white robes symbolize sinless perfection or holiness in the Bible, which can only be given to people by the death of the sinless Lamb of God on our behalf. This is one of the greatest pictures in the Bible of how we are saved through faith. The Old and New Testaments give us scripture to clarify this.

Isaiah 1:18: *"Come now, let us argue this out," says the LORD. No matter how deep the stain of your sins, I can remove it. I can make you as clean as freshly fallen snow. Even if you are stained as red as crimson, I can make you as white as wool".*

Psalm 51:7: *"Purify me from my sins, and I will be clean; wash me, and I will be whiter than snow".*

Romans 3:25-26: *"We are made right with God when we believe that Jesus shed his blood, sacrificing his life for us. God was being entirely fair and just when he did not punish those who sinned in former times. And he is entirely fair and just in this present time when he declares sinners to be right in his sight because they believe in Jesus".*

Notice when the Apostle John is asked by one of the elders who these people are, in vs. 13, he said you are the one who knows. I do not know. I just got here. John looked at this group of people and he did

159

not recognize any of them, they were too great to count, and John knew many people in the church before he had that vision while he was exiled on the Isle of Patmos. The reason he did not recognize any of them is they were saved during the seven-year tribulation.

Here in this scripture, we see prophecy fulfilled when our Lord Jesus Christ foretold in Matthew 24:14 that the Gospel will be preached throughout the world and then the end will come. It is easy to visualize this in our world today.

With all the tremendous technology in communications we now have available to us, we have instant TV broadcasts, XM satellite radios, Internet, smart phones, satellites, and newspapers that cover news over the entire world. Once the Gospel is preached worldwide, people will be saved by the multitudes, and the greatest revival ever known to mankind would have occurred, and then the end will come.

God delivered Jews and Gentiles from the wrath of the antichrist during the tribulation period on earth, and the palm branches express the joy of total and complete deliverance. That is exactly why the Jews laid palm branches in front of Jesus Christ while riding on a donkey down the streets of Jerusalem. They mistakenly assumed He was going to be their military leader to deliverer from the oppression of the Roman Empire so they could be a nation again. Instead, they rejected Him as the Son of God, the Savior of the World.

Revelation 7:15-17

Next, we see our Lord depicted as the Shepherd who shelters his flock in heaven. Many times in the Bible, our Lord Jesus Christ described Himself as the shepherd of the flock. Let us take a look at examples.

Isaiah 49:8-11: "This is what the LORD says: "*At just the right time, I will respond to you. On the day of salvation, I will help you. I*

160

will give you as a token and pledge to Israel. This will prove that I will reestablish the land of Israel and reassign it to its own people again.

Through you I am saying to the prisoners of darkness, 'Come out! I am giving you your freedom!' They will be my sheep, grazing in green pastures and on hills that were previously bare. They will neither hunger nor thirst. The searing sun and scorching desert winds will not reach them anymore. For the LORD in his mercy will lead them beside cool waters. And I will make my mountains into level paths for them".

Psalm 23: *"The LORD is my shepherd; I have everything I need. He lets me rest in green meadows; he leads me beside peaceful streams. He renews my strength. He guides me along right paths, bringing honor to his name. Even when I walk through the dark valley of death, I will not be afraid, for you are close beside me. Your rod and your staff protect and comfort me.*

You prepare a feast for me in the presence of my enemies. You welcome me as a guest, anointing my head with oil. My cup overflows with blessings. Surely your goodness and unfailing love will pursue me all the days of my life, and I will live in the house of the LORD forever".

John 10:1-8: *"I assure you, anyone who sneaks over the wall of a sheepfold, rather than going through the gate, must surely be a thief and a robber! For a shepherd enters through the gate. The gatekeeper opens the gate for him, and the sheep hear his voice and come to him. He calls his own sheep by name and leads them out.*

After he has gathered his own flock, he walks ahead of them, and they follow him because they recognize his voice. They won't follow a stranger; they will run from him because they don't recognize his voice." Those who heard Jesus use this illustration didn't understand what he meant, so he explained it to them. "I assure you, I am the gate for the sheep," he said. "All others who came before me were thieves and robbers. But the true sheep did not listen to them".

The last phrase in this chapter is a blessing and a message of hope to all of us, as you may have heard it recited in funerals to encourage the families of the one they have lost. Our Lord will wipe away every tear from their eyes. The phrase does not say the tears are just wiped away, they are wiped out of their eyes, so no tears are left in their eyes. In other words, there is no possibility to cry anymore. Our Lord does not just wipe the tears away; He takes them out of our eyes forever because there will be no sorrow in heaven.

I want to close Revelation 7 with this thought. Sometime people ask me if someone did not get saved before the rapture, will he or she have a second chance to be saved during the seven-year tribulation. The answer is yes, but they will have to endure persecution, starvation, hatred and even martyrdom for their faith in Christ. We just saw a multitude of Gentile people that got saved during the seven-year tribulation during the great revival of the 144,000 Jewish evangelists.

Another question people ask me: What happens if a believer witnesses to a group of unbelievers about Jesus Christ, just like on a mission trip for example, and they deliberately reject the truth of the Bible about Christ during their lifetime? They would possibly say we are going to continue to live our lives as we wish and enjoy it to the fullest, and if and when the rapture comes, we will accept Christ as our Savior at that time.

There is one thing wrong with that thinking. The Bible says in 2 Thessalonians 2:11-12 that God will send a great delusion (deception) upon them to blind their minds, and they will be greatly deceived by the works of Satan so that they will believe his lies, and they will not be saved. In other words, if they reject Christ now, there is no second chance for them. They are destined to go to hell to be with Satan and the antichrist forever apart from God.

You may ask what lies they will believe. Revelation 13 tells us the antichrist is going to be allowed to perform satanic miracles, and he is going to appear to come back from the dead after being shot and killed. Satanically he is going to counterfeit the resurrection of Jesus Christ. He will try to counterfeit everything our Lord Jesus Christ did in an effort to deceive people and gain popularity.

Chapter Eight
The Lamb Breaks the Seventh Seal

Revelation 8 begins with our Lord Jesus Christ breaking the seventh and the last seal judgment that will be poured out on this earth, which will usher the seven-trumpet judgments.

Let us recap what is going to happen during the great tribulation. When our Lord removes the seventh seal from the scroll that He holds in His hands, He unfolds the seven trumpet judgments. When we get to the end of the trumpet judgments, we will see the seven bowl judgments unfold within the seventh trumpet judgment. So, in essence, when our Lord removes the seventh seal from the scroll, He unravels God's remaining judgments on this earth. This brings us to the time when the world is about to be ruled by Satan, the antichrist and the false prophet including all their followers.

As the various trumpets sound in Revelation 8, our Lord releases the leash he had on Satan up to this point, and he hands the earth over to the antichrist and the false prophet, the devil's messengers, who begins to take control of it. There are seven trumpet judgments in Revelation, and four of them are given to us in Revelation 8.

Revelation 8:1

Notice immediately what happens next after our Lord Jesus Christ breaks the seventh seal on the scroll: There is silence throughout heaven for about half an hour. I want you to know that what is about to happen is so devastating, the Bible says before it can happen, there is a period of silence and awe for half an hour in heaven.

The Bible tells us there is a day coming during the great tribulation when all the angels, the raptured church, men, women, and children who died and went to be with the Lord, and Old Testament prophets and saints, all will be silent for about thirty minutes. Until now in Revelation 7, the heavens were filled with sounds of worship, choirs and angels who have been praising God. But now judgment is about to come on this earth, and for a half hour, the scripture says there will be silence in heaven as if everyone is anticipating what is about to happen.

It is the silence that is experienced just before the storm hits, just like being in the eye of a hurricane. It is as if all heaven is waiting to see what is about to happen next. It seems like half an hour is a short time, but it seems like eternity.

Revelation 8:2-4

Next, we are reminded that the angels in Revelation have an important role. They carry out and execute God's commands. The seven angels were given the authority by our Lord to announce the execution of judgment upon this earth through the sounding of the first four trumpets.

In the Bible trumpets were used in several ways in the Old Testament. For instance, in Exodus 19:16-20, when the angels blew the trumpets (ram's horns), Moses and Aaron summoned the Israelites to the foot of Mount Sinai to meet with God and receive His Ten Commandments.

In Numbers 10:1-8, the Lord instructed Moses to make two trumpets of beaten silver to summon people to assemble and to break camp. In Numbers 10:9-10, Joshua 5-6, Judges 7 and Nehemiah 4:15-20, the trumpets were used to prepare the Israelites for war. Here in Revelation 8, we first see an angel standing before God performing priestly duties similar to what the Levites performed at the altar of the Tabernacle and Temple in Jerusalem. We are not told who this angel is, but the scripture says this angel is presenting the prayers of the saints

(God's holy people) mixed with incense and brought before the Lord.

Revelation 8:5

Here the scripture tells us the angel filled the incense burner with fire from the altar and threw it down on earth. Thunder crashed, lightning flashed, and there was a terrible earthquake. This is all an indication that God's judgment upon this earth has resumed. Remember now, we are in the great tribulation as God's wrath is being poured out upon this earth.

Revelation 8:6

Next, we are told the seven angels with the seven trumpets prepared to blow their mighty blasts unfolding further judgments on earth.

Revelation 8:7

In this passage of scripture, our Lord Jesus Christ is about to answer the prayers of the saints we read about in the previous chapter, Revelation 6:10. Their prayers are about to be answered in the punishment of the unbelieving people left behind on earth after the rapture of the church.

What we have in the rest of this chapter is the result of the sounding of the first four trumpets. The last three trumpet judgments are given to us in the next chapter, Revelation 9, but I want you to know once again here in Revelation 8 we see the number seven again indicating God's number of completion. First there is a division of four followed by the remaining three: The four seals and the three seals; the four trumpets and the three trumpets; when we get to the bowl judgments in Revelation 15, it is the same way, they are divided into four and three with special significance to each.

In <u>Joshua 6</u> when the priests blew their trumpets on the seventh day, the walls of Jericho collapsed, and Joshua and the Israelites took control of the city. There is a strong parallel here forecasting these final trumpet judgments. There is coming a day when the seventh trumpet will sound again, and this time the walls of the world will come crashing down before our Lord sets up His Millennium Kingdom on earth.

Now let us look at the first trumpet judgment. At the sounding of this first trumpet, the scripture tells us the earth will go through a terrible ecological devastation. One third of all vegetation will be destroyed, a bleak picture of desolation caused by hail and fire. Widespread judgment will be poured out upon this earth. I do not know what the consequences will be, but it is going to be devastating.

Revelation 8:8-9

After the first trumpet is sounded, a second trumpet sounds. When that happens, a great mountain of fire (volcanic eruption) is cast into the sea. When Mount St. Helen erupted in 1980, a large portion of the side of the mountain rolled into Spirit Lake and buried Harry Truman and all his belongings after he refused to evacuate the area when the local rangers gave him multiple warnings. Similar volcano eruptions happened in Hawaii, in Europe and all over the world.

In the judgments upon the earth many things will happen that have never happened before in the history of the world. We are seeing many of these events already happening in our lifetime. Then we are told a third part of the sea will become blood causing the death of a third part of life in the sea, and the destruction of the third part of the ships of the world including oil tankers that bring oil to western countries from the Middle East and South America.

The far-reaching implications of these judgments are beyond description and beyond my understanding and comprehension. We all know that bodies of water occupy about three fourths of the earth's surface area, so you can imagine the extent of this judgment. The pollution of the water and death of so many land and sea creatures would greatly affect the balance of life and the ocean.

If you have ever been around a body of water, and some pollution has come in contact with it from dead-sea creatures washed up on shore, there is that awful smell that you cannot tolerate and you want to run away from it as fast as you can. This will happen according to the scripture to a third of the salt-water bodies of the world. That is what is going to happen when the second trumpet is blown, and the scripture says when the second trumpet has been silenced, the third trumpet sounds.

Revelation 8:10-11

The judgment of the third trumpet affects all the fresh water supplies of the world compared to the second trumpet which affects the oceans and seas which have salt water. The Bible says when that trumpet is sounded, these fresh water supplies will become bitter with the result that many will die, and the instrument of judgment will be a great star named here bitterness or the Greek name for it is wormwood as in some Bible translations. The great star most likely refers to a meteorite soaring through space, because the Bible says it burned like a torch.

Wormwood, if you have never heard that name before, is a plant that is native to the region of Israel and Northern Africa, and there are many species of Wormwood that grow in Israel (www.wikipedia.com), and they have a strong bitter taste, leading to the use of the plant as a symbol of bitterness, sorrow and calamity.

In Deuteronomy 29:18 Moses summoned the Israelites and gave them the following command from God: "*so that there may not be among you man or woman or family or tribe, whose heart turns away today from the Lord our God, to go and serve the gods of these nations, and that there may not be among you a root bearing bitterness or wormwood*".

169

The prophet Jeremiah warned the Israelites about wormwood in Jeremiah 9:15 when the Lord instructed him: "*Therefore thus says the LORD of hosts, the God of Israel; Behold, I will feed them, even this people, with wormwood, and give them water of gall to drink*".

Revelation 8:12

Next is the sounding of the fourth trumpet. The Bible tells us the fourth judgment will affect the sun, the moon and the stars, and the cycle of day and night as we know it today. The twenty-four-hour cycle that we are accustomed to will be shortened to a sixteen-hour cycle, because of the darkening that will take place for eight hours.

Our Lord Jesus Christ foretold this would happen in His Olivet Discourse in Luke 21:25-26: "*And there will be strange events in the skies -- signs in the sun, moon, and stars. And down here on earth the nations will be in turmoil, perplexed by the roaring seas and strange tides. The courage of many people will falter because of the fearful fate they see coming upon the earth, because the stability of the very heavens will be broken up*".

Perhaps this shortening of the days is what is referred to in Matthew 24:22: "*In fact, unless that time of calamity is shortened, not a single person will survive. But it will be shortened for the sake of God's chosen ones*".

Revelation 8:13

Then John looks and hears an eagle (or an angel as described in the KJV) announcing the calamity yet to come: "*Terror, terror, terror to all who belong to this world because of what will happen when the last three angels blow their trumpets*". In other words, the sounding of the fourth trumpet is simply the warning of the trumpets that are yet to sound, which we will discuss in the next chapter.

Chapter Nine
The Fifth Trumpet Brings the First Terror

Revelation 9 is a continuation of Revelation 8 as evidenced by the opening with the word "then".

Revelation 9:1

In the opening of this chapter, we get a glimpse of hell described as the bottomless pit and its inhabitants. This is a temporary holding cell for the souls of all unbelievers who reject our Lord Jesus Christ as their Savior and put their trust and faith in someone else other than Him. They include:

-The Jewish people and religious leaders who rejected Jesus Christ as their Messiah and continue to put their faith in the Old Testament Law of Moses

-The sinners and those who choose to follow their evil desires

-Atheists and agnostics

-People of different religions of the world other than Christianity: Islam, Hinduism, Buddhism, New Age Movement, Mormonism, Scientology, Bahai, Confucianism, Sikh, Shinto, Tao, and others.

Here, the Bible tells us that hell is real and Satan and his followers dwell in it. For unbelievers and atheists who argue and dispute the fact that hell does not exist, here is evidence that it does. The bottomless pit is given different names in the Bible depending on which translation you read. It is known as a place of torment. Some of the names given to it in the Bible are:

-Abode of the Dead	-Hades
-Abyss	-Realm of the dead
-Bottomless pit	-Sheol
-Gehenna	-Tartarus

The bottomless pit should not be confused with the lake of fire, which is the permanent dwelling of the souls of all unbelievers mentioned in the scripture in Revelation 20:10: *"The devil, who deceived them, was cast into the lake of fire and brimstone where the beast and the false prophet are. And they will be tormented day and night forever and ever"*.

I want to take a few minutes to talk to you about what Jesus said about this dreadful place in Luke 16:19-26. Most of you are familiar with the parable of the rich man and the beggar Lazarus. Let me explain.

In the Old Testament before Christ's resurrection, there were two compartments for the dead that were divided by a fixed gulf, pit, or chasm where one cannot cross from one side to the other. One upper compartment was for the saints, a temporary place of rest called paradise or Abraham's Bosom. The other lower compartment was for Satan and his followers, the ungodly and the sinners, a place of torment called Sheol in Hebrew or Hades in Greek.

Note the following passage in Psalms in the Old Testament which speaks of *Sheol* as a place of torment, and then observe how in Acts in the New Testament the Hebrew *Sheol is* replaced by the Greek *Hades*:

Psalm16:10: *"For You will not leave my soul in Sheol, Nor will You allow Your Holy One to see corruption"*.

Acts 2:27: *For You will not leave my soul in Hades, nor will You allow Your Holy One to see corruption"*.

We see here that the Hebrew *Sheol* and the Greek *Hades* are synonymous terms in the Bible. Think of Hades as the state penitentiary with several holding cells. The criminal is held in the cell until he must go to trial before the judge. Once the judge rules, the criminal is either sent home free or he is sentenced for life in the "state penitentiary" or put to death. The Bible tells us in Luke 16:23 that the rich man was in torment in Hades, but he could see in the far distance Lazarus with Abraham in paradise.

You may remember in Luke 23:39-43 before Jesus died on the cross there were two criminals that were crucified with Him. One of the criminals scoffed at Jesus saying, "prove it by saving yourself" and he did not repent or ask Jesus for forgiveness of his sins. The other criminal repented and asked Jesus to remember him when He comes into His Kingdom. Jesus said to the criminal who repented "*today you will be with me in paradise*".

Many people ask what happened to our Lord Jesus Christ from the time he died on the cross on Friday afternoon till the third day when He rose from the dead on Sunday. The answer to this question is Jesus went into Hades to proclaim His victory over Satan and death and declared final condemnation to the fallen angels imprisoned there since Noah's days.

This is given to us in 1Peter 3:19-20: "*So He went and preached to the spirits in prison - those who disobeyed God long ago when God waited patiently while Noah was building his boat. Only eight people were saved from drowning in that terrible flood*". 2 Peter 2:4: "*For God did not spare even the angels when they sinned; he threw them into hell, in gloomy caves and darkness until the judgment day*".

Matthew 27:50-54 tells us when Jesus cried out again with a loud voice on the cross and yielded up His spirit, He went to paradise (Abraham's Bosom) with the repentant criminal on the cross, and when He rose from the dead on the third day, He took with Him to heaven the repentant criminal and all the saints, who were in paradise (Abraham's Bosom). Matthew 27:52 tells us when the graves were opened many of these saints rose from their graves after Jesus' resurrection and went into Jerusalem and appeared to many people.

Today many people use paradise and heaven interchangeably,

175

including the Apostle Paul who described it as the third heaven in
2 Corinthians 12:2-4: *"I was caught up into the third heaven fourteen years ago. Whether my body was there or just my spirit, I don't know; only God knows. But I do know that I was caught up into paradise and heard things so astounding that they cannot be told"*.

Our Lord foretold of what would happen to Him after he died on the cross through the story of the Prophet Jonah in the Old Testament. Jonah 1:17 tells us he went into the belly of a great fish, most likely a whale, and was there for three days and three nights before God made the whale spit him onto the beach.

Jonah 2:5-6 describes what it is like to be in Hades and be rescued by our Lord: *"I sank beneath the waves, and death was very near. The waters closed in around me, and seaweed wrapped itself around my head. I sank down to the very roots of the mountains. I was locked out of life and imprisoned in the land of the dead. But you, O LORD my God, have snatched me from the yawning jaws of death!"*

In Matthew 12:40 Jesus Christ tells us: *"For as Jonah was in the belly of the great fish for three days and three nights, so I, the Son of Man, will be in the heart of the earth for three days and three nights"*.

In Jude 1:6: *"And I remind you of the angels who did not stay within the limits of authority God gave them but left the place where they belonged. God has kept them chained in prisons of darkness, waiting for the Day of Judgment"*.

The Apostle Paul in Ephesians 4:8-10 says this: *"Therefore He says: "When He ascended on high, He led captivity captives, And gave gifts to men." (Now this, "He ascended"- what does it mean but that He also first descended into the lower parts of the earth?)"*.

To summarize, when our Lord Jesus Christ descended into Hades after His crucifixion, He proved to Satan and all the sinners in

Hades that He conquered death and sin, and He is in control of everything in this world, as Revelation 1:18 tells us: "*I am He who lives, and was dead, and behold, I am alive forevermore. Amen. And I have the keys of Hades and of Death.*"

Before we continue, let us review for just a moment where we are in our study. The next prophetic event on the horizon is the Rapture of the church of Jesus Christ. Following that moment when the church is taken out of this world, there will be a period of seven years of tribulation upon this earth. The first three-and-a half years are simply called the tribulation. The last three-and-a half years are called the great tribulation, which will culminate in the second coming of Christ with His saints at the battle of Armageddon. His second coming should not be confused with the Rapture of the church, which takes place seven years earlier.

The second coming of Christ will usher His Millennial Kingdom on this earth. He will reign as King of kings and Lord of lords for a thousand years. At the end of the Millennium Kingdom, the Great White Throne Judgment will take place for all the unbelievers, those who rejected Christ as their Lord and Savior.

In vs. 1, as the fifth angel blew his trumpet, John saw a star that had fallen from the sky to the earth, and he was given the key to the shaft of the bottomless pit held up to this point by our Lord Jesus Christ.

In Revelation 8:10 we saw a great flaming star falling from heaven to the earth when the third angel blew his trumpet. But the star in vs. 1 is different. He was given the key to the bottomless pit, the lowest point at the center of the earth, where Satan and his demons reside.

If you recall from Revelation 1:16-20 when I discussed the seven churches in Asia Minor, I stated that our Lord Jesus Christ held seven stars in His right hand, and the seven stars represented the angels of the seven churches that were represented by seven lampstands. Here the scripture tells us the star represents a fallen angel.

You may ask: who is this star that falls to the earth? The answer is no other than Satan, the fallen angel Lucifer. Three times in the Bible we are told Lucifer and his demons were expelled from heaven, and the demons were locked up in prisons of darkness.

The first time is <u>Isaiah 14:12-15:</u> "*How you are fallen from heaven, O shining star, son of the morning! You have been thrown down to the earth, you who destroyed the nations of the world. For you said to yourself, 'I will ascend to heaven and set my throne above God's stars. I will preside on the mountain of the gods far away in the north. I will climb to the highest heavens and be like the Most High.' But instead, you will be brought down to the place of the dead, down to its lowest depths*".

Jesus commented on that in <u>Luke 10:17-18:</u> "*When the seventy-two disciples returned, they joyfully reported to him, "Lord, even the demons obey us when we use your name!" Yes," he told them, "I saw Satan falling from heaven as a flash of lightning!*".

The second time is in <u>Revelation 12:7-9:</u> "*Then there was war in heaven. Michael and the angels under his command fought the dragon and his angels. And the dragon lost the battle and was forced out of heaven. This great dragon -- the ancient serpent called the Devil, or Satan, the one deceiving the whole world -- was thrown down to the earth with all his angels.* The ancient serpent is in reference to his deception and temptation of Eve in <u>Genesis 3:1</u>.

The third time is in <u>Jude 6:</u> "*And I remind you of the angels who did not stay within the limits of authority God gave them but left the place where they belonged. God has kept them chained in prisons of darkness, waiting for the Day of Judgment*".

To summarize, God gives Satan the key to Hades to let his demons loose for a specific period. They are described as giant locusts that sting like scorpions. All the demonic creatures who have been locked up in the bottomless pit since the beginning of time are about to be let loose on this earth.

It is important that we stop for a moment and remember that God is in control of this world and holds back the powers of Satan and his demons in this day and age. If He did not hold back these powers, our world would be turned upside down. But during the seven-year tribulation God is going to unleash Satan to be free with his demons to inflict harm on anyone they choose.

Revelation 9:2

When Satan unlocks the bottomless pit, all his demons ascend out of that pit like a big black cloud of smoke thick enough to darken the air and the sun just like a lunar eclipse when the moon blocks the sun. A swarm of locusts can cover a field in a matter of minutes, and they can totally consume it and destroy it. We saw an example of that in Exodus 10 when our Lord sent a plague of locusts on Pharaoh and the Egyptians who refused to let the Israelite slaves go.

In March 2013 Egyptian farmers suffered millions of dollars in damage after a swarm of about thirty million locusts hit Cairo and then descended on Israel's Negev desert causing tremendous damage. A desert locust lives a total of about three to five months although this is extremely variable and depends mostly on weather and ecological conditions. The life cycle comprises three stages: egg, hopper, and adult. Eggs hatch in about two weeks, hoppers develop in five to six stages over a period of about forty days, and adults mature in about three weeks to nine months but more frequently from two to four months (http://en.wikipedia.org).

Revelation 9:3-4

When Satan unlocks the bottomless pit, demonic creatures that look like locusts come out upon the earth, and they were given power by our Lord to sting like scorpions. These locusts are not the ones we are accustomed to seeing in the fields, because they were told not to harm grass, plants, or trees, but to attack the people who did not have the seal of God on their foreheads.

This means the only people they can sting are the followers of the antichrist who have his mark 666 on their foreheads. We know from Revelation 7:3, 144,000 Jews sealed with the name of God were chosen from the twelve tribes of Israel to proclaim the Gospel to the world during the great tribulation. These demonic creatures are not allowed to harm them.

Revelation 9:5-6

These demonic creatures were told not to kill but to torture people who did not have the seal of God on their foreheads for five months with pain like the pain of a scorpion sting. In those days people will seek death but will not find it. They will long to die, but death will flee from them.

I want you to notice what vs.6 says: "*In those days people will seek death but will not find it. They will long to die, but death will flee from them!*" What this scripture tells us is when people try to take their own lives to escape the horrible suffering from these demons, they will try to kill themselves, but they will not die. No matter what they try to do to kill themselves they cannot die, and they will not be able to get any relief from these stings. They will keep on living in pain and suffering just like it will be for people who end up in hell after the Great White Throne Judgment.

Revelation 9:7

The Bible says these demonic creatures looked like horses prepared for battle, wearing crowns of gold to look like earthly kings, and having human faces, hair like women's hair and teeth like the teeth of lions, and wearing breastplates of iron just like Roman soldiers. The sounds of their wings are like sounds of chariots running to battle. This is a very painful time for all the people left behind on this earth.

Our Lord gave us a parallel picture of His judgment on earth for that same period when he sent the flood on this earth and water covered the earth for five months in Genesis 7:17-24: *"For forty days the floods prevailed, covering the ground and lifting the boat high above the earth. As the waters rose higher and higher above the ground, the boat floated safely on the surface. Finally, the water covered even the highest mountains on the earth, standing more than twenty-two feet above the highest peaks.*

All the living things on earth died -- birds, domestic animals, wild animals, all kinds of small animals, and all the people. Everything died that breathed and lived on dry land. Every living thing on the earth was wiped out -- people, animals both large and small, and birds. They were all destroyed, and only Noah was left alive, along with those who were with him in the boat. And the water covered the earth for 150 days".

I do not know what you are thinking right now, but if you have not accepted our Lord Jesus Christ as your Savior and you are reading this book, I urge you to turn to Him and ask Him to come into your heart and save you. I thank God every day for saving me, because I live every day looking forward to that glorious day as He promised, when the trumpets will sound and the voice of the archangel will be heard, Christ will descend through the clouds at the rapture, and He will take His church to be in heaven with Him forever.

Those who are His will be caught up to meet Him in the clouds to meet Him in the air and remain with Him forever (1 Thessalonians 4:15), and we will escape the terrible judgments that will come upon this earth.

Revelation 9:8-10

Here we see a detailed description of these demonic creatures. The Bible says they had hair like women's hair and teeth like the teeth of a lion. They wore armor made of iron, and their wings roared like an army of chariots rushing into battle. They had tails that stung like scorpions, and for five months they had the power to torment people.

Revelation 9:11

Let us see what the Bible says about the king of these demonic creatures. He is referred to as the angel of the bottomless pit, and he is known by three names: His name in Hebrew is *Abaddon*, in Greek it is *Apollyon* and in English it is the *Destroyer*.

In the Hebrew Bible, *Abaddon* is used with reference to a dwelling place of the dead, often appearing alongside the better-known term *Sheol* (http://en.wikipedia.org). Here in vs. 11 *Abaddon* is the name given to the king of an army of demonic locusts which means to exterminate or destroy. It is no other than Satan, the devil himself, the king of all these demonic creatures that he sets loose out of the bottomless pit. They go throughout the earth to sting and hurt every person on the earth who is not marked with the seal of God.

Every unbeliever, every Jew, every atheist, every Muslim, every Hindu, every Buddhist, every person who mocked the name of Jesus in public and denied Him as their Lord and Savior and as the Son of God, every person who heard the Gospel preached and turned down the opportunity to receive Jesus Christ, is going to be subject to the torment of these demonic creatures when hell breaks loose on the earth.

Revelation 9:12

Here the scripture gives us a warning that the first terror had passed, but two more terrors are coming: The first when the sixth trumpet sounds in Revelation 9:13, and the second when the seventh trumpet sounds in Revelation 11:15.

Revelation 9:13

With the sounding of the sixth trumpet, the first half of the seven-year tribulation comes to an end. The sixth trumpet judgment is about to bring the second terror on earth. The Apostle John hears a voice speaking from the four horns of the golden altar that stands in the presence of God. What does this scripture mean? The answer is given to us in Revelation 6:9-11.

In this passage of scripture, when Jesus broke the fifth seal, the prayers of those who had been martyred for His Word during the seven-year tribulation are answered here. These martyred saints are trying to figure out when God is going to avenge their souls and bring justice. They were saying Lord, we gave our lives for you, and yet down on the earth the wickedness of Satan seems to be triumphing over the good; how long is it going to be before you avenge our souls?

The Lord said in Revelation 6:11 just wait a little while longer; the time is not here yet for the judgment that you want to come until the full number of your brothers and sisters have been martyred. When the time is right, I will do it, and then we come to Revelation 9:13-16 when our Lord answers the prayers of the saints who were martyred in Revelation 6. Our Lord answered and said it is time for the judgment to begin.

I want to stop for a minute and talk about this, as there is an important lesson for us here. We all have been through difficult times in our lives, recently or in the past, whether they were health-related issues, surgeries, cancer and cancer treatments, job losses, financial

183

struggles, family-related issues such as problems with children who are going through a divorce, children or grandchildren who are alcoholics or drug addicts, or loss of loved ones.

We pray and pray continuously, but we do not see the fruits of our prayers for a long time. God promised us many times in the Bible He answers our prayers, but His answer will come according to His timetable that is in line with what is best for us.

Revelation 9:14

God tells the angels *"Release the four angels who are bound at the great Euphrates River, and they were turned loose to kill one-third of all the people on earth"*. It is important to know in the Bible there are good angels and bad angels. In Revelation 7:1-3, the scripture describes four good angels standing at the four corners of the earth ready to carry on God's commands. The job of these good angels is to restrain evil. In this passage, the scripture describes four bad (fallen) angels who are bound in chains at the Euphrates River. They are commanded by God to release evil and kill one third of the earth's population.

You may ask: How do you know these angels in Revelation 9 are fallen angels? Throughout the entire Bible there is no record of good angels being bound or chained by God. These fallen angels have been detained by God and now they are set free, and they are told to release the judgment of God at the Euphrates River. This is confirmed to us in Jude 6: *"And I remind you of the angels who did not stay within the limits of authority God gave them but left the place where they belonged. God has kept them chained in prisons of darkness, waiting for the Day of Judgment"*.

We have a parallel passage which describes the duration of these events as three-and-a half years in Daniel 12:5-7: *"Then I, Daniel, looked and saw two others standing on opposite banks of the river. One of them asked the man dressed in linen who was now standing above*

184

the river, "How long will it be until these shocking events happen?"
The man dressed in linen, who was standing above the river, raised
both his hands toward heaven and took this solemn oath by the one
who lives forever: "It will go on for a time, times, and half a time.
When the shattering of the holy people has finally come to an end, all
these things will have happened".

Now the Bible says these four demonic angels will unleash
God's judgments upon this earth at the Euphrates River, which flows
geographically through the Arab countries of Syria and Iraq. I want you
to know the Euphrates and Tigris Rivers in Iraq are important rivers in
the Bible. The Jordan River comes next as the Israelites crossed the
Jordan under the leadership of Joshua on the way to the Promised Land,
and because Jesus was baptized in that river by John the Baptist.

My wife Jacquetta and I had the unique opportunity to be
baptized in the Jordan River in March 2011 when we went on a ten-day
tour of the Holy Land with our church group. The peace we felt and the
blessing we received after this baptism were indescribable.

Revelation 9:15-16

Here in this passage we are about to witness the four demonic
angels getting ready to lead an army of two-hundred million mounted
troops into battle which will destroy one third of the world population.

Some Bible translations refer to this army as 200 x 1000 x
1000. That is about 60% of the U.S. population (329 million according
to 2019 estimates). Can you imagine an army of two hundred million
soldiers? This has never happened before in the history of our world.

Revelation 16:12-14 tells us these troops represent united world
rulers driven by demonic spirits and are headed to the valley of
Megiddo in Israel to battle against God and his angelic armies:" *Then
the sixth angel poured out his bowl on the great Euphrates River, and it
dried up so that the kings from the east could march their armies*

westward without hindrance".

One of the great questions that students of Bible prophecy ask, and you may be wondering about it as well, is where would it be possible to have such a great army? If you had an army of two hundred million soldiers, how would you ever get that many of them to battle? There has never been such a sizeable army in the history of mankind, but it is not difficult to look at the growth in Asian population and armies in countries such as India, China, North Korea, Pakistan, Afghanistan, Kazakhstan, Iran, and Russia. Some day they will unite their armies to reach the two hundred million troops.

Revelation 9:17

When John's vision continues, he sees demonic creatures that looked like horses having heads like lions. Fire, smoke, and brimstone billowed from their mouths. In vs. 19 he says their power is in their mouth and in their tails; for their tails are like serpents, having heads; and with them they do harm. Then John continues to describe the riders of these demonic creatures. He says they wore armor that was fiery red, dark blue and yellow. These colors are typical of army uniform colors of Chinese and North Korean troops in our world today.

When the apostle John wrote the Book of Revelation, nuclear weapons did not exist and were unheard of at that time, so the closest description he could give us here is horses having heads like lions billowing fire and smoke and brimstone from their mouths.

With today's advanced technology in warfare, it is possible what John saw were either demonic creatures that looked like satanic fiery dragons in Hollywood movies, or armored vehicles with cannons and tanks going into battle and spewing fire, smoke and possibly nuclear missiles and nuclear warheads referred to in vs. 19 as heads like serpents or snakes.

Revelation 9:18-19

The apostle John tells us in this verse a third of mankind will be killed by three plagues: By the fire, the smoke and the brimstone which come out of the mouths of these demonic creatures. In this particular time of the tribulation period, there is going to be so much destruction, death, and chaos much like would have happened in the aftermath of the war of Gog and Magog described in Ezekiel 38 and 39 but at a much larger scale.

To summarize, when the seven seal judgments began, we were told in Revelation 6:8 one fourth of the world population will be killed by the four horsemen of the apocalypse. As of 2019, the world population is 7.7 billion. About 2.4 billion are Christians, and assuming all of them are raptured prior to the seven-year tribulation, that leaves 5.3 billion unbelievers on earth who will go through the seven-year tribulation.

The apostle John tells us one third of those 5.3 billion unbelievers in the world will be killed at that moment by fire, smoke, and brimstone (burning sulfur) that come out of the mouths of the demonic creatures. If we do the math correctly, by the time we get to the sixth trumpet judgment at the half-way point of the seven-year tribulation, more than one-half of the world population would have been wiped out as a result of God's judgments. Never since the time of Noah's flood has a substantial number of the earth population come under God's wrath.

Revelation 9:20

As we come to the conclusion of Revelation 9, the Bible says unbelievers who did not die in these plagues still refused to turn from their evil deeds. They continue to worship demons and idols made by their hands, demons of gold, silver, bronze, stone, and wood—idols that can neither see nor hear nor walk!

Revelation 9:21

Here we are told four sins will be rampant during the seven-year tribulation: Murder, witchcraft, sexual immorality, and theft. You may wonder how that could be? How could someone rebel against God and experience the awful judgments of God on earth and not repent? The answer is his/her heart is hardened and he/she will not believe. The Bible tells us in 2 Thessalonians 2:11 if those who have heard the Word of God and did not believe during this age of grace, God will send them a strong delusion during the seven-year tribulation, so they would be deceived, and they will believe the lies of Satan.

Chapter Ten
The Angel and the Small Scroll

This chapter presents a prelude to the ending of the seven years of tribulation on earth and the beginning of the Millennial Kingdom of Christ. John has seen the opening of the seven-sealed scroll and the seven seals themselves, and now he views it totally opened and disclosed.

So far, we have witnessed the horrors of the six trumpet judgments with one more trumpet yet to sound to complete the seven judgments.

Here in Revelation 10 and part of Revelation 11 there is a break in the action, call it the calm before the next storm, which happens between the blowing of the sixth trumpet and the blowing of the seventh trumpet. I call it glimmer of hope similar to the one we witnessed in Revelation 7 with the commissioning of the 144,000 Jews from the twelve tribes of Israel.

The purpose of this break in the action is to witness the sovereignty and love of God. Some of you might think from the horrors of evil, death and destruction we have witnessed so far, that Satan is winning, and he will preside over this earth forever.

But the interludes remind us that God is still sovereign and in control of all the events in Revelation, and He has not forgotten His people, and ultimately, He will be victorious. I do not want you to lose perspective of this. If you are wondering if perhaps God is losing this battle and evil is winning, these two chapters answer that question with an encouraging reminder.

Revelation 10:1

The first thing we notice in this chapter is the Apostle John's vision shifts from heaven to earth when he sees a messenger from heaven. Then he goes on to describe this heavenly messenger as a mighty or strong angel coming down from heaven, surrounded by a cloud, with a rainbow over his head. His face shone like the sun, and his feet were like pillars of fire. And in his hand was a small scroll, which he had unrolled. Who is this mighty angel?

Some say he is Michael the Archangel. Others say he is another unknown angelic being sent by God to announce the final judgments on earth. According to Drs. David Jeremiah, Henry Morris, and Joseph Chambers, and I personally agree with all of them, this mighty angel of God is none other than our Lord Jesus Christ Himself. Let me explain. He is pictured here as mighty and strong, with authority, laying claim over the land and sea as His own, and ready to establish His Millennium Kingdom on earth

Notice the description of this mighty angel of God. 1. As he comes down from heaven, He is clothed with a cloud, has a rainbow over His head, his face shone like the sun, and has feet like pillars of fire.

The Prophet Daniel had a similar vision of this mighty angel in Daniel 10:5-6: "*I looked up and saw a man dressed in linen clothing, with a belt of pure gold around his waist. His body looked like a dazzling gem. From his face came flashes like lightning, and his eyes were like flaming torches. His arms and feet shone like polished bronze, and his voice was like the roaring of a vast multitude of people*". What is the significance of these attributes?

The Bible says first as He comes down from heaven he is surrounded by a cloud. Throughout the Old Testament scripture, the clouds were always associated with the presence of God.

When the Lord descended on Mount Sinai to give Moses the Ten Commandments, the Bible says in Exodus He came down in a thick cloud of smoke. God guided the Israelites through the wilderness with a pillar of cloud by day and with a pillar of fire by night. When God appeared to Moses in Exodus 24:15, it was in a cloud of glory. It was in a cloud that the glory of the Lord was seen in the tent of the Tabernacle.

Psalm 68:4 says: *"Sing praises to God and to his name! Sing loud praises to him who rides the clouds. His name is the LORD -- rejoice in his presence"*.

Psalm 104:3-4 says: *"you lay out the rafters of your home in the rain clouds. You make the clouds your chariots; you ride upon the wings of the wind. The winds are your messengers; flames of fire are your servants"*.

In Mark 9:7, we see God the Father speaking from a cloud: *"Then a cloud came over them, and a voice from the cloud said, "This is my beloved Son. Listen to him."*

In Acts 1:9 our Lord Jesus ascended to heaven in a cloud.

The Bible says in Revelation 1:7 that He comes with the clouds of heaven. So, when we see in vs. 1 the description of this mighty angel coming down from heaven in a cloud, it is a first indication that is our Lord Jesus Christ.

The second thing we notice in vs. 1, He is not only surrounded by a cloud, but He is crowned with a rainbow. In Genesis 9:12 the rainbow was God's promise to the people of the world that He would never again destroy the world through a flood.

In Ezekiel 1:28 the prophet Ezekiel describes our Lord as follows: *"All around him was a glowing halo, like a rainbow shining*

191

through the clouds. This was the way the glory of the LORD appeared to me".

In Revelation 4:3 the Apostle John describes our Lord with the glow of an emerald circling His throne like a rainbow.

When we see this rainbow around the head of the One who comes down from heaven, it is a preview of our Lord Jesus Christ getting ready to re-claim the earth as His own, to reign on earth, and to establish His Millennial Kingdom on this renovated earth, which I will discuss in more detail in Revelation 20. He sets one foot over the land and one foot over the sea, claiming complete dominion over both. He comes clothed in a cloud wearing a rainbow as His crown.

The third thing we notice in vs. 1 is His face shone like the sun and His feet were as pillars of fire. This is again a description that is only fit for our Lord Jesus Christ, and it is not the first time we see Him described as such in the Bible.
The prophet Malachi describes Him as follows in Malachi 4:2: *"But for you who fear my name, the Sun of Righteousness will rise with healing in his wings".*

The prophet Daniel describes Him as follows in Daniel 10:4-6: *"On the 24th day of Nisan (on the Hebrew calendar, equivalent to March-April on the Gregorian calendar), as I was standing beside the great Tigris River, I looked up and saw a man dressed in linen clothing, with a belt of pure gold around his waist. His body looked like a dazzling gem. From his face came flashes like lightning, and his eyes were like flaming torches. His arms and feet shone like polished bronze, and his voice was like the roaring of a vast multitude of people".*

Matthew 17:1-2: *"Six days later Jesus took Peter and the two brothers, James and John, and led them up a high mountain. As the men watched, Jesus' appearance changed so that his face shone like the sun, and his clothing became dazzling white".*

During Paul's conversion in <u>Acts 9:3-4,</u> he describes our Lord as a brilliant light from heaven: *"As he was nearing Damascus on this mission, a brilliant light from heaven suddenly beamed down upon him! He fell to the ground and heard a voice saying to him, "Saul! Saul! Why are you persecuting me?"*.

In <u>Revelation 1:15-16</u> the Apostle John describes the brilliance of our Lord in His glory: *"His feet were as bright as bronze refined in a furnace, and his voice thundered like mighty ocean waves. He held seven stars in his right hand, and a sharp two-edged sword came from his mouth. And his face was as bright as the sun in all its brilliance"*.

Dr. Henry Morris in his book "The Revelation Record" puts it this way: "This mighty angel can be none other than the Lord Jesus Christ".

Dr. Joseph Chambers explains it this way in his book "The Masterpiece": "When we start reading each verse of chapter ten and studying it in its order, we will see that John is on earth and no longer caught up to heaven. He now witnesses the Lord coming down to earth. He even speaks of his vision differently and in a more physical sense. The Lord is called a messenger, but John's description leaves no doubt as to who He is".

In the Old Testament, our lord Jesus Christ in His pre-incarnate state is presented in many passages of scripture as the angel of the Lord. Let us review some of the passages.

In <u>Genesis 1:26,</u> God said *"Let <u>us</u> make man in our own image"*. In this passage the plural use "us" confirms Christ existed with God the Father and with The Holy Spirit before the world was created. He existed before creation and before time. He is referred to as the pre-incarnate Christ. This simply means he existed as the Second Person of the Godhead prior to His incarnation. When he was conceived by the Virgin Mary, He became human in the flesh, but as he was growing up,

193

He always referred to His Father as God the Father and not Joseph, Mary's husband.

In Exodus 3:14, God identifies Himself to Moses as "I AM WHO I AM." In John 8:58 "*Jesus said to them, "Truly, truly, I say to you, before Abraham was born, I am.*"

We also know Jesus Christ existed before the angels because He created them. The Bible tells us in Colossians 1:16: "*For by him were all things created, that are in heaven, and that are in earth, visible and invisible, whether they be thrones, or dominions, or principalities, or powers: all things were created by him, and for him*".

The Bible has many references to angels. Some are "good" angels as we have already discussed (e.g. our guardian angels), some are "bad" angels (e.g. fallen angels and Satan) and some are "archangels" (e.g. Gabriel and Michael).

But there is also reference to a very special angel known as "The Angel of The Lord" Who alone guided the Israelites through the Exodus out of Egypt and into the Promised Land, and He was in control of key events throughout the Old Testament. He is also addressed as the "Commander of the Lord's Army", "My Lord" with a capital "L" compared to other angels or archangels addressed as "My lord" with a lower case "l". Who is The Angel of The Lord? Let us look at a few examples in The Bible.

Genesis 16:7-13: "*The angel of the LORD found Hagar beside a desert spring along the road to Shur. The angel said to her, "Hagar, Sarai's servant, where have you come from, and where are you going?"" I am running away from my mistress," she replied. Then the angel of the LORD said, "Return to your mistress and submit to her authority." The angel added, "I will give you more descendants than you can count.*"

194

And the angel also said, "You are now pregnant and will give birth to a son. You are to name him Ishmael, for the LORD has heard about your misery. This son of yours will be a wild one -- free and untamed as a wild donkey! He will be against everyone, and everyone will be against him. Yes, he will live at odds with the rest of his brothers." Thereafter, Hagar referred to the LORD, who had spoken to her, as "El Roi, the God who sees me," (See Appendix A) for she said, "I have seen the One who sees me".

In Genesis 18:1-5 the Son of God came down from heaven accompanied by two angels who also appear as men to visit with Abraham and Sarah by the oaks of Mamre:"*Now the LORD appeared to him by the oaks of Mamre, while he was sitting at the tent door in the heat of the day.*

When he lifted up his eyes and looked, behold, three men were standing opposite him; and when he saw them, he ran from the tent door to meet them and bowed himself to the earth, and said, "My Lord, if now I have found favor in Your sight, please do not pass your servant by. "Please let a little water be brought and wash your feet and rest yourselves under the tree; and I will bring a piece of bread, that you may refresh yourselves; after that you may go on, since you have visited your servant".

Genesis 22:11-12: "*But The Angel of The Lord called out to him from heaven, "Abraham! Abraham!" "Here I am," he replied. "Do not lay a hand on the boy," He said. "Do not do anything to him. Now I know that you fear God, because you have not withheld from Me your son, your only son."*

Genesis 32:22-32 tells us about Jacob's experience when he faced a situation that caused him great fear. Years before, Jacob had tricked his older hungry brother Esau out of his birthright by giving him a bowl of lentil soup, and later, he tricked his father Isaac who was blind at his old age into believing he was Esau to receive his blessings. His mother Rebecca had encouraged him to do so.

195

When Esau found out about this, he became terribly angry and plotted to murder Jacob. Jacob then fled from Esau and stayed with his uncle Laban. While there Jacob married two wives and had twelve children from them and his concubines. He also became wealthy with livestock because God had blessed him.

Now Jacob was returning to his father's land with all that God had given to him. He was about to come face to face with his brother Esau for the first time since he had deceived him and fled from him. Jacob sent messengers ahead to greet Esau and to see if Esau still wanted to murder him.

Esau came to meet Jacob with four hundred men, so this caused Jacob to have great fear. The situation did not look good for him and his family. But Jacob prayed to God and he reminded God of His promises to him. So, he sent his wives, children, and servants out of the camp. This was probably to hide them in case they were attacked.

Jacob was left alone in the camp that night. Then a man came and wrestled with him. That man was Jesus Christ, because Jacob named the place *Peniel* in Hebrew meaning *the face of God*, and he said I have seen God face to face yet my life has been spared. God saw that Jacob was determined with his whole heart and all his strength to hold on to Him.

Then God struck him in the hip socket and changed his name from Jacob to Israel. Why did He do that? So that He could bless him. God humbled Jacob into total dependence upon Him. It is when we are humble and not proud that God can trust us with His strength and with His blessing.

Exodus 3:2-6: *"There The Angel of The Lord appeared to him in flames of fire from within a bush. Moses saw that though the bush was on fire it did not burn up. So, Moses thought, "I will go over and see this strange sight - why the bush does not burn up." When The Lord saw that he had gone over to look, God called to him from within the*

196

bush, *"Moses! Moses!" And Moses said, "Here I am." "Do not come any closer," God said. "Take off your sandals, for the place where you are standing is holy ground." Then He said, "I Am The God of your father, The God of Abraham, The God of Isaac and the God of Jacob." At this, Moses hid his face, because he was afraid to look at God".*

Joshua 5:13-15: *"As Joshua approached the city of Jericho, he looked up and saw a man facing him with sword in hand. Joshua went up to him and asked, "Are you friend or foe?" "Neither one," he replied. "I am commander of the LORD's army." At this, Joshua fell with his face to the ground in reverence. "I am at your command," Joshua said. "What do you want your servant to do?" The commander of the LORD's army replied, "Take off your sandals, for this is holy ground." And Joshua did as he was told".*

1 Kings 19:7-9: *"The Angel of The Lord came back a second time and touched him and said, "Get up and eat, for the journey is too much for you." So, he got up and ate and drank. Strengthened by that food, he traveled forty days and forty nights until he reached Horeb, the mountain of God. There he went into a cave and spent the night. And The Word of The Lord came to him: "What are you doing here, Elijah?"*

In Psalm 34:6-7: *"In my desperation I prayed, and the Lord listened; he saved me from all my troubles. For the angel of the Lord is a guard; he surrounds and defends all who fear him".*

To summarize, the description of the Lord as a strong and mighty angel in this chapter is not a mistranslation. The son of God was called the *"Angel of the Lord"* often in the Old Testament". This mighty angel is our Lord Jesus Christ revealing Himself to the world, after he conquered all His enemies at the end of the seven-year tribulation.

Revelation 10:2

When He comes down from heaven, the scripture says He had in his hand a small scroll which He had unrolled. The fact that the scroll is unrolled means that all the judgments written in the scroll have been fulfilled.

He then sets His right foot on the sea and His left foot on land, and He gave a great shout like the roar of a lion. When he shouted, the seven thunders answered.

The Apostle John here describes our Lord shouting like a roaring lion, who has executed His judgment on his enemies and conquered. This fits His description as the Lion of the tribe of Judah. Back in Revelation 5:5 one of the twenty-four elders told the Apostle John: "*Stop weeping! Look, the Lion of the tribe of Judah, the heir to David's throne, has conquered. He is worthy to open the scroll and break its seven seals*". This is evident that this mighty angel is our Lord Jesus Christ.

Revelation 10:3

Notice what happens next. When our Lord shouts like a roaring lion something amazing happens: The seven thunders respond from heaven in honor of our Lord. This majestic event was foretold by King David in Psalm 29:1-3: "*Honor the Lord, you heavenly beings; honor the Lord for his glory and strength. Honor the Lord for the glory of his name. Worship the Lord in the splendor of his holiness. The voice of the Lord echoes above the sea. The God of glory thunders. The Lord thunders over the mighty sea*".

Revelation 10:4

When the seven thunders spoke, the Apostle John hears a message from God telling him to keep secret what the seven thunders said, just as Daniel was instructed to keep the message and vision revealed to him secret in <u>Daniel 12</u>. Note this is the only place in Revelation where John is not allowed to write what he sees.

<u>Revelation 10:5-6</u>

This mighty angel, our Lord Jesus Christ, while standing with one foot on the sea and one foot on the land, raises his hand up towards heaven, and he swears an oath in the name of our God the Father Who created the heaven, the sea, and the earth and everything in between them, that God will wait no longer. The time is now to fulfill God's plan with no more delay.

When I was teaching this chapter in my Sunday school class at Northeast Baptist Church, a couple in my class members disagreed with me on the identity of this mighty angel. Their argument was God does not swear by His own name. I did not have a good answer at that time, so I researched this topic and as always, the answer is in the Bible, where our Lord Jesus Christ is referred to as the Angel of the Lord, and our God the Father swears by His own name.

In <u>Genesis 22:15-18</u>: "*Then <u>the Angel of the LORD</u> called again to Abraham from heaven, "This is what the LORD says: Because you have obeyed me and have not withheld even your beloved son, <u>I swear by my own self</u> that I will bless you richly. I will multiply your descendants into countless millions, like the stars of the sky and the sand on the seashore. They will conquer their enemies, and through your descendants, all the nations of the earth will be blessed -- all because you have obeyed me*".

In <u>Psalm 95:10-11</u>:" *For forty years I was angry with them, and I said, 'They are a people whose hearts turn away from me. They refuse to do what I tell them.' <u>So, in my anger I took an oath</u>: 'They will never enter my place of rest*". The place of rest stated in this passage is the Promised Land of Canaan.

199

In Hebrews 6:13-17: *"For example, there was God's promise to Abraham. Since there was no one greater to swear by, God took an oath in his own name, saying: "I will certainly bless you richly, and I will multiply your descendants into countless millions." Then Abraham waited patiently, and he received what God had promised. When people take an oath, they call on someone greater than themselves to hold them to it. And without any question that oath is binding. God also bound himself with an oath, so that those who received the promise could be perfectly sure that he would never change his mind"*.

Our Lord Jesus Christ is a member of the Triune God, the Holy Trinity, and He can swear an oath by His own self or by the name of His own Father. At the end of this verse, our Lord Jesus Christ says, *"There will be no more delay"*.

Revelation 10:7

The scripture says *"When the seventh angel blows his trumpet, God's mysterious plan will be fulfilled. It will happen just as he announced to his servants the prophets"*. The next question you may ask: What is God's mysterious plan? According to Dr. David Jeremiah, this mysterious plan includes all of God's promises to the Old Testament prophets concerning His ultimate defeat of evil and His victorious reign on earth.

For six thousand years. Satan has been allowed to roam the earth, to inflict evil, and to create doubt in people's minds about who God is. In 2 Corinthians 4:4 the Apostle Paul tells us: *"Satan, the god of this evil world, has blinded the minds of those who don't believe, so they are unable to see the glorious light of the Good News that is shining upon them. They don't understand the message we preach about the glory of Christ, who is the exact likeness of God"*.

In Ephesians 2:2 Satan is described as the prince of the power of the air: *"You used to live just like the rest of the world, full of sin, obeying Satan, the mighty prince of the power of the air. He is the spirit at work in the hearts of those who refuse to obey God"*.

So, God's mysterious plan is the answer to the question "why evil seems to triumph while we suffer for our faith in our Lord Jesus Christ". It is about to end, and God will renovate the earth and make it the way He intended it to be before Adam and Eve committed their first sin in the Garden of Eden. That is why we have hope and encouragement. God will do away with evil; He will establish righteousness, justice, and holiness on earth forever as we will see in Revelation 20-22.

Revelation 10:8-10

As we approach the end of Revelation 10, a command from heaven is given to the Apostle John to take the unrolled scroll from our Lord Jesus Christ and eat it. I want you to know this is not the first time this happened in the Bible. It happened to the Prophet Ezekiel almost exactly like that in Ezekiel 2:8-10: *"Son of man, listen to what I say to you. Do not join them in being a rebel. Open your mouth and eat what I give you." Then I looked and saw a hand reaching out to me, and it held a scroll. He unrolled it, and I saw that both sides were covered with funeral songs, other words of sorrow, and pronouncements of doom"*.

Then in Ezekiel 3:1-3: *"The voice said to me, "Son of man, eat what I am giving you -- eat this scroll! Then go and give its message to the people of Israel." So, I opened my mouth, and he fed me the scroll. "Eat it all," He said. And when I ate it, it tasted as sweet as honey"*. In those verses the scroll first tasted as good as honey, but then it made John's stomach sour.

What the Apostle John is being asked to do here is fully understand what is in the scroll. The word "eat" here has to do with not so much with physically eating it but taking it and assimilating it, learning it, and understanding what it says. When you first begin to do

201

that, it may taste as sweet as honey, but as you allow it to settle down, and you begin to meditate on it, it will become sour.

The message to us here is this: God's Word is sweet to us believers because it brings us hope and encouragement, but it sours our stomach because of the coming judgment we know is coming on unbelievers. That is why Jesus Christ emphasized the importance of spreading the Gospel to all four corners of the earth.

Revelation 10:11

Here the Apostle John is told by our Lord "*You must prophesy again about many peoples, nations, languages, and kings.*" What the Lord is telling John, once you assimilated all this information, I have given you and understood its meaning, then go and prophecy about the coming judgments to all the nations of the world.

Chapter Eleven
The Two Witnesses and the Seventh Trumpet Judgment

Revelation 11 begins with the adverb "then" meaning "soon after" indicating it is a continuation of the events in Revelation 10 until we reach vs. 14, at which time the seventh trumpet is sounded and brings the third terror on earth.

This chapter is focused on the nation of Israel as the scripture makes references to the Millennial Temple of God, to the altar, to the worshippers, to the outer courtyard, to the Holy City of Jerusalem, to the two prophets, to the clothes of the two prophets (sackcloth symbolizing suffering and grief), to the olive trees and to the lampstands.

It is the time of Jacob's (Israel's) trouble, which is the great tribulation as foretold by the Prophet Jeremiah in Jeremiah 30:7: *"Alas! For that day is great, so that none is like it; And it is the time of Jacob's trouble, But he shall be saved out of it"*.

Jesus spoke of this time of trouble that would come upon the nation of Israel in Matthew 24:21: *"For then there will be great tribulation, such as has not been since the beginning of the world until this time, no, nor ever shall be"*.

Revelation 11:1-2

The Apostle John is given a command to go and measure the Tribulation Temple of God in Jerusalem. When this chapter was written by the Apostle John around 95 A.D., there was no temple in existence. If you recall, the first Jewish Temple was built and completed by King Solomon in 959 B.C. It was destroyed in 586 B.C. by King

Nebuchadnezzar of Babylon. The second Jewish Temple was built in 515 B.C. by Zerubbabel & Ezra when the Jews were allowed to return to Jerusalem by King Cyrus II of Persia. This Temple was remodeled by King Herod the Great in 20 B.C. at which time the outer court was marked off for the gentiles and the inner court marked off for the Jews. This Temple was later destroyed by the Romans in 70 A.D.

Today the Orthodox Jews in control of the Temple Institute are preparing to rebuild the third Jewish Temple in Jerusalem which I mentioned in the first chapter of this book. It is called the "Tribulation Temple" by Bible prophecy scholars.

This Temple will be built at a time in the near future before or during the reign of the antichrist as we are told in 2 Thessalonians 2:3-4: *"Let no one deceive you by any means; for that Day will not come unless the falling away comes first, and the man of sin is revealed, the son of perdition, who opposes and exalts himself above all that is called God or that is worshiped, so that he sits as God in the temple of God, showing himself that he is God"*.

In this passage of scripture, the apostle Paul tells us the Day of the Lord, which is the beginning of the seven-year tribulation on earth, will not come until four events take place:

1. There is a global falling away from the faith referred as apostasy or the great rebellion in other Bible translations.
2. The antichrist is revealed to the whole world.
3. The Tribulation Temple is rebuilt.
4. The antichrist sits in this Temple and declares himself to be God, which is called the abomination of desolation.

Notice next the apostle John is given a measuring rod with specific instructions to measure the Tribulation Temple and the altar and to count the number of Jewish worshippers. He is also asked not to measure the outer courtyard, because it was turned over to the gentile nations who will trample the Holy City of Jerusalem for forty-two months (3 ½ years).

In Luke 21:20 and 21-24, Jesus said: *"But when you see Jerusalem surrounded by armies, then know that its desolation is near.... And Jerusalem will be trampled by Gentiles until the times of the Gentiles are fulfilled"*.

The times of the gentile nations will be fulfilled when our Lord Jesus Christ judges them at His second coming, as we are told in the parable of the sheep and the goats in Matthew 25:31-33: *"When the Son of Man comes in His glory, and all the holy angels with Him, then He will sit on the throne of His glory. All the nations will be gathered before Him, and He will separate them one from another, as a shepherd divides his sheep from the goats. And He will place the sheep at His right hand, but the goats at His left"*.

Then the King will say to those on His right, 'Come, you who are blessed by my Father, inherit the Kingdom prepared for you from the foundation of the world. For I was hungry, and you fed me. I was thirsty, and you gave me a drink. I was a stranger, and you invited me into your home. I was naked, and you gave me clothing. I was sick, and you cared for me. I was in prison, and you visited me".

In this passage the sheep are the believers who will come to Jesus Christ during the seven-year tribulation and will enter the Millennium Kingdom. The goats are the unbelievers who will reject Him and will not be allowed to enter the Millennium Kingdom, as we are told in Matthew 25:41-43: *"Then the King will turn to those on the left and say, 'Away with you, you cursed ones, into the eternal fire prepared for the devil and his demons. For I was hungry, and you didn't feed me. I was thirsty, and you didn't give me a drink. I was a stranger, and you didn't invite me into your home. I was naked, and you didn't give me clothing. I was sick and in prison, and you didn't visit me"*.

The final destination of the righteous is The New Jerusalem. The final destination of the unrighteous is the Lake of Fire. Matthew 25:46: "*And they will go away into eternal punishment, but the righteous will go into eternal life*".

To summarize, the Lord will gather all the armies of the world in the last days at the battle of Armageddon, He will defeat them at His second coming, and He will execute His judgment on them for how they treated the apple of His eye, the nation of Israel. Did they aid them during the Great Tribulation, or did they turn against them and followed the leadership of the antichrist knowing Israel needed their help?

Revelation 11:3

The Lord tells the Apostle John He will give power to His two witnesses; they will be clothed in sackcloth, and they will prophecy for one thousand two hundred and sixty days (three-and-a half years). Who are these two witnesses?

We know they are Hebrews by their description in this verse, but there is disagreement among Bible scholars on their identities. Some say they are Moses and Elijah, and others say they are Enoch and Elijah. Let us examine the two views.

I want to remind you in Deuteronomy 29:29 Moses tells us "*The secret things belong to the Lord our God, but those things which are revealed belong to us and to our children forever, that we may do all the words of this law*". If our Lord wanted to reveal the identity of these two witnesses to the Apostle John and to us, he would have done so, but He chose not to do it. Instead, He gives us clues and facts in the Bible about them so we can decide for ourselves.

There is no mention in the Bible of Enoch being one of the two prophets. People spiritualize the scripture by saying, because both Enoch and Elijah were taken alive from this earth (raptured), they will come back to earth as the two witnesses in <u>Revelation 11</u>. This is not biblical. Enoch is mentioned three times in the Bible:

<u>Genesis 5:22-24</u>: "*When Enoch was 65 years old, he became the father of Methuselah. After the birth of Methuselah, Enoch lived in close fellowship with God for another 300 years, and he had other sons and daughters. Enoch lived 365 years, walking in close fellowship with God. Then one day he disappeared, because God took him*".

<u>Jude 1:14</u>: "*Now Enoch, the seventh from Adam, prophesied about these men (false teachers) also, saying, "Behold, the Lord comes with ten thousands of His saints, to execute judgment on all, to convict all who are ungodly among them of all their ungodly deeds which they have committed in an ungodly way, and of all the harsh things which ungodly sinners have spoken against Him*".

<u>Hebrews 11:5</u>: "It was by faith that Enoch was taken up to heaven without dying - "he disappeared, because God took him." For before he was taken up, he was known as a person who pleased God".

<u>Genesis 5</u> and <u>Hebrews 11</u> tell us before the flood Enoch walked in close fellowship with God, and then he was taken alive to heaven (raptured) when he was 365 years old. <u>Jude 1</u> tells us Enoch prophesied about the second coming of Christ with His saints, and the judgment that will fall on false teachers and sinners who infiltrate the church and try to influence the congregation with their evil ways and doctrines.

The prophet Elijah was taken alive in a chariot of fire before the prophet Elisha became his successor. <u>2 Kings 2:9-11</u>: "*When they came to the other side, Elijah said to Elisha, "Tell me what I can do for you before I am taken away". And Elisha replied, "Please let me inherit a double share of your spirit and become your successor." "You have asked a difficult thing," Elijah replied. "If you see me when I am taken from you, then you will get your request. But if not, then you won't." As they were walking along and talking, suddenly a chariot of fire*

209

appeared, drawn by horses of fire. It drove between the two men, separating them, and Elijah was carried by a whirlwind into heaven".

I personally believe these two witnesses are Moses and Elijah based on what the Bible tells us about their actions. Let me explain.

In Exodus 7-10 Moses called ten plagues to come down on the nation of Egypt and in one of the plagues he turned the Nile River water into blood.

Elijah in 1Kings18 killed 450 prophets of Baal and defeated 400 prophets of Asherah who were supported by King Ahab and his wife Jezebel. We know from 1Kings 17 and 18 Elijah had the power from God to stop the rain and bring the rain down on earth after three years of drought.

In Malachi 4:4-5 the Prophet Malachi reminds us about the coming Day of Judgment and the fate of believers and unbelievers on that day. He also reminds us to obey the Law of Moses and listen to the preaching of the prophet Elijah.

In Zechariah 4:1-14 the prophet Zechariah had a vision of a solid gold lampstand with seven golden spouts that is continually kept burning by an unlimited reservoir of olive oil. He also saw two olive trees (symbolic of two prophets), one on each side of the bowl. He then asked the angel who had been talking to him what the vision meant.

In Zechariah 4:14 the angel tells the prophet Zechariah the two olive trees represent the two anointed ones (Moses and Elijah) who will assist the Lord of all the earth in the last days.

Another reason why I believe these two witnesses are Moses and Elijah is they both appeared with Jesus Christ as He was transfigured on Mount Tabor in Matthew 17:1-7. They will return to the streets of Jerusalem during the great tribulation to prophesy to the world.

Revelation 11:4-6

The scripture tells us the two witnesses have supernatural power from God. They have supernatural fire-breathing ability to defend themselves in case someone tries to harm them. The antichrist cannot kill them until they have prophesied and completed their testimony for one thousand two hundred and sixty days (three-and-a half years), and then God will allow the antichrist to kill them. Think about it, these two witnesses will be missionaries on the streets of Jerusalem for one thousand two hundred and sixty days preaching the Gospel, warning people about the antichrist and bringing Jewish people to Christ.

Revelation 11:7-9

After the two witnesses complete their testimonies, the antichrist will be allowed to kill them, and their bodies will be put on public display on the main street of Jerusalem for three-and-a half days. The great city where our Lord was crucified, Jerusalem, is now compared to Sodom & Egypt, both well known for their evil and corruption, because during those days the character of Jerusalem will be like those two cities, full of sin and immorality.

Can you imagine if this were to happen today, the photographers and TV cameras of all the media and news networks, national and international, would compete for the coverage and that would be headline news in all the newspapers. It is like watching this event live on CNN or FOX News; there will be many updates saying "we will take you live now to the streets of Jerusalem for an update". That is what vs. 9 says, and it says no one is allowed to bury them.

Revelation 11:10

The scripture says the enemies of the two witnesses, referred to as the people who belong to this world, the people who rejected Jesus Christ as their Savior and followed Satan and his demons, will rejoice and celebrate by giving gifts to each other in celebration of this event,

211

because they have been tormented by the two prophets with their message of repentance and judgment.

Revelation 11:11-12

We are told after three-and-a half days, the Spirit of life from God enters the two witnesses who were lying down dead on the main street of Jerusalem, and suddenly, they will come back to life and stand up. Then they hear the voice of God from heaven shouting *"Come up here"* similar to the voice the Apostle John heard in Revelation 4:1 *"Come up here, and I will show you what must happen after these things"*.

Notice what happens immediately after this miraculous event. Terror struck all who were staring at the two prophets as they watched in disbelief. Then the two witnesses are raptured to heaven in the same manner that Jesus ascended to heaven before His disciples.

Revelation 11:13-14

That same hour, there was a terrible earthquake that destroyed a tenth of the city of Jerusalem. Seven thousand people died in that earthquake, and everyone who did not die was terrified and gave glory to God. This is what happened just before the seventh trumpet is about to blow, which brings the third terror on earth.

Revelation 11:15

When the seventh angel blew his trumpet, there were loud voices shouting in heaven declaring the whole world has now become the kingdom of our Lord Jesus Christ, and He will reign forever and ever.

Revelation 11:16-18

Then we see the twenty-four elders sitting around the throne of

God falling on their faces and worshipping Him. They give us a preview of all the things that our Lord is going to do:

-Assume His great power
-Begin to reign as King of kings and Lord of lords
-Judge the nations of the world who oppressed the nation of Israel
-Reward all His followers, the saints
-Judge the dead at the Great White Throne Judgment
-Destroy all the enemies of Israel, including Satan and his demons who came out of the bottomless pit, the antichrist, the false prophet and their followers who caused destruction on the earth.

Revelation 11:19

Here the apostle John has a glimpse of The Temple of God in heaven. It was open so he could see what is inside of it, and the first thing he sees is the Ark of the Covenant (some translations refer to it as the Ark of the Testament), which is symbolic of the presence of God enthroned between two Cherubim angels; it was the Holy of holies from which the pattern was given to Moses in the Old Testament to build for the Israelites.

Wherever the Israelites left Egypt, they took the Ark of the Covenant ahead of them symbolic of God leading them to the Promised Land. Only the high priest could enter the Holy of holies, and then only after he had undergone ceremonial cleansing, made sacrifices to atone for his sins and the sins of the Israelites. No one could enter or touch the Ark, and if they did, they would die (1 Samuel 6:19 and 2 Samuel 6:1-8).

So, The Ark of the Covenant was an embodiment of God's presence with the Israelites. It was the Ark of the Covenant that went ahead of the Israelites under Joshua's leadership across the Jordan River into the Promised Land in Joshua 3:9-17.

After the Babylonians destroyed the Jewish Temple in Jerusalem in 586 B.C., the Ark of the Covenant disappeared, and no one knows even today where it is located. There have been many speculations about its location, but no one really knows for sure where it is.

Some people say it was taken to Ethiopia and hidden in Saint Mary of Zion's Church in the ancient city of Aksum. Some of the Jewish religious leaders say the prophet Jeremiah hid the Ark in a cave in Mt. Nebo before the Babylonian invasion. Others say it was hidden beneath the Temple Mount inside a cave.

The fact that we are told in this passage that the apostle John sees the Ark of the Covenant inside the Temple of God in heaven, tells us that God wants to reveal His glory to the Jewish people on earth at the halfway point of the seven-year tribulation when the seventh Trumpet is sounded in judgment, giving them one more opportunity to turn to Him, and to remind them of His presence with them during the Exodus. The earthly Ark of the Covenant described in Exodus 37 was modeled after this heavenly Ark.

If we go back to the beginning of Revelation 11, we were given a vision of the Millennial Temple often referred to as Ezekiel's Temple. In vs. 19, we are given a glimpse of God's Temple in heaven. In other words, God is telling us let me give you another glimpse of heaven to give you hope and encouragement during the great tribulation. Notice what happens next: Lightening flashed, thunder crashed and roared; there was a great hailstorm, and the world was shaken by a mighty earthquake indicating the whole world has now become the Kingdom of our Lord Jesus Christ.

Chapter Twelve
The Woman and the Dragon

In Revelation 12 the apostle John witnesses an event of great significance in heaven: Spiritual warfare, the conflict between good and evil, between God and Satan. He sees the source of all sin, evil, immorality, persecution and suffering on earth, and he understands why the great battle between the forces of God and Satan must soon take place.

The apostle Paul gives us a great explanation of the battle between good and evil in the heavenly realm in Ephesians 6:10-18, which I referred to in the "Overview" section of my book. He encourages us to put on the full armor of God to be able to protect ourselves against the schemes and attacks of Satan and his demons.

Revelation 12:1-2

In these verses, we are right away introduced to a woman clothed with the sun, the moon beneath her feet, and a crown of twelve stars on her head. This woman was pregnant, and she cried out in the pain of labor as she awaited her delivery.

The prophets Isaiah and Micah foretold about this woman and her son in Isaiah 26:17: "*We were like a woman about to give birth, writhing and crying out in pain*", and in Micah 5:2-3: "*But you, O Bethlehem Ephrathah, are only a small village in Judah. Yet a ruler of Israel will come from you, one whose origins are from the distant past. The people of Israel will be abandoned to their enemies until the time when the woman in labor gives birth to her son*".

Here is what the Apostle John saw in his vision:

1. A pregnant woman (a symbol of the nation of Israel) dressed with the sun (which we will discuss shortly), is about to give birth to a male child (our Lord Jesus Christ) who would rule all the nations on earth with perfect judgment with a rod of iron (Revelation 19:15; Psalm 2:7-9) during His Millennium Kingdom. But His own people, the Jews, rejected Him and they crucified Him as foretold by the prophet Daniel in Daniel 9:26. The woman had the moon beneath her feet and a crown of twelve stars on her head.

2. In vs. 5, the scripture says, "And her child was snatched away from the dragon and was caught up to God and to his throne". Clearly, this is describing our Lord Jesus Christ when He rose from the dead and ascended to heaven in Acts 1:9-11.

3. A large red dragon (a symbol of Satan) with seven heads and ten horns with seven crowns on his heads (representing his rule over seven kingdoms through his right-hand man, the antichrist during the seven-year tribulation). His tail dragged down one third of the stars (a symbol of Lucifer's fall from heaven and his demons or fallen angels), which he dragged down to the earth with him.

4. In vs. 6 and again in vs. 14, we are told God's faithful people in Israel will flee into the wilderness during the great tribulation for 1260 days, where God prepared a place to care for them. We will discuss that in more detail shortly.

I want you to know in Revelation there are five references to women that the Lord revealed to the Apostle John. Let us look at them one at a time: In Revelation 2:20-22, our Lord warns the church of Thyatira about a woman named Jezebel who is leading His servants astray by calling herself the prophetess, the high priestess of paganism and sexual sin.

In Revelation 12:1-2, the Apostle John sees a pregnant woman clothed with the sun and wearing a crown of twelve stars. That woman is a symbol of the nation of Israel. It includes all the remnant Jewish people who converted from Judaism to Christianity, the ones who were saved because of the evangelism of the 144,000 Jews we learned about in Revelation 7, and the evangelism of the two witnesses sent by God, whom we just studied in the previous chapter.

In Revelation 12:14, the Apostle John tells us when Satan realized he had been thrown down to earth, he pursued the woman who had given birth to the child. That woman is the nation of Israel and the child is our Lord Jesus Christ. The woman was given two wings like those of a great eagle. This is not the first time we see reference to the nation of Israel as carried on wings like those of a great eagle in the Bible.

In Exodus 19:4 our Lord reminded the Israelites: "*You have seen what I did to the Egyptians. You know how I brought you to myself and carried you on eagle's wings*".

In Isaiah 40:31: "*But those who trust in the Lord will find new strength. They will soar high on wings like eagles. They will run and not grow weary. They will walk and not faint*".

In Revelation 17:3 the Apostle John sees a woman sitting on a scarlet beast representing Babylon, the center of corruption and immorality on earth in the last days.

In Revelation 19:7, we read about the bride of Jesus Christ, the purified church consisting of all the believers who were raptured before the seven-year tribulation, ready to share a feast with our Lord.

We first learned about the curse God put on Satan in Genesis 3:14-15: "*So the LORD God said to the serpent, "Because you have done this, you will be punished. You are singled out from all the domestic and wild animals of the whole earth to be cursed. You will*

219

grovel in the dust as long as you live, crawling along on your belly. From now on, you and the woman will be enemies, and your offspring and her offspring will be enemies. He will crush your head, and you will strike his heel".

The passage *"From now on, you and the woman will be enemies, and your offspring and her offspring will be enemies"* refers to Satan (you) and the nation of Israel (the woman).

The phrase "You will strike his heel" refers to Satan's repeated attempts to defeat Christ during His life on earth. "He will crush your head" foreshadows Satan's defeat when Christ rose from the dead. A strike on the heel is not deadly, but a crushing blow to the head is. Already in Genesis, the first book in the Bible, God reveals his plan to defeat Satan and offer salvation to the world through His Son Jesus Christ.

In vs. 1 the crown of twelve stars represents the twelve tribes of Israel. Our Lord Jesus Christ, according to His genealogy given to us in Matthew 1, is a descendant of King David whose ancestors came from the tribe of Judah, one of the twelve tribes of Israel.

Next, let us examine the significance of the woman being clothed with the sun. According to Dr. Henry Morris in his book "The Revelation Record" the glory of the sun is a picture of the glory of Jesus Christ who is the light of the world (John 8:12).

What is the significance of the sun, the moon and the twelve stars? The answer to this question is in Genesis 37:9-11 when Joseph the son of Jacob had two dreams: *"One night Joseph had a dream and promptly reported the details to his brothers, causing them to hate him even more. "Listen to this dream," he announced. "We were out in the field tying up bundles of grain. My bundle stood up, and then your bundles all gathered around and bowed low before it!" "So, you are going to be our king, are you?" his brothers taunted. And they hated him all the more for his dream and what he had said. Then Joseph had another dream and told his brothers about it. "Listen to this dream," he said. "The sun, moon, and eleven stars bowed low before me!" This time he told his father as well as his brothers, and his father rebuked him. "What do you mean?" his father asked. "Will your mother, your brothers, and I actually come and bow before you?" But while his brothers were jealous of Joseph, his father gave it some thought and wondered what it all meant".*

Joseph had a special gift of interpreting dreams that would serve him well after he was sold into slavery in Egypt by his brothers. However, as a seventeen-year-old, he did not yet have a very well-developed sense of wisdom. Instead of boasting about his dreams he should have humbled himself and quietly watched to see what God would do in his life.

Sometimes God gives us information that he just wants us to keep to ourselves. He watches to see if we are trustworthy with the information he gives us, and if we truly are, he empowers us to do bigger and bigger things. Joseph eventually grew to great maturity and wisdom, but he did so through great suffering and persecution.

The two dreams that Joseph had were not ordinary dreams like the ones you and I have; they were part of God's plan to foretell about future events that would come to fruition.

Joseph's eleven brothers may have understood the significance of the first dream in Genesis 37:8: *"So you are going to be our king, are you?" his brothers taunted. And they hated him all the more for his dream and what he had said".*

Joseph's father Jacob did not fully understand the meaning in Genesis 37:10: *"What do you mean? his father asked. Will your mother, your brothers, and I actually come and bow before me?"* He assumed the sun was Rachel, the moon was Jacob himself and the eleven stars were his sons. The time would come in Genesis 42 when these things would come true.

Joseph used the words "sun and moon" to describe his dreams in terms his brothers and father would not have understood, because they represent the celestial planets which the Egyptians worshipped as pagan gods. The Egyptians worshipped many pagan gods of the sun, moon, and stars. They worshipped Pharaoh as their pagan god, and they addressed him as "Ra" meaning "the god of the midday sun". What Joseph was foretelling is all the people in Egypt one day will bow down to him, including Jacob, his wife Rachel and his eleven brothers.

The Bible tells us Rachel died after giving birth to Benjamin and years later Joseph rose to power and became the second in command under Pharaoh. The eleven stars in Genesis 37:9 represent Joseph's brothers who would submit to his authority and bow down to him. They formed the eleven tribes of Israel. Joseph's two sons Ephraim and Manasseh represent him as the twelfth tribe.

To this day, many Muslim countries in the Middle East and in Asia display the sun, the moon, and the stars on their national flags. They are symbolic of their pagan gods whom they worship.

The Prophet Zephaniah in Zephaniah 1:4-6 confirms it when he speaks about the coming judgment against Judah: "*I will crush Judah and Jerusalem with my fist and destroy every last trace of their Baal worship. I will put an end to all the idolatrous priests, so that even the memory of them will disappear. For they go up to their roofs and bow to the sun, moon, and stars. They claim to follow the LORD, but then they worship Molech, too. So now I will destroy them! And I will destroy those who used to worship me but now no longer do*".

Revelation 12:3

The Apostle John witnesses another significant event in heaven: He sees Satan pictured as a red dragon having seven heads, ten horns, and seven crowns representing his dominion over seven kingdoms of the world, which he rules through his right-hand man, the antichrist. For us to understand the meaning of this scripture, we need to turn our attention to the book of Daniel. In Daniel 7:7 God reveals to the Prophet Daniel the fourth beast or kingdom that will be in power in the last days. This fourth beast was terrifying, dreadful, and strong, and it had ten horns. This beast with ten horns symbolizes the revived Roman Empire. The ten horns represent ten kings yet to arrive on the world stage. Today the European Union (EU) has become a consolidation of world powers consisting of twenty-eight nations united with common goals and common currency, the Euro.

Since the fall of the Roman Empire in 476 A.D. no nation has been able to achieve world dominance, even though some people believe the U.S. controls the world today. There will be a time in the future however, before the Lord comes back to set up His Millennial Kingdom, a revived Roman Empire represented by European Union nations will be in control of this world which will be unified under one man, the antichrist.

Here in vs. 3, we are told the apostle John witnesses in heaven another significant event. He sees a large red dragon with seven heads and ten horns, with seven crowns on his heads. This is the same fourth beast that the prophet Daniel saw in Daniel 7:7. Satan the dragon, through his right-hand man the antichrist, will initially rule over ten kingdoms of the revived Roman Empire. He will subdue three of them, most likely because they disagree with his plan, and will rule over the remaining seven kingdoms.

Revelation 12:4

We are told here when Lucifer (Satan) rebelled because of his pride, God expelled him from heaven and his tail dragged one third of the stars (the angels) with him to earth. They became his demons.

Isaiah 14:12-19 gives us more details about Satan's doom: *"How you are fallen from heaven, O shining star, son of the morning! You have been thrown down to the earth, you who destroyed the nations of the world. For you said to yourself, 'I will ascend to heaven and set my throne above God's stars. I will preside on the mountain of the gods far away in the north. I will climb to the highest heavens and be like the Most High.' But instead, you will be brought down to the place of the dead, down to its lowest depths.*

Everyone there will stare at you and ask, 'Can this be the one who shook the earth and the kingdoms of the world? Is this the one who destroyed the world and made it into a wilderness? Is this the king who demolished the world's greatest cities and had no mercy on his prisoners?' "The kings of the nations lie in stately glory in their tombs, but you will be thrown out of your grave like a worthless branch. Like a corpse trampled underfoot, you will be dumped into a mass grave with those killed in battle. You will descend to the pit".

When Satan was expelled from heaven, he stood in front of the woman (nation of Israel) as she was about to give birth, ready to devour her baby (Jesus Christ) as soon as He was born.

Satan was ready to attack as soon as Jesus was born. He deceived king Herod into issuing a decree to kill all boys younger than two years, but he did not succeed. An angel of the Lord appeared to Joseph in a dream and told him to flee to Egypt (Matthew 2:13-16). Herod's desire to kill the newborn King Jesus, whom he saw as a threat to his throne, was motivated by Satan the red dragon.

Revelation 12:5

The scripture tells us here Israel gave birth to Jesus Christ who will rule all nations during the Millennium Kingdom with a rod of iron. Jesus was snatched away from the dragon when He ascended to heaven after His resurrection, and He was caught up to God and to his throne, where He now sits at the right hand of God the Father.

Revelation 12:6

Here in vs. 6 and again in vs.14 we are told God's faithful people will fly to a place God prepared for her in the wilderness for 3 ½ years (1260 days), where God will protect them supernaturally and will take care of them. The Bible does not give us the location of this wilderness, but the most likely location in the wilderness is the fortified city of Petra built on Mount Hor in southern Jordan, which my wife and I had the privilege to visit during our trip to the Holy Land in March 2011.

Revelation 12:7-9

Here we see Michael the Archangel and the angels under his command engaged in a spiritual battle in the heavenly realm with Satan and his demons (Ephesians 6:12), and Satan lost that battle, was forced out of heaven and thrown down to earth with all his demons. John goes on to describe Satan as the ancient serpent who deceived Eve in the Garden of Eden at the beginning of the Bible in Genesis 3:1.

Then suddenly, the Apostle John hears a loud voice shouting across the heavens saying "The salvation, power, authority, and Kingdom of our Lord Jesus Christ has happened at last, and the accuser, Satan, was thrown down to earth. The name "Satan" means "Accuser or Adversary".

Revelation 12:10-11

The scripture says the critical blow to Satan came when our Lord Jesus Christ triumphed over him by the shedding of His blood on the cross for our sins, and because of the testimonies of the martyrs in the Old and New Testaments who were not afraid to die for their faith in our Lord.

We had a preview of these martyrs in Revelation 6:9-11. Even though God permits Satan to do his work in this world, God is still in control, and Jesus has complete power over him. One day Satan will be bound for a thousand years (Revelation 20:1-3) and then forever as we will see in Revelation 20:10, never again to be able to do his evil work.

Revelation 12:12

The scripture tells us Satan will step up his persecution because he knows that he has little time left on this earth. We are living in the last days, and we are already experiencing Satan's attacks on our families and friends, which have become more and more intense. This is especially true as we learn more and more about his doom in this book.

I want you to know one of the reasons God allows Satan to do his evil work and bring temptations in our lives is to test our faith in Him. He wants to weed out those who pretend to be Christ followers from those who are true followers and believers. Many times, those who pretend to be Christ followers, when they go through the storms of life, tend to blame God for what happens by saying "why did God allow this to happen to me?" or "where was God when all this happened?"

By contrast true believers stay the course, endure the storms of life, praise God, remain joyful, and nothing shakes their faith in our Lord. By doing so, they become stronger and stronger in their personal walk with Him.

The apostle Peter addressed this issue facing the believers in 1Peter 1:6-7: "*So be truly glad. There is wonderful joy ahead, even though you must endure many trials for a little while. These trials will show that your faith is genuine. It is being tested as fire tests and purifies gold—though your faith is far more precious than mere gold. So when your faith remains strong through many trials, it will bring you much praise and glory and honor on the day when Jesus Christ is revealed to the whole world*".

Ephesians 1:4-5 tells us God loved us and chose us to do His work on this earth before the world was created: "*Long ago, even before he made the world, God loved us and chose us in Christ to be holy and without fault in his eyes. His unchanging plan has always been to adopt us into his own family by bringing us to himself through Jesus Christ. And this gave him great pleasure*".

Before God decides to use us, He must make us tough enough and strong enough to endure and stand up to the difficulties we will encounter in this world. When we use our muscles to do hard work, whether working out at a gym or doing physical work, at the end of the day these muscles become sore. As we get older, we feel the hurt more often than when we were younger. But this is how we know our muscles are getting stronger.

In the same way, God puts us in situations that are difficult for us to handle on our own, and as a result we hurt. But these situations make our faith, our mind, and our attitude stronger. As we become stronger, we are better able to serve God. That is God's way of preparing us to serve Him.

Revelation 12:13-14

When Satan realized he had been expelled from heaven and thrown down to earth, he pursued the nation of Israel who had given birth to our Lord Jesus Christ through the Virgin Mary. The Apostle John goes on to describe the nation of Israel as having two wings like those of a great eagle. Note this is not the first time we see in the Bible Israel being carried on eagle's wings.

In Exodus 19:3-6 when God rescued the Israelites from slavery, He gave the following instructions to Moses: "*The LORD called out to him from the mountain and said, "Give these instructions to the descendants of Jacob, the people of Israel: 'You have seen what I did to the Egyptians. You know how I brought you to myself and carried you on eagle's wings. Now if you will obey me and keep my covenant, you*

will be my own special treasure from among all the nations of the earth; for all the earth belongs to me. And you will be to me a kingdom of priests, my holy nation.' Give this message to the Israelites."
God wanted Israel to be an example for all the nations of the world to follow. This was the reason God chose the Israelites because they were the least of all nations (Deuteronomy 7:1-11).

Revelation 12:15

Satan begins to step up his persecution of the Jewish people in the form of a flood, because he knows that his time on earth is short. We see Satan here trying to drown the nation of Israel by sending torrential rain by satanic means. This is in retaliation for what our Lord did at the parting of the Red Sea to save the Israelites from Pharaoh and his army of chariots who were determined to drown the Israelites.

We see the enemy here coming like a flood in an all-out effort to destroy all the Jewish people who refused the mark of the beast and converted to Christianity, just like Hitler tried to do so in Germany during the Holocaust, the genocide of approximately six million Jews during World War II.

Revelation 12:16

Here we see our Lord Jesus Christ defeating Satan one more time to protect His people by miraculously opening the earth by creating an earthquake and swallowing the flood caused by Satan.

Revelation 12:17

In this verse, we see Satan becoming angry at the nation of Israel and all the Jewish people who accepted Jesus Christ as their Lord and Savior during the seven-year tribulation, and he declares war against them. We will see in the next chapter how Satan's right-hand man and political leader, the antichrist, and his religious leader, the false prophet, will rise to power during the great tribulation, and impose the mark 666, called the mark of the beast, on all those who refuse to worship the antichrist as God.

Revelation 12:18

The Bible New Living Translation says in this verse the dragon took his stand on the shore beside the sea ready for the big moment in the next chapter. The apostle Peter warns us about the schemes of the devil in 1 Peter 5:8: *"Stay alert! Watch out for your great enemy, the devil. He prowls around like a roaring lion, looking for someone to devour"*.

Chapter Thirteen
The Beasts out of the Sea and out of the Earth

As we begin our study of Revelation 13, we are right away introduced to Satan's two evil accomplices: The beast out of the sea, the antichrist in vs. 1 and the beast out of the earth, the false prophet in vs. 11.

The antichrist has political/commercial authority to manipulate the masses and the commerce. The false prophet has religious authority to enforce a false religion and perform satanic miracles on behalf of the antichrist. Together with Satan, the three evil beings form an unholy trinity in direct conflict and opposition to the Holy Trinity of God the Father, God the Son and God the Holy Spirit. This is a clear picture of the final battle on earth that will take place in the last days between the forces of good and the forces of evil.

There are twenty or more titles of the antichrist in the Bible as shown in the following scriptures:

The Offspring of Satan	(Genesis 3:15)
The Little Horn	(Daniel 7:8)
The Fierce King	(Daniel 8:23)
The Master of Intrigue	(Daniel 8:23)
The Prince That Shall Come	(Daniel 9:26)
The Ruler	(Daniel 9:27)
The Defiler	(Daniel 9:27)
The Desolate	(Daniel 9:27)
The Despicable Man	(Daniel 11:21)
The King	(Daniel 11:36)
The Worthless Shepherd	(Zechariah 11:17)

The Man of Lawlessness (sin)	(2 Thessalonians 2:3)
The Son of Perdition	(2 Thessalonians 2:3)
The Lawless One	(2 Thessalonians 2:8)
The One Who Comes In His Own Name	
	(John 5:43)
The Great Liar	(1 John 2:22)
The Deceiver	(2 John 1:7)
The Rider on the White Horse	(Revelation 6:2)
The Beast from the Bottomless Pit	(Revelation 11:7)
The Beast out of the Sea	(Revelation 13:1)

Revelation 13:1

The sea mentioned by the Apostle John in his vision is most likely in reference to the sea of humanity consisting of people from the Mediterranean nations surrounding the Mediterranean Sea. This is consistent with the vision of the four beasts the prophet Daniel saw in Daniel 7:2: *"Daniel spoke, saying, "I saw in my vision by night, and behold, the four winds of heaven were stirring up the Great Sea (Mediterranean Sea).* The sea, or sea of humanity, is a common term often used for the nations of the earth.

In Matthew 4:1-11 Satan wanted to gain world dominance by tempting Jesus in the wilderness after He fasted for forty days and forty nights. Satan wanted Jesus to worship him, to perform miracles by turning stones into bread and by jumping from a high mountain. Satan's plan was to rule the world through Jesus if Jesus would only bow down to him and worship him. But Jesus even in His weakest moment knew what Satan's motives were, so He rebuked him by quoting the Word of God from the book of Deuteronomy three times and then He commanded him to leave.

Here in Revelation 13, we see Satan the dragon as more powerful taking his standby the seashore and waiting for his two evil accomplices to emerge on the world stage. To the beast out of the sea, the antichrist, he gives political and commercial power (vs. 7), and to

232

the beast of the earth, the false prophet, he gives religious power to enforce the mark of the beast and perform satanic miracles (vs. 13). This unholy trinity, the dragon and the two beasts unite and work together in the last three-and-a-half years of the seven-year tribulation in a desperate attempt to gain control over the whole world.

The Apostle John in his first letter 1 John 2:18 warns us about the coming of the antichrist: *"Dear children, the last hour is here. You have heard that the Antichrist is coming, and already many such antichrists have appeared. From this we know that the end of the world has come"*.

Revelation 11:7 tells us the antichrist will originate his journey from the underworld, the abyss, or the bottomless pit: *"When they (the two witnesses) complete their testimony, the beast that comes up out of the bottomless pit will declare war against them, and he will conquer them and kill them"*. In other words, he will emerge on the world scene as a demonic spirit who will indwell in a human body.

The apostle Paul tells us in 2 Thessalonians 2:9: *"This man will come to do the work of Satan with counterfeit power and signs and miracles"*.

Paul goes on the say in 2 Thessalonians 2:10 the antichrist will deceive unbelievers left behind during the seven-year tribulation: *"He will use every kind of evil deception to fool those on their way to destruction, because they refuse to love and accept the truth that would save them"*

The prophet Daniel tells us in Daniel 7:25 during the great tribulation, the antichrist will defy God and persecute the believers who accepted Christ as a result of the preaching of the 144,000 Jews and the two witnesses Moses and Elijah: *"He will defy the Most High and oppress the holy people of the Most High (the Jews). He will try to change their sacred festivals and laws, and they will be placed under his control for a time, times, and half a time (3 ½ years)"*.

233

Daniel goes on to tell us in <u>Daniel 9:27</u>: *"He will make a treaty with the people (of Israel) for a period of one set of seven (7 years), but after half this time (3 ½ years), he will put an end to the sacrifices and offerings"*.

Revelation 13:1-2

The Apostle John describes the antichrist as having seven heads and ten horns, with ten crowns on its horns indicating his initial rule over ten kingdoms. But apparently three of these kingdoms will disagree with his plans, so he defeats them. The seven heads portray the remaining kingdoms over which the antichrist will reign over during the seven-year tribulation.

The antichrist will then begin to wage war against the followers of Jesus Christ. The Apostle John's vision in <u>vs. 1</u> is parallels the vision in <u>Daniel 2:41-42</u>, where Daniel sees the final world government consisting of ten kingdoms represented by the ten toes of the colossal statue that King Nebuchadnezzar saw in his dream. The scripture does not tell us who these ten kingdoms will be in the last days, but when they come to power, the scripture is clear that the antichrist will immediately defeat three of them, and he will rule over the remaining seven.

Today it is not difficult to envision ten kingdoms rising out of the G10 or G20 nations, a group of ten or twenty nations including the U.S., consisting of finance ministers and Central Bank governors from the European Union, Middle East, North and South America. Their mission is to bring together important industrialized and developing economies, and possibly one-world currency.

Revelation 13:3

In this passage, the Apostle John witnesses a satanic miracle: the antichrist is shot in the head and seems wounded beyond recovery. Everyone believes he is dead, but in an attempt to counterfeit the resurrection of our Lord Jesus Christ, he satanically stages his resurrection, and he appears to come back to life from the dead. As a result, the whole world marvels at this satanic miracle and gives allegiance to the antichrist.

Revelation 13:4

Here we are told as a result of this satanic miracle, people who rejected our Lord Jesus Christ will follow the antichrist and worship him as a god, because they are awed by his power and satanic miracles. These people do not realize by following the antichrist, they are only deceiving themselves, because he will use his power to manipulate them and promote his evil plans.

Revelation 13:5-6

The scripture tells us the power given to the antichrist will be limited by God. He will be allowed to exercise his authority only for a short time. The antichrist will be allowed to speak great blasphemies against God slandering His name and the names of His followers and all who dwell in heaven.

Revelation 13:7

The scripture tells us the antichrist was allowed to wage war against God's saints and to conquer them. And he was given authority to rule over every tribe and people and language and nation. This means God gave him permission and authority to rule over the entire world.

Revelation 13:8

Here we are told all the people who were left behind after the rapture, referred to here as the people who belong to this world, worshiped the antichrist as god. They are described here as the ones whose names were not written in the Book of Life that belongs to our

Lord and Savior Jesus Christ who was slaughtered as lamb when He was crucified for sins on the cross.

In Chapter three, I discussed the Book of Life and we will revisit it again in Revelation 20. But here in this passage, our lord Jesus Christ tells us everyone who worships the antichrist as god, his/her name will be erased from His Book of Life, and they will not inherit eternal life in heaven. Instead, they will join Satan, the antichrist, and the false prophet in the lake of fire, where they will be tormented forever.

Revelation 13:9-10

In this passage the apostle John gives words of encouragement to the saints who come to Christ during the seven-year tribulation. He says: "*If anyone has an ear, let him hear. If anyone is to be taken captive, to captivity he goes; if anyone is to be slain with the sword, with the sword must he be slain. Here is a call for the endurance and faith of the saints*".

In other words, he tells the saints some of you may be taken captive, some of you may be killed for your faith in Christ with the sword but remain faithful and endure for your reward is great in heaven". Jesus told His followers during the Sermon on the Mount in Matthew 5:11-12: "*Blessed are you when they revile and persecute you and say all kinds of evil against you falsely for My sake. Rejoice and be exceedingly glad, for great is your reward in heaven, for so they persecuted the prophets who were before you*".

I want to point refusal to worship the antichrist will result in suffering and persecution for God's holy people, but they will be rewarded with eternal life in the end. Vs.10 tells us in this time of persecution, being faithful to Christ would most likely lead to imprisonment and death.

The Apostle James tells us in James 1:2-4: "*Count it all joy when you encounter various trials, knowing that the testing of your*

236

faith produces endurance. And let endurance have its perfect result, so that you may be perfect and complete, lacking in nothing."

The Apostle Peter tells us in 1 Peter 4:12-13: "*Dear friends, don't be surprised at the fiery trials you are going through, as if something strange were happening to you. Instead, be very glad -- because these trials will make you partners with Christ in his suffering, and afterward you will have the wonderful joy of sharing his glory when it is displayed to all the world*".

Revelation 13:11

The Apostle John sees a second beast that comes out of the earth. He is identified in Revelation 16:13 as the false prophet. He is a false religious leader and a counterfeit of the Holy Spirit. He had two horns like those of a lamb, but he spoke with the voice of a dragon (Satan). This lamb is depicted as if it were our Lord Jesus Christ, while in reality, it is a counterfeit of Jesus Christ, disguised to look like him.

In Matthew 7:15-16, our Lord Jesus Christ warns us about false prophets when they come on the scene, and how to identify them: "*Beware of false prophets who come disguised as harmless sheep but are really vicious wolves. You can identify them by their fruit, that is, by the way they act... Yes, just as you can identify a tree by its fruit, so you can identify people by their actions*".

Just like the antichrist is depicted as a counterfeit of Jesus Christ riding on a white horse in Revelation 6, the two horns on the lamb refer to two kings with authority and power to make and enforce laws, with punishment to those who disobey them. I want you to know Bible prophecy contains many symbols and illustrations, which are often explained in other passages of scripture. Here is an example that parallels the one we are studying about the lamb with two horns.

In Daniel 8, the prophet Daniel while exiled in Babylon sees in his vision a male goat coming from the west and crossing the land swiftly. This goat had one exceptionally large horn between its eyes and was headed toward a two-horned ram that was standing beside the river. The goat charged furiously at the ram and struck him, breaking off both his horns.

In Daniel 8:20-21 we are given an explanation of this symbolism. The male goat represents the king of Greece, and the large horn between his eyes represents the first king of the Greek Empire, Alexander the Great. The two-horned ram represents the kings of Media and Persia.

Revelation 13:12

The apostle John tells us here the false prophet will exercise all the authority of the antichrist. He will stage a counterfeit resurrection of the antichrist after he is shot and appears to be dead, and he will require all the earth and its people to worship him as god, when his fatal wound appears to be healed by satanic deception.

Revelation 13:13

The false prophet goes on to perform astounding miracles, such as making fire flash down to earth from heaven to counterfeit what the prophet Elijah did on Mount Carmel, but the purpose of his miracles is to deceive people who belong to this world so they will be deceived into worshipping the antichrist. Here is a good illustration of it:

1 Kings 18:38-40	Revelation 13:13
Elijah kills 450 prophets for false worship of pagan god Baal	The false prophet requires all the earth and its people to worship the antichrist as a god. Anyone who refuses to worship him must die
Elijah calls for fire from the Lord to flash down from heaven and burn up the young bull, the wood, the stones, and the dust of the altar	The false prophet will do astounding miracles, even making fire flash down to earth from the sky while everyone was watching

If you recall from Exodus 4, Pharaoh's magicians Jannes & Jambres tried to duplicate Moses' signs given to him by God in Egypt. When Moses threw his rod on the floor and changed it into a snake, Pharaoh's magicians tried to counterfeit it. They also tried to duplicate the bloody water from the Nile River after Moses turned it into blood. So here the false prophet tries to gain influence through wonders and deception that he can perform on behalf of the antichrist.

The Apostle Paul in his second letter to Timothy warns us about the deception and immorality that will take place in the last days in 2 Timothy 3:1-5: *"You should also know this, Timothy, that in the last days there will be very difficult times. For people will love only themselves and their money. They will be boastful and proud, scoffing at God, disobedient to their parents, and ungrateful. They will consider nothing sacred.*

They will be unloving and unforgiving; they will slander others and have no self-control; they will be cruel and have no interest in what is good. They will betray their friends, be reckless, be puffed up with pride, and love pleasure rather than God. They will act as if they are religious, but they will reject the power that could make them godly".

Then in 2 Timothy 3:8-9, Paul compares these corrupt people to Jannes and Jambres: *"And these teachers oppose the truth just as Jannes and Jambres opposed Moses. They have depraved minds and a counterfeit faith. But they won't get away with this for long. Someday everyone will recognize what fools they are, just as with Jannes and Jambres"*.

Revelation 13:14-15

The deception continues when the false prophet orders the people of the world to worship a statue of the antichrist that was given life by deception through the power of Satan. You may ask how this is possible. With today's computer technology and artificial intelligence, it is very possible to create an image of the antichrist that appears to be real, and through robotics, make it look animated seemingly alive and speaking.

The statue commanded that anyone refusing to worship it must die, in the exact same fashion king Nebuchadnezzar ordered all the people in Babylon to worship his statue that he built after he had his dream which the prophet Daniel interpreted.

Saddam Hussein followed king Nebuchadnezzar's footsteps and built a similar statue of himself in Baghdad. This is a direct violation of God's second commandment in Exodus 20:4-6: *"Do not make idols of any kind. You must never worship or bow down to them"*.

So how do we keep from getting deceived by false miraculous signs and false prophets in our world today? By allowing the Word of God in the Bible and the Holy Spirit to penetrate our hearts, control our lives and strengthen our faith in the Lord. Knowledge of the Word of God will keep us from being deceived by false signs and wonders, no matter how convincing they appear to be. Just remember any scientific or worldly teaching that contradicts the Word of God is false.

Revelation 13:16-17

The Apostle John tells us the antichrist will require everyone great and small, rich and poor, slave and free to be given a satanic mark on the right hand or on the forehead, and no one can buy or sell anything without this mark. This means anyone who refuses the mark will be unable to buy food, clothing, or other necessities of life. No doubt the vast majority of people in the world will accept the mark simply to survive.

There is a great deal of speculation as to how exactly this mark will be affixed, but with the technologies that are available to us right now, such as RFID microchips as small as a grain of rice, which can be implanted in the right hand under the skin, or barcodes stamped or tattooed on the forehead, we can see how easily it can be implemented on a worldwide scale.

Those who are left behind after the rapture of the church will be faced with a difficult choice, accept the mark of the beast to survive or face starvation and horrific persecution by the antichrist and his followers. But those who come to Christ during this time will face persecution even to the point of martyrdom.

I want you to note this mark of the beast, 666, is intended to counterfeit the seal of God, the Holy Spirit (Ephesians 1:13), God places on the foreheads of his followers (Revelation 7).

Just as God marks his people with the seal of the Holy Spirit to save them from the persecution that Satan will inflict on God's followers during the great tribulation, so does the antichrist with his mark 666 to identify his people as his own.

I want you to note identifying his people with this particular mark 666 is not as important as understanding the purpose of the mark. Those who accept it show their allegiance to the antichrist and his satanic agenda, their willingness to operate within the economic system he promotes, and their rebellion against God. To refuse the mark means to commit yourself entirely to God, preparing yourself to die rather than compromise your faith in Christ.

Revelation 13:18

The New Living Bible translation reads: "*Wisdom is needed here. Let the one with understanding solve the meaning of the number of the beast, for it is the number of a man. His number is 666*". The King James Bible translation reads: "*Here is wisdom. Let him that hath understanding count the number of the beast: for it is the number of a man; and his number is six hundred threescore (three times 20=sixty) and six*".

Over the years many Bible scholars have attempted to decipher the numbers 666 and applying them to many known figures that have already come and gone. Others have attempted to tie them in to values of Hebrew and Latin letters based on names of well-known political or religious leaders, such as:

- Antiochus IV Epiphanes, one of the four generals of Alexander the Great
- Nero, the evil Roman Emperor who persecuted Christians
- The Pope, head of the Catholic church
- Napoleon Bonaparte, Emperor, and ruler of France
- Adolf Hitler, who ordered the genocide of six million Jews during WWII
- Benito Mussolini, head of government of Italy and leader of the National Fascist Party
- Former president of Iran Mahmoud Ahmadinejad. He wanted to wipe Israel off the map

Others used Roman numerals such as "V =5", "VIII = 8", or "X = 10" that add up to numbers 666, but no one has been able to explain the numbers biblically.

After many hours of researching this topic, I was led by the Holy Spirit to come to the conclusion this number 666 is associated with no other than king Nebuchadnezzar in the book of Daniel. Let me explain.

King Nebuchadnezzar built a statue of himself made of gold. Its height was <u>sixty cubits</u> (ninety-feet tall), and its width was <u>six cubits</u> (nine feet wide), as we are told in <u>Daniel 3:1-7</u>: *"Nebuchadnezzar the king made an image of gold, the height of which was <u>sixty cubits</u> and its width <u>six cubits;</u> he set it up on the plain of Dura in the province of Babylon.*

Then Nebuchadnezzar the king sent word to assemble the satraps (regional governors), the prefects (people in authority) and the governors, the counselors, the treasurers, the judges, the magistrates and all the rulers of the provinces to come to the dedication of the image that Nebuchadnezzar the king had set up.

Then the satraps, the prefects and the governors, the counselors, the treasurers, the judges, the magistrates and all the rulers of the provinces were assembled for the dedication of the image that Nebuchadnezzar the king had set up; and they stood before the image that Nebuchadnezzar had set up.

Then the herald loudly proclaimed: "To you the command is given, O peoples, nations and men of every language, that at the moment you hear the sound of the horn, flute, lyre, trigon, psaltery, bagpipe, and all kinds of music, you are to fall down and worship the golden image that Nebuchadnezzar the king has set up.

"But whoever does not fall down and worship shall immediately be cast into the midst of a furnace of blazing fire." Therefore at that time, when all the peoples heard the sound of the horn, flute, lyre, trigon, psaltery, bagpipe and all kinds of music, all the peoples, nations and men of every language fell down and worshiped the golden image that Nebuchadnezzar the king had set up".

The rest of this passage in the book of Daniel (Daniel 3:19), tells us that three young Jewish men by the names of Shadrach, Meshach and Abednego refused to bow down to this statue, and as a result, they were thrown into a fiery furnace to be burned to death, but instead, they were miraculously delivered by our Lord Jesus Christ.

To summarize, the number **666** in Revelation 13:18 is the number associated with king Nebuchadnezzar and the statue he built:
-The first number **6** of the mark of the beast represents the number of a man, as God created man on the sixth day and rested on the seventh.
-The second and third set of numbers **60** and **6** represent the height (**sixty cubits**.) and width (**six cubits**) of the golden statue king Nebuchadnezzar built. This is the only biblical explanation associated with the mark 666. In the same manner, the antichrist will duplicate what king Nebuchadnezzar attempted to do but at a much larger scale. He will declare himself to be God, and through his right-hand man the false prophet, he will demand everyone to worship his statue. Refusal to worship the statue of the antichrist will result in death. Revelation 13:15 tells us: *"Then the statue of the beast commanded that anyone refusing to worship it must die"*.

Chapter Fourteen
The Lamb and the 144,000 Jews

Before we begin our study of Revelation 14, I want to take a few minutes to point out the contrasts between Revelation 13 and Revelation 14 in the following table:

Revelation 13	Revelation 14
Vision of two beasts, one of out of the sea and the other out of the earth	Vision of the Lamb of God, Jesus Christ on Mount Zion with 144,000 celibate Jews, redeemed from the earth
False religion of the antichrist, requiring everyone on earth to worship him as God	The one and only true religion of Jesus Christ
Idolatry and evil worldwide	Praise and worship worldwide
The mark of the beast 666 imposed on all unbelievers left behind after the rapture	The marks of God the Father and God the Son on the foreheads of the 144,000 Jews

Back in Revelation 5:11-14, we saw thousands and millions of angels gathered around the throne of God and of the living beings and the twenty-four elders singing praises to our God. They all sang in chorus.

Revelation 14:1-3

In this passage the apostle John sees the same 144,000 Jews we saw in Revelation 7, 12,000 from each tribe of Israel, preserved, redeemed from the earth, standing on Mount Zion in Jerusalem. Notice here, John identifies the seal of the living God on the foreheads of the 144,000 Jews. The Bible tells us in vs. 1 "the 144,000 had the name of

Jesus and His Father's name written on their foreheads". The Bible does not tell us what these names are, but we know from the Old and New Testaments, the names of Jesus and God the Father the Jewish people are familiar with are "YESHUA" and "YHWH" (see Appendices A & B).

After the seven-year tribulation, our Lord Jesus Christ God will rule and reign during the Millennium Kingdom from Mount Zion. It will be the highest point o earth in Jerusalem after the earth is renovated by fire (2 Peter 3:10). How do we know that? The answer is in the following scripture:

Psalm 48:1-2: "*How great is the LORD, and how much we should praise him in the city of our God, which is on his holy mountain! It is magnificent in elevation -- the whole earth rejoices to see it! Mount Zion, the holy mountain, is the city of the great King!*"

Isaiah 24:23: "*Then the LORD Almighty will mount his throne on Mount Zion. He will rule gloriously in Jerusalem, in the sight of all the leaders of his people. There will be such glory that the brightness of the sun and moon will seem to fade away*".

Micah 4:1-2: "*In the last days, the Temple of the LORD in Jerusalem will become the most important place on earth. People from all over the world will go there to worship. Many nations will come and say, "Come, let us go up to the mountain of the LORD, to the Temple of the God of Israel. There he will teach us his ways, so that we may obey him." For in those days the LORD's teaching and his word will go out from Jerusalem*".

Revelation 14:4-5

The scripture tells us these 144,000 Jews are spiritually undefiled, celibate, and pure as virgins, which means they did not commit sin or idolatry, which will be rampant during the reign of the antichrist. They have remained faithful to Christ, they have followed

248

Him exclusively, and they have received God's reward for staying committed to Him, despite the persecution by the antichrist.

Revelation 14:6-7

The Apostle John sees an angel in heaven preaching the Gospel to the people of this world for the last time before God's final judgment on earth. This is probably the only place in the Bible where we see an angel preaching the Good News to the world. He warns the people to fear God and give glory to Him while there is still time.

Revelation 14:8

The Apostle John hears another angel in heaven shouting "Babylon that great city is fallen, because of her great sin and immorality". What do we know about Babylon and where will it be located?

The answers are in Revelation 17 and 18, but it is mentioned here for the first time in the book of Revelation. It is a preliminary announcement by an angel of the Lord saying "Fallen, fallen is Babylon the great, she who made all nations drink the wine of the passion of her sexual immorality".

Let us go back to the Old Testament in the book of Genesis to find out what the Bible says about ancient Babylon.

Babylon was first mentioned in Genesis 10 and 11. It was founded by a warrior by the name of Nimrod. It was at Nimrod's city of Babel that a towering structure was first built in defiance of God. Other than Genesis 10:6-10, the Bible does not give us much information on Nimrod, so I Googled it and here is what I found out about him.

After the Flood, Noah had a great-grandson, a descendant of Ham and Cush named Nimrod. The Bible says that he was a mighty warrior in the Lord's sight (Genesis 10:6-10). However, history tells us

249

Nimrod was a dictator who encouraged all the people on earth to rebel against God. Nimrod was not only a political leader, but also the lead priest of a form of occultic worship (http://en.wikipedia.org, the free encyclopedia).

Nimrod founded the Babylonian Empire. The Bible tells us in Genesis 10:10-12 that it included the cities of Babel, Erech, Akkad, and Calneh. From there he extended his reign to Assyria, where he built Nineveh, Rehoboth-ir, Calah and Resen. When we read the Old Testament, we see how most of these cities thrived with great occultic worship, human sacrifices, sexual practices, and perversion.

When Nimrod died, the Babylonian occultic religion which he led continued on. Nimrod's wife, Queen Ishtar, declared him as the sun-god. In various cultures, he later became known as Baal, which the Bible mentions many times in the Old Testament. Nimrod was also known by other names such as the great life giver, the god of fire, Baalim and Molech. If you recall, God condemned King Solomon when he fell into idolatry to these detestable gods in 1 Kings 11:1-13.

Today the ruins of Nimrod's fortress still exist in the Golan Heights in Israel. In the valley below Nimrod's fortress is Caesarea-Philippi and Banias in the region where the tribe of Dan settled, which my wife Jacquetta and I toured in March 2011.

Both Babel and Babylon were in the land of Babylonia (the plain of Shinar in Hebrew, the country of Iraq in today's geography). This was a time when the whole world spoke a single language. So here the name Babylon is associated with both an evil, adulteress immoral society, a world center for idol worship from God's point of view.

Isaiah the prophet said this about her in Isaiah 13:19-22: *"Babylon, the most glorious of kingdoms, the flower of Chaldean culture, will be devastated like Sodom and Gomorrah when God destroyed them. Babylon will never rise again. Generation after generation will come and go, but the land will never again be lived in.*

250

Nomads will refuse to camp there, and shepherds will not allow their sheep to stay overnight. Wild animals of the desert will move into the ruined city. The houses will be haunted by howling creatures. Ostriches will live among the ruins, and wild goats will come there to dance. Hyenas will howl in its fortresses, and jackals will make their dens in its palaces. Babylon's days are numbered; its time of destruction will soon arrive".

In Isaiah <u>21:9</u>: *"Now at last -- look! Here come the chariots and warriors!" Then the watchman said, "Babylon is fallen! All the idols of Babylon lie broken on the ground!"*

In <u>Jeremiah 50:35-40</u>: *"The sword of destruction will strike the Babylonians, says the LORD. "It will strike the people of Babylon -- her princes and wise men, too. And when it strikes her wise counselors, they will become fools! When it strikes her mightiest warriors, panic will seize them! When it strikes her horses and chariots, her allies from other lands will become as weak as women. When it strikes her treasures, they all will be plundered. It will even strike her water supply, causing it to dry up.*

And why? Because the whole land is filled with idols, and the people are madly in love with them. "Soon this city of Babylon will be inhabited by ostriches and jackals. It will be a home for the wild animals of the desert. Never again will people live there; it will lie desolate forever. I will destroy it just as I destroyed Sodom and Gomorrah and their neighboring towns," says the LORD. "No one will live there anymore".

In <u>Jeremiah 51:54-56</u>: *"Listen! Hear the cry of Babylon, the sound of great destruction from the land of the Babylonians. For the LORD is destroying Babylon. He will silence her. Waves of enemies pound against her; the noise of battle rings through the city. Destroying armies come against Babylon. Her mighty men are captured, and their weapons break in their hands. For the LORD is a*

God who gives just punishment, and he is giving Babylon all she deserves".

Based on the Word of God in Isaiah and Jeremiah, the ancient city of Babylon will never rise again and will lie desolate forever just like Sodom and Gomorrah. So, when we see the name Babylon in Revelation, it can only mean one thing: A corrupt religious-political system established by the antichrist and the false prophet with its roots dating back to Nimrod and the Tower of Babel.

It will be booming with sin and idolatry during the great tribulation. It will be the center of false prophets, witchcraft, idolatry, sexual immorality and all the workings of Satan and his accomplices.

Revelation 14:9-12

Next the Apostle John sees a third angel shouting, *"Anyone who worships the beast and his statue or who accepts his mark on the forehead or on the hand must drink the wine of God's wrath".* This is the final warning by this angel who is sent by our Lord Jesus Christ not to accept the mark of the beast 666 or suffer the consequences of doing so. He also encourages God's holy people to endure persecution and remain faithful to Christ.

Revelation 14:13

The Apostle John hears the voice of God from heaven saying *"Write this down: Blessed are those who die in the Lord from now on. Yes, says the Spirit, they are blessed indeed, for they will rest from their hard work; for their good deeds follow them".*

The Bible speaks about finding rest in Jesus Christ in heaven in the following two passages:

Hebrews 4:1-3: *"God's promise of entering his place of rest still stands, so we ought to tremble with fear that some of you might fail to get there. For this Good News -- that God has prepared a place of rest -- has been announced to us just as it was to them. But it did them no good because they didn't believe what God told them. For only we who believe can enter his place of rest"*.

Psalm 95:8-11: *"The LORD says, "Don't harden your hearts as Israel did at Meribah, as they did at Massah in the wilderness. For there your ancestors tried my patience; they courted my wrath though they had seen my many miracles. For forty years I was angry with them, and I said, 'They are a people whose hearts turn away from me. They refuse to do what I tell them.' So, in my anger I made a vow: 'They will never enter my place of rest"*.

God wants us to find rest in him. For the Israelites during the time of Moses and Joshua this rest was the earthly rest to be found in the Promised Land. For Christian believers today, for you and me, we find rest walking with God on earth, obeying His Word, looking forward to the return of His Son Jesus Christ at the rapture to take us to be with Him in heaven.

Revelation 14:14

In this verse, the Apostle John has a vision of our Lord sitting on a white cloud ready to execute judgment on earth in the form of a harvest on the earth: *"Then I saw a white cloud, and seated on the cloud was someone like the Son of Man. He had a gold crown on his head and a sharp sickle in his hand"*.

John's vision parallels that of Prophet Daniel in Daniel 7:13-14: *"I was watching in the night visions, And behold, One like the Son of Man (our Lord Jesus Christ), coming with the clouds of heaven! He came to the Ancient of Days (our Lord God the Father), And they brought Him near before Him. Then to Him was given dominion and glory and a kingdom (the Millennium Kingdom), That all peoples, nations, and languages should serve Him. His dominion is an*

253

everlasting dominion, which shall not pass away, And His kingdom the one which shall not be destroyed".

In the Olivet Discourse in <u>Matthew 24:30-31 (NLT)</u>, Jesus told His disciples: "And then at last, the sign that the Son of Man (Jesus Christ) is coming will appear in the heavens, and there will be deep mourning among all the peoples of the earth. And they will see the Son of Man coming on the clouds of heaven with power and great glory. And He will send out his angels with the mighty blast of a trumpet, and they will gather His chosen ones from all over the world - from the farthest ends of the earth and heaven".

In <u>Revelation 1:7 (NLT)</u>, the apostle John prophecies about the second coming of our Lord Jesus Christ saying: "Look! He comes with the clouds of heaven. And everyone will see him - even those who pierced him (the Jewish people). And all the nations of the world will mourn for him. Yes! Amen!

In this passage, the Jews will mourn because they finally come to realize they had crucified and pierced their own Messiah saying, "what have we done?" They will sprinkle themselves with ashes and beat their own chests in grief.

The unbelieving Gentiles too will mourn as they realize it is too late to repent from their sins and their rejection of the truth of the Gospel of Jesus Christ. Now they have no choice but to face their impending judgment.

Revelation 14:15-16

Here we are given an image of God's judgment: Christ is separating the faithful from the unfaithful like a farmer swinging his sickle harvesting his crops. The harvest is a symbol of divine judgment. The Prophet Jeremiah used this term during the Babylonian invasion of Judah in <u>Jeremiah 51:33</u>: "*This is what the LORD of Heaven's Armies,* the God of Israel, says: "Babylon is like wheat on a threshing floor, about to be trampled. In just a little while her harvest will begin".

The harvest is also explained in detail in Hosea 6:11: "Also, O Judah, a harvest is appointed for you, when I return the captives of My people".

In Joel 3:13: "Put in the sickle, for the harvest is ripe. Come, go down; for the winepress is full, the vats overflow-- For their wickedness is great".

At the end of the Parable of the Weeds given to us in Matthew 13:24-30, our Lord Jesus Christ compares the final judgment on earth, which is the Great White Throne Judgment, to the harvest of the earth: "Let both grow together until the harvest, and at harvest time I will tell the reapers, "Gather the weeds first and bind them in bundles to be burned, but gather the wheat into my barn".

Jesus then explains the Parable of the Weeds in Matthew 13:37-42: "The Son of Man is the farmer who plants the good seed. The field is the world, and the good seed represents the people of the Kingdom. The weeds are the people who belong to the evil one. The enemy who planted the weeds among the wheat is the devil. The harvest is the end of the world, and the harvesters are the angels.

"Just as the weeds are sorted out and burned in the fire, so it will be at the end of the world. The Son of Man will send his angels, and they will remove from his Kingdom everything that causes sin and all who do evil. And the angels will throw them into the fiery furnace (lake of fire), where there will be weeping and gnashing of teeth".

Revelation 14:17-18

The apostle John then sees another angel coming from the Temple of God in heaven, and he also had a sharp sickle. Then another angel, who had the power to destroy with fire, came from the altar. He

255

shouted to the angel with the sharp sickle, *"Swing your sickle now to gather the clusters of grapes from the vines of the earth, for they are ripe for judgment"*. In other words, it is time for the harvest on earth to separate the wheat from the weeds.

Revelation 14:19-20

A winepress during the time of the apostles was a large vat where grapes were collected and then crushed. The word "winepress" is often used in the Bible as a symbol of God's wrath and judgment against sin. A great example of its use as such is at the second coming of our Lord Jesus Christ at the battle of Armageddon, clearly described in Revelation 19:11-16: *"Then I saw heaven opened, and a white horse was standing there. Its rider was named Faithful and True, for he judges fairly and wages a righteous war. His eyes were like flames of fire, and on his head were many crowns. A name was written on him that no one understood except himself.*

He wore a robe dipped in blood, and his title was the Word of God. The armies of heaven, dressed in the finest of pure white linen, followed him on white horses. From his mouth came a sharp sword to strike down the nations. He will rule them with an iron rod. He will release the fierce wrath of God, the Almighty, like juice flowing from a winepress. On his robe at his thigh was written this title: King of all kings and Lord of all lords".

The prophet Isaiah explains God's judgment in Isaiah 63:2-4: *"Why is Your apparel red, And Your garments like one who treads in the winepress? "I have trodden the winepress alone, And from the peoples no one was with Me. For I have trodden them in My anger and trampled them in My fury; Their blood is sprinkled upon My garments, and I have stained all My robes"*.

The prophet Joel also explains God's judgment in Joel 3:12-14: *"Let the nations be wakened and come up to the Valley of Jehoshaphat (Armageddon); For there I will sit to judge all the surrounding nations.*

Put in the sickle, for the harvest is ripe. <u>Come, go down; For the</u>
<u>winepress is full,</u> The vats overflow-- For their wickedness is great."
Multitudes, multitudes in the valley of decision! For the day of the Lord
is near in the valley of decision".

To summarize, the winepress in these passages is the place of reaping, known as the valley of Armageddon or the valley of Megiddo in the Bible. This valley is in the northern part of Israel, and today water from Mount Hermon drains into the Jordan Valley and into the Dead Sea, allowing sufficient distance to literally fulfill this prophecy. We are told here that this battle will be so bloody that it will fill this valley 180-200 miles with blood up to the horse's bridle. This much bloodshed has never happened in the history of mankind, but the Word of God says it is going to happen as a result of God's wrath on his enemies.

Chapter Fifteen
The Song of Moses and of the Lamb and the Seven Bowl Judgments

Our attention is now directed to two events in heaven of great significance.

Revelation 15:1-2

The first event is the vision the apostle John has of seven angels holding the seven last plagues in bowls, which will come down on earth and would bring God's wrath to completion.

The second event is the vision the apostle John has of all the people who refused to accept the mark of the beast and were martyred for their faith during the great tribulation. They were victorious over the antichrist and his statue and the number representing his name. They were all holding harps that God had given them, and they were singing the song of Moses.

The seven last plagues are reminiscent of God's warning to the Israelites in Leviticus 26:14-18 if they refuse to obey His commands and continue to worship idols: "*However, if you do not listen to me or obey all these commands, and if you break my covenant by rejecting my decrees, treating my regulations with contempt, and refusing to obey my commands, I will punish you. I will bring sudden terrors upon you—wasting diseases and burning fevers that will cause your eyes to fail and your life to ebb away.*

You will plant your crops in vain because your enemies will eat them. I will turn against you, and you will be defeated by your enemies. Those who hate you will rule over you, and you will run even when no one is chasing you! "And if, in spite of all this, you still disobey me, I will punish you seven times over for your sins".

The crystal sea of glass in heaven, which the apostle John saw in Revelation 4:6, is now seen by the Apostle John mixed with fire indicating the wrath of God is about to be poured out on earth. We will not actually see the execution of this event until the next chapter, Revelation 16.

I want you to note, unlike the previous seal and trumpet judgments, the seven-bowl judgments will culminate with the ending of all evil in our world and the end of the world as we know it today. Also please keep in mind, the earth will not disappear, but it will be transformed after these events, as we will see in the remaining chapters.

Revelation 15:3-4

In this passage, we see reference to the song of Moses and the song of the Lamb. The song of Moses is given to us in Exodus 15:1-4: *"Then Moses and the people of Israel sang this song to the LORD: "I will sing to the LORD, for he has triumphed gloriously; he has thrown both horse and rider into the sea. The LORD is my strength and my song; he has become my victory. He is my God, and I will praise him; he is my father's God, and I will exalt him! The LORD is a warrior; yes, the LORD is his name! Pharaoh's chariots and armies, he has thrown into the sea. The very best of Pharaoh's officers have been drowned in the Red Sea".*

This song was sung by Moses and celebrated with the Israelites when they were delivered from Egypt after God parted the Red Sea and after the drowning of Pharaoh's army and chariots. In a similar way here the song of the Lamb celebrates the ultimate deliverance of God's people from the power of Satan and his antichrist.

Revelation 15:5

The Apostle John sees the Temple of God in heaven wide open, which he describes as God's Tabernacle. This scripture parallels that of Exodus 25-30 when the Ark of the Covenant, which symbolized God's presence among His people, led the Israelites in the wilderness on the way to the Promised Land and resided in the Tabernacle.

Revelation 15:6

In this passage, the apostle John sees seven angels coming out of Temple in heaven clothed in spotless white linen with gold belts across their chests. They are holding the seven plagues in bowls.

Revelation 15:7

Next John sees one of the four living beings in front of the Throne of God handing each of the seven angels a golden bowls filled with the wrath of God.

Revelation 15:8

In this verse, the smoke that fills the Temple is the manifestation of God's glory and power. No one could enter the Temple until the seven angels have completed the pouring out of the seven plagues, which we will see in the next chapter.

Chapter Sixteen
The Seven Bowls of the Seven Plagues

As we begin our study of Revelation 16, we see right away a repeat of the ten plagues brought by our Lord on Egypt in Exodus 7-10. These plagues preceded the time when Moses led the Israelites into the wilderness. Moses and his brother Aaron approached Pharaoh and demanded to let the people of Israel go and leave Egypt in order to celebrate a feast in the wilderness to honor God. Pharaoh refused to grant them permission.

When Moses and Aaron next approached Pharaoh, by the power of the Holy Spirit they were able to produce a miracle: Aaron threw down his staff and it turned into a snake. This seemed like magic to the Egyptians, so the court sorcerers Jannes and Jambres (2 Timothy 3:8) satanically duplicated this event.

But then, Aaron's snake swallowed up the court sorcerers' snake – a miraculous event which Jannes and Jambres could not do anything about. Following divine orders, Moses then told Pharaoh that his rod would work many miracles in the form of ten plagues that would come down on Egypt. They were a divine demonstration of God's power and displeasure with Pharaoh designed to persuade him to let His people go.

The seven seals and the seven trumpets in Revelation 8 and 11, and the seven bowls in Revelation 16 are three succeeding series of end-times judgments from God on this earth. The judgments get progressively worse and more devastating as the end times progress. They are all connected to one another. The seventh seal introduces the seven trumpet judgments, and the seventh trumpet introduces the seven bowl judgments.

263

You may ask: what is the significance of the seven bowls? As always, the answer is in the Bible. Let us review.

In Revelation 5 our Lord Jesus Christ is described as the Lamb of God who was slain on the cross. But now He is pictured holding a seven-sealed scroll and described as the Heir to King David's throne and the Lion of the tribe of Judah. He is about to bring His wrath on earth in the form of seven-seal judgments, which will begin at the half-way point of the seven-year tribulation.

In Revelation 7 in the midst of the seven seals judgment, Jesus preserves and seals 144,000 Jewish servants with His name, 12,000 from each tribe of Israel, to evangelize and bring the Jewish people to repentance and to a saving knowledge of our Lord Jesus Christ.

In Revelation 12 the seventh seal ushers the seven-trumpet judgments after a period of intermission when God sent his two witnesses to preach the Gospel and give people on earth one more chance to repent and accept Jesus Christ as their Savior.

Revelation 16:1

The apostle John hears a mighty voice from the Temple of God in heaven saying to the seven angels, "*Go your ways and pour out on the earth the seven bowls containing God's wrath.*" It is as if all the angels in heaven were already prepared and ready for this moment.

To understand what the seven bowls represent, we need to turn our Bible to Jeremiah 25:15-26: "*Then the LORD, the God of Israel, said to me, "Take from my hand this cup filled to the brim with my anger, and make all the nations to whom I send you drink from it. When they drink from it, they will stagger, crazed by the warfare I will send against them." So, I took the cup of anger from the LORD and made all the nations drink from it -- every nation the LORD sent me to.*

I went to Jerusalem and the other towns of Judah, and their kings and officials drank from the cup. From that day until this, they have been a desolate ruin, an object of horror, contempt, and cursing.

I went to Egypt and spoke to Pharaoh, his officials, his princes, and his people. They, too, drank from that terrible cup, along with all the foreigners living in that land. So did all the kings of the land of Uz and the kings of the Philistine cities of Ashkelon, Gaza, Ekron, and what remains of Ashdod.

Then I went to the nations of Edom, Moab, and Ammon, and the kings of Tyre and Sidon, and the kings of the regions across the sea. I went to Dedan, Tema, and Buz, and to the people who live in distant places. I went to the kings of Arabia, the kings of the nomadic tribes of the desert, and to the kings of Zimri, Elam, and Media.

And I went to the kings of the northern countries, far and near, one after the other -- all the kingdoms of the world. And finally, the king of Babylon himself drank from the cup of the LORD's anger".

In this passage the Prophet Jeremiah portrays the wrath of God coming down on Judah and surrounding pagan nations enemies of Israel as drinking from a cup filled with God's anger. In vs. 1, we see a parallel to that in the form of a greater judgment being poured out on earth from a bowl instead of a cup, and it answers the prayers of the saints standing under the altar in Revelation 6:9-11 who were martyred for their faith during the seven-year tribulation.

Revelation 16:2-14

The Apostle John describes what he sees as a series of sequential judgments that will come down on earth. These judgments parallel those that came down on Egypt in Exodus 7-10 as shown in the following table:

265

Exodus 9:8-12, soot from a furnace covered Egypt causing boils to break out on people and animals	Revelation 16:2, first bowl, malignant sores break out on everyone who has the mark of the beast
Exodus 7:17-18, the Lord instructed Moses to tell Aaron to point his staff toward the waters of Egypt and water turned into blood	Revelation 16:3-4, second and third bowls, the sea becomes like blood of a corpse and everything in the sea dies; the rivers and springs become blood
	Revelation 16:5, the angel praises the Lord because He sent these judgments.
	Revelation 16:6, the angel praises the Lord because He avenged the souls of all the martyrs
	Revelation 16:7, another angel in heaven praises the Lord saying Hi judgments are true and just
Exodus 9:13-35, a devastating hailstorm covered Egypt	Revelation 16:8-9, fourth bowl, the sun scorches everyone with fire
Exodus 10:21-29, all Egypt fell into darkness	Revelation 16:10, fifth bowl, the kingdom of the antichrist plunges into darkness
	Revelation 16:11, followers of the antichrist curse God for their pains and sores, but they do not repent of their evil deeds and turn to Him

Exodus 14, the Red Sea dried up to allow safe passage of the Israelites Joshua 3:7-17, The Lord also dried up the Jordan River so the Israelites could cross into the Promised Land	Revelation 16:12, sixth bowl, the Euphrates River dries up so the kings from the east could march westward
Exodus 8:1-4, God sent a plague of frogs across the entire land of Egypt	Revelation 16:13-14, three demonic spirits that look like frogs work satanic miracles and go out to all the rulers of the world to gather them for battle against the Lord in the valley of Armageddon
	Revelation 16:15, Jesus Christ announces He will come as unexpectedly as a thief, and blesses are all who are watching for Him
	Revelation 16:16, the demonic spirits gather all the rulers and their armies to the battle of Armageddon
Exodus 15, Moses and the Israelites celebrate their deliverance by singing and praising God John 19:28-30, the Roman soldiers soaked a sponge in sour wine, put it on a hyssop branch, and held it up to Jesus' lips while crucified. When Jesus had tasted it, he said, "It is finished!"	Revelation 16:17, seventh bowl, judgments complete. Angels celebrate in heaven. Jesus shouts "it is done (finished)" just as He said on the cross before he gave up His last breath

The Prophet Isaiah foretold about our Lord drying up the Euphrates River just like He did to the Red Sea to accomplish His plans in Isaiah 11:15: "*The LORD will make a dry path through the Red Sea. He will wave his hand over the Euphrates River, sending a mighty wind to divide it into seven streams that can easily be crossed*". And in Isaiah 11:27: "*When I speak to the rivers and say, 'Be dry!' they will be dry*".

It is important to note here after all these devastating judgments on the earth, you would think the followers of the antichrist who accepted his mark on their foreheads and right hands would repent and turn to God and ask for forgiveness of their sins, but instead, they refuse to repent, they grind their teeth in anguish and curse God for their pains and sores.

Revelation 16:15

I want to remind you during God's twenty-one judgments in Revelation we see evidence of God's mercy and an opportunity to turn to Him. We have seen that in the many parenthetical passages throughout this book. Here before the seventh bowl judgment, God gives a warning to the whole world for the last time to turn to Him followed by beatitude.

He says: "*Look, I will come as unexpectedly as a thief! Blessed are all who are watching for me, who keep their clothing ready so they will not have to walk around naked and ashamed*". In other words, there is a blessing awaiting those who refused the mark of the beast 666 and are ready for His appearance and watching for Him when He comes unexpectedly as a thief in the night.

The apostle Paul reminded us of Jesus' words and His second coming in 1 Thessalonians 5:2: "*For you know quite well that the day of the Lord's return will come unexpectedly, like a thief in the night*".

The apostle Peter also reminded us of Jesus words and His second coming in 2 Peter 3:10: "*But the day of the Lord will come as a thief in the night, in which the heavens will pass away with a great noise, and the elements will melt with fervent heat; both the earth and the works that are in it will be burned up"*.

Revelation 16:16

Here we see the one and only reference to Armageddon in the Bible. The word Armageddon comes from the Hebrew words Har and Megiddo, which mean the mountain or hill of Megiddo located in northern Israel. The valley of Armageddon, also known as the valley of Megiddo and the valley of Jezreel, lies beneath this mountain. It is the site where the kings of the East will march across the dry bed of the river Euphrates to join the antichrist and his army for final battle against God and His army of angels.

We will see in Revelation 19 in an awesome display of a miracle, glory and power, our Lord Jesus Christ speaks the Word, and his enemies will be defeated. He will not lift a literal sword to defeat His enemies. His sword is His Word (John 1:1; Ephesians 6:17; Revelation 19:19-21).

Revelation 16:17

In this verse, we see the seventh and final bowl judgment that will come down on the earth, which indicates God's completion of His judgments. This scripture parallels that of John 19:28-30: *"Jesus knew that everything was now finished, and to fulfill the Scriptures he said, "I am thirsty." A jar of sour wine was sitting there, so they soaked a sponge in it, put it on a hyssop branch, and held it up to his lips. When Jesus had tasted it, he said, "It is finished!" Then he bowed his head and gave up his spirit"*.

Revelation 16:18

Following the Lord's shout, we see in this passage thunder, lightning, and an earthquake greater than ever before in human history.

Revelation 16:19

Then we immediately see our Lord directing our attention to the complete destruction of the sinful and idolatrous city Babylon. It split into three sections. God remembered all of Babylon's sins, and he brought His fierce wrath on her.

Revelation 16:20-21

Right after the destruction of Babylon, we see cataclysmic events on earth never seen before: Cities destroyed all over the world, islands disappeared into the water; mountains leveled, terrible hailstorm; hailstones weighing a talent (seventy-five pounds; thirty-four kilograms) fall from the sky killing millions of people on earth. Again you would think the followers of the antichrist who accepted his mark on their foreheads and right hands would repent and turn to God and ask for forgiveness of their sins, but instead, they refuse to repent and they curse God because of the hailstorm.

Back in Revelation 14:8, we were given a preview of the downfall of the immoral city Babylon, and now in Revelation 16 it is mentioned again as the seat of evil, being split into three sections.

In the Old Testament, the Lord through his prophets Isaiah and Jeremiah prophesied about the destruction of Babylon:

Isaiah 13:19-22: *"Babylon, the most glorious of kingdoms, the flower of Chaldean culture, will be devastated like Sodom and Gomorrah when God destroyed them. Babylon will never rise again. Generation after generation will come and go, but the land will never again be lived in. Nomads will refuse to camp there, and shepherds will not allow their sheep to stay overnight.*

Wild animals of the desert will move into the ruined city. The houses will be haunted by howling creatures. Ostriches will live among the ruins, and wild goats will come there to dance. Hyenas will howl in

270

its fortresses, and jackals will make their dens in its palaces. Babylon's days are numbered; its time of destruction will soon arrive".

Jeremiah 50:35-40: *"The sword of destruction will strike the Babylonians," says the LORD. "It will strike the people of Babylon -- her princes and wise men, too. And when it strikes her wise counselors, they will become fools! When it strikes her mightiest warriors, panic will seize them! When it strikes her horses and chariots, her allies from other lands will become as weak as women.*

When it strikes her treasures, they all will be plundered. It will even strike her water supply, causing it to dry up. And why? Because the whole land is filled with idols, and the people are madly in love with them. "Soon this city of Babylon will be inhabited by ostriches and jackals. It will be a home for the wild animals of the desert. Never again will people live there; it will lie desolate forever. I will destroy it just as I destroyed Sodom and Gomorrah and their neighboring towns," says the LORD. "No one will live there anymore".

When Saddam Hussein rose to power in Iraq in 1979, he conceived a grandiose scheme to rebuild the ancient City of Babylon (http://en.wikipedia.org). He said that Babylon's great palaces and its legendary hanging gardens (one of the seven wonders of the ancient world) would rise from the dust.

Like powerful King Nebuchadnezzar who conquered Jerusalem 2,500 years before, Saddam Hussein ambition was to rule over the world's greatest empire. The boasting ambition of Saddam Hussein found expression in palaces full of gold and expensive architecture.

In 1983, Saddam Hussein's workers began reconstructing Babylon's most imposing building, the 600-room palace of king Nebuchadnezzar. Archaeologists were horrified. Many said that to rebuild on top of ancient artifacts does not preserve history but disfigures it.

271

The original bricks, which rise two or three feet from the ground, bear ancient inscriptions praising Nebuchadnezzar. Above these, Saddam Hussein's workers laid more than 60-million sand-colored bricks inscribed with the words, "In the era of Saddam Hussein, protector of Iraq, who rebuilt civilization and rebuilt Babylon".

I will discuss Babylon in more detail in the next two chapters Revelation 17 and 18.

Chapter Seventeen
The Scarlet Woman and the Scarlet Beast

Back in Revelation 14:8, the Apostle John heard another angel in heaven shouting *"Babylon that great city is fallen, because of her great sin and immorality"*. In Revelation 16:19, the Lord said this about Babylon: *"The great city of Babylon split into three pieces, and cities around the world fell into heaps of rubble. And so, God remembered all of Babylon's sins, and he made her drink the cup that was filled with the wine of his fierce wrath"*.

As we discussed in the previous chapter, the Lord through his Prophets Isaiah and Jeremiah prophesied about the destruction of Babylon in relation to the Babylonian Empire under the rule of King Nebuchadnezzar. Now we see Babylon revived symbolically in relation to future events yet to come. Revelation 17 focuses on the corrupt religious system of Babylon, and Revelation 18 focuses on the commercial aspect of Babylon.

The Lord said this city will never be inhabited again. So, when we see the name Babylon in this chapter, it can only mean one thing: A corrupt religious system within the revived Roman Empire established by the antichrist with its roots dating back to Nimrod and the Tower of Babel in Genesis 10-11. It will be booming with sin, immorality, corruption, and idolatry during the great tribulation. It will be the center of false prophets, witchcraft, idolatry and all the workings of Satan and his accomplices.

If you recall in Revelation 12:1-2, we saw a woman clothed with the sun wearing a crown of twelve stars on her head. This woman is a symbol of the nation of Israel. It represents God's faithful people in Israel waiting for their Messiah. Here in Revelation 17 we see an opposite picture: A harlot woman dressed in purple and scarlet clothing

273

and expensive jewelry sitting on a scarlet beast with seven heads and ten horns representing Babylon's corruption and immorality in the last days.

Revelation 17:1-2

The apostle John tells us one of the seven angels who had poured out the seven bowls comes over and speaks to him saying: *"Come with me,"*, *"and I will show you the judgment that is going to come on the great prostitute, who rules over many waters. The kings of the world have committed adultery with her, and the people who belong to this world have been made drunk by the wine of her immorality"*.

The first thing we learn about Babylon is it sits on many waters, which we are told in vs. 15, represents masses of people of every nation and language. Just like the vision John had in Revelation 13 about the antichrist rising out of the sea, here Babylon is described as sitting on many waters, just like New York City, London, Rome, or Paris.

It is described by our Lord as "Mystery Babylon, the Mother of Harlots and obscenities in the world". This is because Babylon is viewed by God as the root of all evil, false doctrines and false religions of the world. Its roots date back to ancient Babylon when men, in defiance of God, built the Tower of Babel, and our Lord dispersed them and gave them the many languages spoken in our world today.

What the Word of God is telling us here, Babylon, the corrupt religious-political system, one day will be the center of the empire of the antichrist in the last days. Satan has already set up his dark agenda for this world, and he will establish his throne in Babylon from which his right-hand man, the antichrist, will rule in the last days.

Revelation 17:3-4

The angel takes the apostle John in the spirit into the wilderness. There he shows him a woman sitting on a scarlet beast with seven heads and ten horns, and blasphemies against God were written all over it. The apostle John goes on to describe this woman as wearing purple and scarlet clothing and beautiful jewelry made of gold and precious gems and pearls. In her hand she holds a gold goblet full of obscenities.

Revelation 17:5-6

The apostle John notices something unusual about this woman: A mysterious name is written on her forehead: "Babylon the Great, Mother of All Prostitutes and Obscenities in the World". He says she was drunk with the blood of God's saints who were witnesses for Jesus. John is amazed and overwhelmed by what he sees. He sees Babylon as the center of idolatry, fornication, and immorality responsible for murdering Christ's followers during the great tribulation and bragging about it. This is the meaning of being drunk with the blood of the saints.

Revelation 17:7

The angel asks John: Why are you so amazed?" "I will tell you the mystery of this woman and of the beast with seven heads and ten horns on which she sits. The angel is about to explain to John the meaning of the vision that he sees.

Revelation 17:8

The scripture tells us here the beast that John sees, the antichrist, was alive but now he is dead. Then he will come up out of the bottomless pit and will go to eternal destruction.

Back in Revelation 11:7 we are told the antichrist will originate his journey from the underworld, the abyss, or the bottomless pit: *"When they (the two witnesses) complete their testimony, the beast that comes up out of the bottomless pit will declare war against them, and he will conquer them and kill them*". In other words, he will emerge on the world scene as a demonic spirit who will indwell in a human body.

In Revelation 13:3, the Apostle John witnessed a satanic miracle: the antichrist is shot in the head and seems wounded beyond recovery. He appears to be dead, but in an attempt to counterfeit the resurrection of our Lord Jesus Christ, he satanically stages his resurrection, and he appears to come back to life from the dead. As a result, the whole world marvels at this satanic miracle and gives allegiance to the antichrist. This is the meaning of the antichrist, was alive but now he is dead.

Revelation 17:9-10

The Apostle John is now given an explanation by the angel about the antichrist. Just like we are told in Revelation 13:18 that wisdom is needed to understand the meaning of the mark of the beast 666, here the angel tells the apostle John that wisdom is needed again to help him understand what he sees in his vision.

He tells John: The seven heads of the beast represent seven hills, or seven mountains depending on the Bible translation, where the woman rules. They also represent seven kings, five have already fallen, the sixth now reigns, and the seventh is yet to come, but his reign will be brief.

I want you to know there is disagreement among Bible prophecy teachers about these seven kings. Some say the seven hills or mountains represent seven Roman Emperors, five of which had fallen, one reigned during the time of the apostle John, and a future Roman Emperor yet to come.

The first five kings are: (1) Pharaoh (Egypt), (2) Sennacherib (Assyria), (3) Nebuchadnezzar (Babylon), (4) Cyrus the Great (Medo Persia), and (5) Alexander the Great (Greece). The sixth which reigned during the time the apostle John was Emperor Domitian (Rome). The seventh, which is yet to come but his reign will be brief, is the antichrist. He will rule over the ten-nation confederacy of the revived Roman Empire represented by the ten toes of the colossal statue in Daniel 2. I personally agree with this view. Rome is the only European city that sits on seven hills. The names of these hills are: (1) Aventine, (2) Caelian, (3) Capitoline, (4) Esquiline, (5) Palatine, (6) Quirinal, and (7) Viminal.

Revelation 17:11

The scripture tells us the beast that was, and is not, is himself also the eighth, and is of the seven, and is going to perdition. The angel tells the apostle John in this passage there is an eighth king who is yet to come on the scene. He is described as the seventh king that was in power when he was alive, but then he died, but now he is the eighth king. So, who is king number eight?

The eighth king is king number seven, the antichrist, resurrected after he was shot and appeared to be dead! By satanic deception, he was resurrected to counterfeit the resurrection of our Lord Jesus Christ. But soon afterwards he goes to destruction.

From that point on, the antichrist becomes more than just a human being. He becomes a supernatural being in the eyes of his followers, as he comes back to life from the dead after being shot. That is what the Apostle John is telling us; the antichrist becomes the eighth king. Once he is in power, he will command the worship of the masses of people on earth.

Revelation 17:12-14

The scripture tells us here the ten horns of the scarlet beast are ten kings who have not yet risen to power. They will be appointed to their kingdoms for a moment (one hour, KJV) to reign with the beast under his authority. Together they will wage war against our Lord Jesus

Christ, but our Lord will defeat them at the battle of Armageddon by the breath of His mouth.

The Apostle John describes the beast with seven heads and ten horns in the same manner the prophet Daniel describes him as the fourth beast in Daniel 7 as having ten horns, which are ten kings which have not yet risen to power.

What we are given in this scripture is an overall picture of what it is going to be like in the great tribulation: The antichrist will be ruling over the political system. He will be working with his right-hand man the false prophet who will be ruling over the false religious system. Together, they will rule over a coalition of ten kings, which will govern the entire earth which was once controlled by Rome.

Once they are in control, the antichrist will immediately destroy three of them, most likely because they are in opposition to his plans. The remaining seven will wage war against the Jewish people and appear to be defeating them until the time our Lord Jesus Christ comes (Revelation 19 and Zechariah 14), and He defeats his armies and the armies from the East at the battle of Armageddon.

Today we are seeing among the twenty-seven nations of the European Union the beginning stages of this coalition that can easily fulfill this prophecy of ten kings who will be able to rule with the antichrist and false prophet during the last days, and literally reign all over the world.

Revelation 17:15

In this passage, the angel tells the apostle John *"The waters where the prostitute is ruling represent masses of people of every nation and language"*. The waters as I discussed in Revelation 1-2 represent masses of people of every nation and language from all the people of the world. In other words, all the nations of the world who have been deceived by Satan (Revelation 12:9) into worshipping the antichrist as a god are represented here.

Revelation 17:16-17

Here we see a dramatic turn of events. The scripture says in the last days, the antichrist will turn against the harlot woman, the false religious system already in place, strip her naked to the flesh and burn her remains with fire. Up to this point, the antichrist teamed up with this false religious system, because it was useful to him to gain political advantage. Now that he is in power, he turns against the religious system and destroys it.

The scripture tells us in vs. 17 this will all take place so that the Word of God may be fulfilled. There are two key passages of scripture in the Old Testament that clearly tell us that our God is in control over the world events. He judges; He decides who will rise and who will fall; He appoints kings and removes kings to accomplish His purposes.

The first passage is in Psalm 75:2-8: *"At the time I have planned, I will bring justice against the wicked. When the earthquakes and its people live in turmoil, I am the one who keeps its foundations firm. I warned the proud, 'Stop your boasting!' I told the wicked, 'Don't raise your fists! Don't lift your fists in defiance at the heavens or speak with rebellious arrogance.'"*

For no one on earth -- from east or west, or even from the wilderness -- can raise another person up. It is God alone who judges; he decides who will rise and who will fall. For the LORD holds a cup in his hand; it is full of foaming wine mixed with spices. He pours the wine out in judgment, and all the wicked must drink it, draining it to the dregs".

The second passage in Daniel 2:19-22: *"That night the secret was revealed to Daniel in a vision. Then Daniel praised the God of heaven. He said, "Praise the name of God forever and ever, for he has all wisdom and power. He controls the course of world events; he removes kings and sets up other kings. He gives wisdom to the wise and knowledge to the scholars. He reveals deep and mysterious things and knows what lies hidden in darkness, though he is surrounded by light".*

To summarize the events in this chapter, in the second half of the seven-year tribulation period, during the great tribulation, the antichrist is going to try to marry his corrupt political system and the false religious system in place on this earth to gain control, power and wealth. This is how we get the terms "One World Religion" and "One World Government".

The antichrist will use Rome to gain political advantage. Then after he makes a peace treaty with the Jewish people, he will use Jerusalem to gain religious advantage, wealth, and popularity. His evil influence will stretch throughout the whole world. He will lead a ten-king confederacy that will reign over all the earth. He will subdue three of these kings and will rule over the remaining seven.

Revelation 17:18

You may be asking yourself what is the significance of the colors of this false religious system that is represented by a harlot wearing purple and scarlet clothing and dressed up with beautiful gold jewelry indicating its great wealth? The answer is given to us in vs. 18: *"And this woman you saw in your vision represents the great city that rules over the kings of the earth".* The woman is the false religious system, and the great city is Rome.

The Apostle John is talking about Rome. He sees in amazement a vast corrupt and wealthy religious system that is centered in Rome reaching out to the whole world to gain more power. In vs. 9 the Apostle John tells us this corrupt and wealthy religious system where the woman rules, is centered on seven hills and that center is Rome.

Notice the colors of the clothes this woman is wearing: Purple and red. These colors are symbolic of the purple and red robes, belts and hats worn by Catholic bishops, archbishops, and cardinals in Vatican City.

If you have been following the news from around the world, you would have heard about the sexual immorality and corruption that surfaced in the Catholic church among the laity and among the Vatican City staff in the past few years.

The Italian media reported that Pope Benedict XVI resigned on February 28, 2013, after receiving the results of an internal investigation, delivered in a three-hundred-page document that exposed blackmail, corruption, and fornication at the Vatican.

In February 2019 Pope Francis held a four-day meeting on the protection of minors in the church in Vatican City to discuss preventing sexual abuse by Catholic clergy.

If you visited Rome and Vatican City, which my wife and I have, you would immediately notice the staggering wealth in the various churches such as St Peter's Basilica and the Vatican government buildings. Just like the Roman Emperors who ruled from Rome for over four hundred years, the Pope today governs from Rome over the Catholic church with his cardinals, archbishops, bishops, clergy, and laity. In the same manner the antichrist and false prophet will rule from Rome in the last days.

To understand what the Word of God is telling us here, we must look back in the Old Testament to see how God brought His wrath on the Israelites who fell into idolatry and worshipped pagan gods by disobeying His First and Second Commandments given to us in Exodus 20. In the last days, we will see this happening all over again but on a much larger scale.

Chapter Eighteen
The Fall of Babylon

In the previous chapter we were introduced to the corrupt religious system of Babylon. In this chapter, we are introduced to commercial Babylon as a center of world trade.

Revelation 18:1-3

The Apostle John begins with a vision of another angel coming down from heaven with great authority, and it lit up the sky with its splendor as he shouted, *"Babylon is fallen—that great city is fallen"*!

We should not be surprised about the fall of Babylon because the Lord has already warned us about this sudden ending of Babylon in the following passages of scripture:

-Isaiah 13:19-22
-Isaiah 21:9
-Jeremiah 50:35-40
-Jeremiah 51:54-55
-Revelation 14:8
-Revelation 16:19

But before Babylon can be destroyed, it must be rebuilt and prosper as a center of commerce. In Revelation 16 we discussed Saddam Hussein's attempt to rebuild Babylon. The only difference here in this chapter is there is a specific mention of that city, which is already rebuilt and has prospered. The bible tells us in vs. 2-3 it is full of adultery, immorality, wealth and has become the hideout of evil and demonic spirits, but it will be short-lived as its destruction is near.

I want to take a few minutes here to compare the two Babylons (religious and commercial) described in Revelation 17 and 18, because there are significant differences between the two of them as revealed to the Apostle John by the angel of our Lord Jesus Christ:

Revelation 17	Revelation 18
Religious Babylon is called **"Mystery Babylon"**	Commercial Babylon is called **"Babylon the Great"**
Religious Babylon is presented as the mother of all harlots	Commercial Babylon is portrayed as a great city which will be destroyed forever
Religious Babylon is situated on seven hills	Commercial Babylon is visible from the sea
Religious Babylon is destroyed by the antichrist and his coalition of ten kings	Commercial Babylon is destroyed by God
When religious Babylon is destroyed, the kings of the earth rejoice	When commercial Babylon is destroyed, the kings, ship owners and merchants of the earth lament for her

The Lord spoke through the Prophet Zechariah in Zechariah 5:5-11 about the sin, wickedness and immorality that will be rampant in Babylon in the last days: *"Then the angel who was talking with me came forward and said, "Look up! Something is appearing in the sky." "What is it?" I asked. He replied, "It is a basket for measuring grain, and it is filled with the sins of everyone throughout the land." When the heavy lead cover was lifted off the basket, there was a woman sitting inside it.*

The angel said, "The woman's name is Wickedness," and he pushed her back into the basket and closed the heavy lid again. Then I looked up and saw two women flying toward us, with wings gliding on the wind. Their wings were like those of a stork, and they picked up the basket and flew with it into the sky. "Where are they taking the basket?" I asked the angel. He replied, "To the land of Babylonia, where they will build a temple for the basket. And when the temple is ready, they will set the basket there on its pedestal".

The scripture tells us here a basket is typically used in those days for measuring grain, which is a symbol of commerce and trade, with a wicked woman sitting inside it, symbolizing corruption and greed. This is the same harlot woman who sits on many waters mentioned in Revelation 17. That woman is now being transported in a basket by two angels to the Land of Babylonia (Shinar in Hebrew) located in the old region of Mesopotamia, the country of Iraq in the Middle East.

What this passage is telling us is this: In the last days there will be a shift of the center of commerce and economic wealth in the world to the nation of Iraq in the Middle East, a picture of a world that is dependent on the wealth in that region which includes a worldwide currency, gold, silver, precious stones, and most likely Middle Eastern oil. You may ask how this could happen? The answer is look what is happening in our debt-ridden country today.

With over twenty-two trillion dollars in debt in 2019, America has overspent to save its social security system, Medicare and Medicaid programs, housing market, financial institutions, and automobile manufacturers, and in the process, our government has crippled the future of our children and grandchildren, our future generation, with its massive build-up of national debt.

Yet at the same time, across the Pacific Ocean, China has seen decades of economic growth that has driven the country to surpass Germany and Japan to become the second-largest economy in the world, trailing only the United States, but forecast to surpass it soon. A similar shift in wealth will take place in the last days, but it will be centered in Babylon.

When Nimrod and his pagan followers built the Tower of Babel that reached high in the sky back in Genesis 11, they were essentially declaring we are going to do it on our own apart from God, with our own strength and with our own wisdom. God became angry with them, dispersed them, and confused their languages. In the last days, there will be a reversal of the dispersion that took place in Genesis 11.

When commercial Babylon is rebuilt and the merchants of the world converge back to it, it will be called "Babylon the Great". The many false religions of the world will also regather at Babylon.

Today the Babylonian system is still alive and well all over the world. People still think they can go it alone apart from God. They are full of pride and arrogance. Look around in our country, in Europe, and in the Middle Eastern Muslim nations of the world from Dubai in the Middle East to Malaysia and Taiwan in the Far East, skyscrapers and towers are built as high in the sky as the eye can see.

The Bible gives us a great example of that Babylonian pride, boasting and arrogance in the life of king Nebuchadnezzar in Daniel 4:28-34: *"But all these things did happen to King Nebuchadnezzar. Twelve months later, he was taking a walk on the flat roof of the royal palace in Babylon. As he looked out across the city, he said, 'Just look at this great city of Babylon! I, by my own mighty power, have built this beautiful city as my royal residence and as an expression of my royal splendor.' "*

While he was still speaking these words, a voice called down from heaven, 'O King Nebuchadnezzar, this message is for you! You are no longer ruler of this kingdom. You will be driven from human society. You will live in the fields with the wild animals, and you will eat grass like a cow. Seven periods of time (seven years) will pass while you live this way, until you learn that the Most High rules over the kingdoms of the world and gives them to anyone he chooses.' "

That very same hour the prophecy was fulfilled, and Nebuchadnezzar was driven from human society. He ate grass like a cow, and he was drenched with the dew of heaven. He lived this way until his hair was as long as eagles' feathers and his nails were like birds' claws. "After this time had passed, I, Nebuchadnezzar, looked up to heaven. My sanity returned, and I praised and worshiped the Most High and honored the one who lives forever. His rule is everlasting, and his kingdom is eternal".

To summarize, the Babylonian doctrine is synonymous with alienation from our One and only true God, YHWH, the Great I Am. It started with the construction of the Tower of Babel and continued with the descendants of Noah's son Ham, Abraham's son Ishmael and Jacob's son Esau.

It flourished under the reign of king Nebuchadnezzar and continues in our world today with the false religions of the Middle Eastern and Asian countries such as Islam, Hinduism, Taoism, Buddhism and Confucianism, the political correctness in the United States and Europe by allowing removal of God's name from government buildings and schools, infiltration of same-sex marriage and false religions into their societies.

Revelation 18:4-6

Our Lord Jesus Christ gives a warning to his followers who are going through the great tribulation saying: "Do not take part of Babylon's sins, or you will be punished with her" as her judgment is near. God's people are the tribulation saints who accepted Christ as their savior who might be tempted by the Babylonian system.

God is calling them to separate themselves from it, just like he did in the Old Testament when the Israelites, under Joshua's leadership, took over the Promised Land from the Hittites, the Amorites, the Canaanites, the Perizzites, the Hivites and the Jebusites who lived in that region. He warned the Israelites not to marry their pagan women or worship their man-made idols.

Revelation 18:7-8

Here we see a repeat of what king Nebuchadnezzar did when he boasted about his city from the top of his palace. Apparently the rulers of Babylon in the last days will boast about their city, wealth, luxury and pleasure, but the Bible tells us in vs.8 our Lord will send His wrath on Babylon in the form of three plagues, which will destroy her in a single day: Death, famine and mourning, and she will be completely consumed by fire, just like He did to Sodom and Gomorrah.

Revelation 18:9-10

Here the scripture tells us the kings and rulers of the world, the ship owners who took part in her immoral acts and enjoyed her great wealth and luxury, will mourn and weep for Babylon as they see the smoke rising from her charred remains. They will cry out in desperation "How terrible, how terrible for you, O Babylon, you great city! In a single moment God's judgment came on you".

Revelation 18:11-17

The merchants of the world cannot believe what they are seeing. They stand in amazement and shock. They will weep and mourn for Babylon because all their wealth went up in smoke. They cannot find one person left to buy their goods.

The Bible tells us Babylon bought great quantities of gold, silver, jewels, pearls; fine linen, purple, silk, scarlet cloth; spices made of fragrant wood, ivory goods, objects made of expensive wood; bronze, iron, and marble, cinnamon, spice, incense, myrrh, frankincense, wine, olive oil, fine flour, wheat, cattle, sheep, horses, wagons, and even human slaves, which was common in the ancient world and was practiced in ancient Egypt, Greece, and Rome.

The Bible tells us in vs.15-17 the merchants who became wealthy by selling her these things will stand at a distance, terrified by

288

what they see. They will weep and cry out, "How terrible, how terrible for that great city! She was clothed in finest purple and scarlet linens, decked out with gold and precious stones and pearls! In a single moment all the wealth of Babylon is gone!"

Revelation 18:18-19

Here we are told the captains of the merchant ships and ship owners who transported Babylon's great wealth on the seas and became wealthy, their passengers, sailors and crews will all stand at a distance in disbelief. They will cry out as they watch the smoke ascend from Babylon, and they will say, "Where is there another city as great as this? In a single moment it is all gone." They will weep and throw dust on their heads to show their grief, because they lost all their wealth which they invested in Babylon. And they will cry out, "How terrible, how terrible for that great city!

Revelation 18:20

In this passage of scripture, the voice from heaven says: *"Rejoice over her fate, O heaven and people of God and apostles and prophets! For at last God has judged her for your sakes"*.

Revelation 18:21-22

In this passage of scripture, the apostle John sees a mighty angel picking up a boulder as large as a great millstone, and he threw it into the ocean carrying on God's commands that the great city of Babylon will be thrown down as violently as the boulder, and it will disappear forever fulfilling Isaiah 13 and Jeremiah 50-51 prophecies.

Revelation 18:23

We are told in this verse Babylon will fall and will be destroyed because her merchants used deception and sorcery to achieve their prosperity.

Revelation 18:24

In vs. 24 the Lord tells us Babylon must fall because she was the one who slaughtered God's chosen people, the Jews. This fulfills Jeremiah 51:49 prophecy: "*As Babylon has caused the slain of Israel to fall, so at Babylon the slain of all the earth shall fall.*"

Here we see the Lord fulfilling His promise in avenging the blood of the saints by answering their prayers in Revelation 6:10 when they called out to Him and said: "*O Sovereign Lord, holy and true, how long will it be before you judge the people who belong to this world for what they have done to us? When will you avenge our blood against these people?*"

In closing, I personally believe the efforts and sacrifices of our U.S. and Allies troops in *Operation Desert Storm in 1991* and *Operation Iraqi Freedom* in 2003 have set the stage for the fulfillment of the prophecy of rebuilding and destruction of Babylon in Revelation 17-18.

Chapter Nineteen
Songs of Victory in Heaven and the Rider on the White Horse

Revelation 19 is a continuation of Revelation 17 and 18 as it opens with "after this or after these things" depending on the Bible translation. What happens after the destruction of Babylon?

Songs of Victory in Heaven

Revelation 19:1-2

The Apostle John says after the destruction of false religious and political systems of commercial Babylon, he hears the sound of a vast crowd in heaven praising our Lord shouting *"Hallelujah" and saying "salvation is from our God. Glory and power belong to him alone. His judgments are just and true. He has punished the great harlot who corrupted the earth with her immorality, and He has avenged the murder of his servants"*. He has fulfilled His promise by answering the prayers of the saints in Revelation 6:10. This brings up a question. Who is represented in this vast crowd?

This vast crowd in heaven is composed of all those who remained faithful to God throughout the Old and New Testaments plus the saints martyred during the seven-year tribulation. They were martyred for their faith in Jesus Christ because they refused to accept the mark of the beast 666. They are praising our Lord because He has punished Babylon, the great harlot who corrupted the earth with her immorality, and He has avenged the murder of his servants."

Revelation 19:3

Here we see this vast crowd rejoicing and praising God because the smoke from the destruction of Babylon can be seen rising in the sky, and it is visible from heaven. This fulfilled Isaiah's prophecy about the destruction of Babylon in Isaiah 13:19-20: *"Babylon, the most glorious of kingdoms, the flower of Chaldean pride, will be devastated like Sodom and Gomorrah when God destroyed them. Babylon will never be inhabited again. It will remain empty for generation after generation"*.

Revelation 19:4

Here the twenty-four elders sitting around the throne of God and the four living beings we saw in Revelation 4 fall and worship God Who is sitting on His throne. They cry out "Amen, Hallelujah". In Hebrew, an Alleluia chorus means "Praise YHWH", "Praise Jehovah" or "Praise the Lord."

Revelation 19:5

The voice that came from the throne of God is an angel encouraging the angelic host to continue praising our Lord. Here we see the fulfillment of the prophecy in Revelation 11:16-18: *"And the twenty-four elders sitting on their thrones before God fell on their faces and worshiped him. And they said, "We give thanks to you, Lord God Almighty, the one who is and who always was, for now you have assumed your great power and have begun to reign. The nations were angry with you, but now the time of your wrath has come. It is time to judge the dead and reward your servants. You will reward your prophets and your holy people (saints), all who fear your name, from the least to the greatest. And you will destroy all who have caused destruction on the earth"*.

Revelation 19:6

Here, we see a repeat of what the Old Testament prophets saw and heard when God communicated directly with them. They described these events as roars of ocean waves, clouds and crash of loud thunder and fire by night. The vast crowd continues to praise God in heaven saying: *"Praise the Lord! For the Lord our God, the Almighty, reigns"*.

Revelation 19:7-8

In this verse we see the fulfillment of Psalm 118:24 *"This is the day the Lord has made, let us rejoice and be glad in it"*. The day is in reference to the wedding feast (marriage supper) of the Lamb. The bride of Christ, which includes all the saints who put their trust and faith in Jesus Christ, has prepared herself for this special moment talked about throughout the Bible: The wedding feast of Jesus Christ!

I want to take a few minutes to discuss four passages in the scripture where our Lord gives us a preview of this wedding feast:

Genesis 43:19-34. Joseph, displaying the character of Jesus Christ, forgave his eleven brothers who humiliated him and threw him into a pit then sold him into slavery to Ishmaelite traders. Joseph afterwards invited his brothers to Egypt to have a feast with him before he revealed his identity to them, and then told them the famous words in Genesis 50:20: *"God turned into good what you meant for evil. He brought me to the high position I have today so I could save the lives of many people"*.

Matthew 8:5-12. A Roman officer demonstrates his amazing faith by telling Jesus:
"Lord, my young servant lies in bed, paralyzed and in terrible pain". Jesus said, *"I will come and heal him"*. But the officer said, *"Lord, I am not worthy to have you come into my home. Just say the word from where you are, and my servant will be healed"*.

When Jesus heard this, he was amazed. Turning to those who were following him, he said, "I tell you the truth, I haven't seen faith like this in all Israel! And I tell you this, that many Gentiles will come from all over the world—from east and west—and sit down with Abraham, Isaac, and Jacob at **the feast in the Kingdom of Heaven**".

Matthew 22:1-14. Jesus tells the parable of the wedding feast. In this passage there are two messages for us:
(1) In the Jewish culture, two invitations were expected when banquets were given at a wedding, which often lasts a full week. The first invitation asked the guests to attend. The second invitation announced that all was ready. In this parable the King is our Lord Jesus Christ who invited his guests three times, and each time they rejected His invitation. God sends us invitations again and again through many people to join Him at His banquet, but sadly many have rejected His invitation.

(2) In the Jewish culture, it was customary for wedding guests to be given wedding clothes to wear to the banquet. Refusal to wear these clothes would be an insult to the host, implying he did not want to take part of the wedding celebration.

The wedding clothes picture the righteousness needed to enter God's Kingdom pure and sin free. The application to our life is Christ has provided these clothes of righteousness to every believer by shedding His blood for us on the cross. Each person must choose to put them on in order to enter the Kingdom of God.

This brings up a question: Where has the church been during the seven-year tribulation which I covered in Revelation 6 through 18? The church was not mentioned one time in these chapters. The answer is in Heaven! You see, the church was raptured in Revelation 4:1 and has not been mentioned again until this point in time for preparation for the wedding feast of the Lamb.

Revelation 19:9

In this verse we see the fourth beatitude in Revelation: "*And the angel said, "Write this: Blessed are those who are invited to the wedding feast of the Lamb." And he added, "These are true words that come from God*".

Revelation 19:10

The Apostle John is overwhelmed by this prophetic event. He falls on his knees and begins to worship the angel giving him the prophetic message. So, the angel tells him, do not worship me, I am a servant of God just like you. Worship God.

Then the angel gives John a particularly important message. He tells him "*For the testimony of Jesus is the spirit of prophecy*". In other words, the essence of Bible prophecy is to give a clear testimony about our Lord Jesus Christ. I have memorized this verse to remind me what the book of Revelation is all about.

Revelation 19:11

The Rider on the White Horse

In this passage, the vision of the apostle John shifts again. He sees the door of heaven open for the second time. If you recall, the first time the door of heaven opened was in Revelation 4:1. Here he sees our Lord Jesus Christ, not riding on a donkey like He did on Palm Sunday down the streets of Jerusalem, but as a warrior and a King riding on a white horse. His name is Faithful and True. He is ready to judge the world and conquer Satan's forces of evil.

This is the glorious event we have been waiting for since Revelation 4 when the church was raptured into heaven. It is the moment when our Lord Jesus Christ returns with His angels and with His saints to reclaim the earth for Himself. This event is called "The

Revelation of Jesus Christ" among Bible prophecy teachers because it is the moment the Lord reveals himself to the inhabitants of earth.

There are seven passages in the Bible which portray the second coming of our Lord Jesus Christ to earth. Let us examine them one by one:

Zechariah 14:1-4: "*Watch, for the day of the LORD is coming when your possessions will be plundered right in front of you! On that day I will gather all the nations to fight against Jerusalem. The city will be taken, the houses plundered, and the women raped. Half the population will be taken away into captivity, and half will be left among the ruins of the city. Then the LORD will go out to fight against those nations, as he has fought in times past. On that day his feet will stand on the Mount of Olives, which faces Jerusalem on the east. And the Mount of Olives will split apart, making a wide valley running from east to west, for half the mountain will move toward the north and half toward the south*".

Daniel 7:13-14: "*As my vision continued that night, I saw someone who looked like a man coming with the clouds of heaven. He approached the Ancient One and was led into his presence. He was given authority, honor, and royal power over all the nations of the world, so that people of every race and nation and language would obey him. His rule is eternal -- it will never end. His kingdom will never be destroyed*".

Matthew 24:30-31: "*And then at last, the sign of the coming of the Son of Man will appear in the heavens, and there will be deep mourning among all the nations of the earth. And they will see the Son of Man arrive on the clouds of heaven with power and great glory. And he will send forth his angels with the sound of a mighty trumpet blast, and they will gather together his chosen ones from the farthest ends of the earth and heaven*".

<u>2 Peter 3:9-10:</u> *"The Lord isn't really being slow about his promise to return, as some people think. No, he is being patient for your sake. He does not want anyone to perish, so he is giving more time for everyone to repent. But the day of the Lord will come as unexpectedly as a thief. Then the heavens will pass away with a terrible noise, and everything in them will disappear in fire, and the earth and everything on it will be exposed to judgment".*

<u>Jude14-15</u>: *"Now Enoch, the seventh from Adam, prophesied about these men also, saying, "Behold, the Lord comes with ten thousands of His saints, to execute judgment on all, to convict all who are ungodly among them of all their ungodly deeds which they have committed in an ungodly way, and of all the harsh things which ungodly sinners have spoken against Him".*

<u>Revelation 11:15-18</u>: *"Then the seventh angel blew his trumpet, and there were loud voices shouting in heaven: "The whole world has now become the Kingdom of our Lord and of his Christ, and he will reign forever and ever." And the twenty-four elders sitting on their thrones before God fell on their faces and worshiped him. And they said, "We give thanks to you, Lord God Almighty, the one who is and who always was, for now you have assumed your great power and have begun to reign.*

The nations were angry with you, but now the time of your wrath has come. It is time to judge the dead and reward your servants. You will reward your prophets and your holy people, all who fear your name, from the least to the greatest. And you will destroy all who have caused destruction on the earth".

<u>Revelation 19:11-16</u>: *"Then I saw heaven opened, and a white horse was standing there. And the one sitting on the horse was named Faithful and True. For He judges fairly and then goes to war. His eyes were bright like flames of fire, and on his head were many crowns. A name was written on him, and only he knew what it meant.*

He was clothed with a robe dipped in blood, and his title was the Word of God. The armies of heaven, dressed in pure white linen, followed him on white horses. From his mouth came a sharp sword, and with it he struck down the nations. He ruled them with an iron rod, and he trod the winepress of the fierce wrath of almighty God. On his robe and thigh was written this title: King of kings and Lord of lords ".

Jesus came to earth the first time as the Lamb of God ready to be sacrificed on the cross for our sins, and through Him and Him only he brought forgiveness of our sins as foretold by John the Baptist in John 1:29: *"The next day John saw Jesus coming toward him and said, "Look! There is the Lamb of God who takes away the sin of the world!"*

When Christ rose from the dead on the third day and ascended to heaven, He gave us the opportunity to receive eternal life. But someday He will return as the Lion of the tribe of Judah, as King of kings and Lord of lords to execute judgment against His enemies and the enemies of Israel at the battle of Armageddon. The saints and the angels in heaven will accompany our Lord Jesus Christ on white horses to witness His power and glory, as he defeats the evil forces of the antichrist and all the nations of the world who came to fight against Jerusalem.

Revelation 19:12-13

The apostle John goes on to describe our Lord Jesus Christ in His glory. He says: *"His eyes were like flames of fire, and on his head were many crowns. A name was written on him that no one understood except himself. He wore a robe dipped in blood, and his title was the Word of God".*

If you recall from Revelation 1:13-16 Jesus appeared to the apostle John standing among the seven churches in Asia Minor. John described Him as follows: He was clothed with a garment going down to His feet and a golden sash around His chest. His head and hair are white like wool, as white as snow. His eyes are like flames of fire.

John sees Jesus holding seven stars in His right hand, and His feet look like highly polished brass from a furnace. His voice thundered like mighty ocean waves. Jesus' face shines like the sun in its brilliance.

In Daniel 10:5-6, the prophet Daniel had a similar vision of our Lord Jesus Christ. He describes Him as follows: "*I looked up and saw a man dressed in linen clothing, with a belt of pure gold around his waist. His body looked like a precious gem. His face flashed like lightning, and his eyes flamed like torches. His arms and feet shone like polished bronze, and his voice roared like a vast multitude of people*".

John 1:1-2 tells us: "*In the beginning was the Word, and the Word was with God, and the Word was God. 2 He was in the beginning with God*". This is the title that John sees in Revelation 19:13. He is telling us the Word in the Bible is another title for our Lord Jesus Christ.

In vs.13, we are told Jesus was clothed with a robe dipped in blood. Why is the Lord's garment dipped in blood before the battle of Armageddon? The answer is in Isaiah 63:1-6: "*Who is this who comes from Edom, from the city of Bozrah, with his clothing stained red? Who is this in royal robes, marching in his great strength? "It is I, the Lord, announcing your salvation! It is I, the Lord, who has the power to save!"* **Why are your clothes so red, as if you have been treading out grapes**?

"*I have been treading the winepress alone; no one was there to help me. In my anger I have trampled my enemies as if they were grapes. In my fury I have trampled my foes.* **Their blood has stained my clothes.** *For the time has come for me to avenge my people*".

What Jesus is saying in this passage, His clothes are stained by the blood of His enemies in the capital city of Edom: Bozrah, whom He defeated by Himself without anyone helping Him. By doing so, He will save the Jewish people who fled to Petra seeking shelter there from the persecution of the antichrist during the seven-year tribulation.

You may ask why Bozrah and Edom? Because it is the land where Esau settled after he separated from his brother Jacob, and the Edomites would not allow the Israelites safe passage through their land on their way to the Promised Land. In fact, the Moabites and Edomites were enemies of Israel. They were allies of the Assyrian invaders (Psalm 83:6), and they attacked Judah in the days of king Ahaz (2 Chronicles 28:17) and carried away captives.

At His second coming, Jesus will first go to Bozrah to bring judgment on the Edomites, before he goes on to defeat the armies of His enemies at the battle of Armageddon.

Isaiah's prophecy is confirmed by the prophet Jeremiah in Jeremiah 49:22: "Behold, He shall come up and fly like the eagle, and spread His wings over Bozrah; the heart of the mighty men of Edom in that day shall be like the heart of a woman in birth pangs". In other words, before Jesus appears at the battle of Armageddon, He will spread His wings over Bozrah like an eagle swooping down on his prey.

Revelation 19:14

The apostle John is saying here the armies of heaven, who are the angels dressed in white linen, followed him on white horses. In Jude14-15 we are also told the saints, that's you and I, will accompany the angels as well to witness the mighty power of the Lord at the battle of Armageddon: "*Now Enoch, the seventh from Adam, prophesied about these men also, saying, "Behold, the Lord comes with ten thousands of His saints, to execute judgment on all*".

We have already seen in Revelation 17:14 the promise that His called, chosen, and faithful followers, that's you and I and all the saints that preceded us, will accompany him at His second coming. This describes the church saints returning with the armies of angels when the Lord appears in glory.

300

Revelation 19:15

John continues to describe our Lord Jesus Christ by saying: *"From his mouth came a sharp sword to strike down the nations. He will rule them with an iron rod. He will release the fierce wrath of God, the Almighty, like juice flowing from a winepress"*.

How will our Lord defeat His enemy nations? According to this verse, there will be no hand-to-hand combat with the sword. The sword here is in reference to the Word of God. Jesus will speak the Word just as He did many times in the Old Testament, and His Word will defeat His enemies by causing earthquakes, landslides, floods, and confusion among them. During the Millennium Kingdom He will rule the nations with a rod of iron meaning with discipline, authority, and justice.

Hebrews 4:12 says: *"For the word of God is living and powerful, and sharper than any two-edged sword, piercing even to the division of soul and spirit, and of joints and marrow, and is a discerner of the thoughts and intents of the heart"*.

Jesus will order Michael the archangel and His angels to rule His enemies with a rod of iron and to defeat the antichrist and the false prophet. The antichrist and the false prophet will be eternally cast into the Lake of Fire with Satan, and the armies of the kings of the earth will be destroyed with their flesh and bodies eaten by vultures.

Revelation 19:16

John continues to describe our Lord at His second coming by saying *"On his robe at his thigh was written this title: King of all kings and Lord of all lords"*. In other words, the whole world will know who He is, and they will recognize Him as King of kings and Lord of lords.

Revelation 19:17-18

Then John sees an angel standing in the sun, shouting to the vultures flying high in the sky: "Come! Gather together for the great banquet God has prepared. Come and eat the flesh of kings, generals, and strong warriors; of horses and their riders; and of all humanity, both free and slave, small and great". Even though this description of the carnage that will result in the defeat of the enemies of God is graphic, it tells us vultures and desert condors which are native to the Negev desert in the land of Israel, will be summoned by God to clean up the land by eating the flesh of dead humans and animals.

Revelation 19:19-21

As we come to the end of this chapter, the apostle John sees the antichrist (the beast) and the kings of the world and their armies gathered in the valley of Megiddo in Israel to fight against our Lord Jesus Christ and his army of angels.

It is no contest as our Lord defeats them with the breath of His mouth. He captures the antichrist and the false prophet who did mighty miracles that deceived all who had accepted the mark of the beast 666, and who worshiped his statue. Both the antichrist and his false prophet were thrown alive into the lake of fire to be tormented forever. The vultures all gorged themselves on the dead bodies.

In closing, Christ will return at His second coming with His saints and His angels, not only to defeat His enemies, but to judge the nations that wanted to divide up His land, and the nations that oppressed Israel since it became a nation in the Middle East on May 14, 1948. This includes the leaders of our nation, the leaders of the European Union nations, and the leaders of the Middle Eastern nations, who continue to this day to put pressure on Israel to divide Jerusalem to give parts of it to the Palestinians.

The prophet Joel gives us a warning about dividing the land of Israel in Joel 3:1-2: *"At that time, when I restore the prosperity of Judah and Jerusalem, says the LORD, "I will gather the armies of the world into the valley of Jehoshaphat. There I will judge them for harming my people, for scattering my inheritance among the nations, **and for dividing up my land"***.

Chapter Twenty
The Millennium Kingdom and the Defeat of Satan

This chapter is a continuation of the previous chapter, as it begins with the word "Then". It gives us a glimpse of the most beautiful, peaceful, and rewarding age this world will ever know, the Millennium Kingdom, or one-thousand-year reign of our Lord Jesus Christ on earth as King of kings and Lord of lords, and King David will be the second in command to assist our Lord Jesus Christ in His reign, as we are told by the prophets Isaiah and Jeremiah:

Isaiah 9:7: "*His ever expanding, peaceful government will never end. He will rule forever with fairness and justice from the throne of his ancestor David*".

Jeremiah 30:9: "*For my people will serve the LORD their God and David their king, whom I will raise up for them.*"

The word Millennium is not in the Bible, but it originates from the Latin word "mille" in Latin meaning "one thousand" and from the Latin word "annum" meaning "years". Just like the word "annual" means "yearly", the word "annum" means years.

Ever since May 14, 1948 when Israel became a nation in the Middle East, the U.S. and European Union leaders have tried without success to establish peace in the Middle East. As I am writing this book, our U.S. government is pursuing a peace plan in the Middle East, which includes partioning Israel to give part of its territory captured during the 1967 six-day war to the Palestinians, which is in direct defiance of the Word of God in Joel 3:2 I mentioned at the end of the previous chapter.

However, there will come a time in the future when peace prevails, when nations will no longer be in conflict with each other, when they will beat their weapons into plowshares for agriculture use, when military power is no longer needed, when peace will finally take place in the Middle East between Israel and its Arab neighbors, when diseases, rioting, hatred and racial tension will disappear, when poverty and world hunger will end. That time is the Millennium Kingdom of our Lord Jesus Christ.

During the Millennium Kingdom, the earth is restored to its origins in the Garden of Eden. People's life span will again increase like it was after our Lord flooded the earth and spared Noah and his family as we are told in Isaiah 65:20-22: *"No longer will babies die when only a few days old. No longer will adults die before they have lived a full life. No longer will people be considered old at one hundred! Only sinners will die that young! In those days, people will live in the houses they build and eat the fruit of their own vineyards. It will not be like the past, when invaders took the houses and confiscated the vineyards. For my people will live as long as trees and will have time to enjoy their hard-won gains"*.

I need to clarify what the prophet Isaiah is saying in this passage.

At the end of the seven-year tribulation on earth, many Jews and Gentiles who accepted Jesus Christ as their Lord and Savior will be ushered into the Millennium Kingdom in their earthly bodies. These people will multiply and will have many children, but they will all still carry the sin of Adam and Eve in their earthly mortal bodies. They have not been raptured nor received their immortal heavenly bodies, but they will cohabitate with us the believers who were raptured and received our immortal heavenly bodies.

The prophet Isaiah is saying these people will live as long as trees to be 600 or 700 years old, just like it was during the days of Noah and his sons before the flood. Their children will still be called children when they are 100-years old. However, we the raptured believers in our heavenly immortal bodies will never die. We will be with the Lord forever.

During the Millennium Kingdom Jesus will once again walk with us on this earth that was cleansed by fire, just like he did with Adam and Eve before their fall. The earth will be at peace, and the knowledge of God will spread throughout the world. The population of the earth will multiply just like it did after the flood. Old and New Testament saints, and tribulation saints, will receive authority from our Lord to rule and reign over the earth.

Psalm 2:6-7 foretells about Christ's reign on earth: "*For the LORD declares, "I have placed my chosen king on the throne in Jerusalem, my holy city". The king proclaims the LORD's decree*"".

Psalms 98 put this period into perspective: "*Sing a new song to the LORD, for he has done wonderful deeds. He has won a mighty victory by his power and holiness. The LORD has announced his victory and has revealed his righteousness to every nation! He has remembered his promise to love and be faithful to Israel.*

The whole earth has seen the salvation of our God. Shout to the LORD, all the earth; break out in praise and sing for joy! Sing your praise to the LORD with the harp, with the harp and melodious song, with trumpets and the sound of the ram's horn. Make a joyful symphony before the LORD, the King! Let the sea and everything in it shout his praise! Let the earth and all living things join in. Let the rivers clap their hands in glee! Let the hills sing out their songs of joy before the LORD. For the LORD is coming to judge the earth. He will judge the world with justice and the nations with fairness".

Psalm 99:1-5 foretells about the Lord reigning from Jerusalem during the Millennium Kingdom: "*The LORD is king! Let the nations tremble! He sits on his throne between the cherubim. Let the whole earth quake! The LORD sits in majesty in Jerusalem, supreme above all the nations. Let them praise your great and awesome name. Your name is holy! Mighty king, lover of justice, you have established fairness. You have acted with justice and righteousness throughout Israel. Exalt the LORD our God! Bow low before his feet, for he is holy!"*

Psalm 102:18-22 foretells about the nations gathering together to worship the Lord on Mount Zion during the Millennium Kingdom:*" Let this be recorded for future generations, so that a people not yet born will praise the Lord. Tell them the Lord looked down from his heavenly sanctuary. He looked down to earth from heaven to hear the groans of the prisoners, to release those condemned to die. And so, the Lord's fame will be celebrated in Zion, his praises in Jerusalem, when multitudes gather together and kingdoms come to worship the Lord".*

Daniel 2:44 says this about the Millennium Kingdom: *"And in the days of these kings shall the God of heaven set up a kingdom, which shall never be destroyed... and it shall stand for ever".*

Daniel 7:13-14: *"As my vision continued that night, I saw someone like a Son of Man (Jesus Christ) coming with the clouds of heaven. He approached the Ancient One (God the Father) and was led into his presence. He was given authority, honor, and sovereignty over all the nations of the world, so that people of every race and nation and language would obey him. His rule is eternal - it will never end. His kingdom will never be destroyed".*

Matthew 19:27-28: *"Then Peter said to him (Jesus), "We've given up everything to follow you. What will we get out of it?" And Jesus replied, "I assure you that when I, the Son of Man, sit upon my glorious throne in the Kingdom (Millennial Kingdom), you who have been my followers will also sit on twelve thrones, judging the twelve tribes of Israel".*

Another question we may ask ourselves: Who will occupy the Millennial Kingdom? The answer is there will be four distinct groups

308

of people:

1. The New Testament saints who received their glorified bodies at the rapture.
2. The saints (Jews and Gentiles) who were martyred for their faith during the seven-year tribulation and resurrected when Christ returns to earth.
3. The saints with earthly bodies who survived the seven-year tribulation and did not accept the mark of the beast.
4. The Old Testament saints

The people who survive the seven-year tribulation are going to have children and grandchildren who will populate the earth just like it was in Noah's days. Many of these children are going to grow up and embrace the faith in Jesus Christ. But also, the scripture tells us in vs. 7, many of them are not going to embrace the faith by their own choice, even though Satan is locked up and sin is non-existent. These are the nations from every corner of the earth mentioned in vs. 8. They are as numberless as sand along the seashore. Our Lord refers to them as Gog and Magog, in reference to the vast armies, enemies of Israel, mentioned in Ezekiel 38-39.

Revelation 20:1-2

As we read the scripture, we are told the apostle John has another amazing vision. He sees an angel coming down from heaven with a key to the bottomless pit (the abyss), the place of confinement for Satan and his demons, which is one of the compartments of Hades, and a heavy chain in his hand ready to capture and bind Satan the dragon, the old serpent.

If you recall from Revelation 19:20, both the antichrist and the false prophet were cast into the lake of fire that burns with sulfur. I want you to know the lake of fire is not the same as the bottomless pit mentioned in Luke 8:31 and Revelation 9:1. It is a temporary prison cell in Hades where Satan is locked up for a thousand years. The lake of fire is the eternal dwelling place of the wicked ones who rejected Jesus Christ as their Lord and Savior. It is the place of torment where the wicked will suffer everlasting separation from God at the Great White Throne Judgment (Revelation 20:11). It is the second death mentioned in Revelation 20:6.

Revelation 20:3

The scripture tells us the angel threw Satan into the bottomless pit, which he shut and locked, so that he is unable to deceive the nations anymore for a thousand years, and afterwards he will be released for a short time. This brings up a question: Will the Millennium Kingdom be free of sin and deception with Satan being locked up in the bottomless pit? Let us take a look.

The answer is no. If you recall from our study of Revelation 11 and 14, during the seven-year tribulation, many Jews and Gentiles will turn to God and accept His Son Jesus Christ as their Lord and Savior. This will take place when the 144,000 chosen and sealed Jews from the twelve tribes of Israel evangelize all over the world, and the two witnesses Moses and Elijah preach the Gospel on the streets of Jerusalem.

These converted Jews and Gentiles will be ushered into the Millennium Kingdom of Christ in their earthly, sinful mortal bodies. However, the raptured believers will reign with Christ in their immortal heavenly bodies that are free of sin. That is how sin will infiltrate the Millennium Kingdom.

After the thousand-year reign of Christ on earth, and just before the New Jerusalem comes down from heaven as we will see in Revelation 21, God wants to make sure none of the new generation of people born during the Millennium Kingdom will be tempted to follow Satan and rebel against God, just as the Israelites did during the Exodus. That is why He will release Satan from the bottomless pit for a little while to see if anyone from the new generation on earth will

310

follow him. The scripture does not give us the duration of Satan's release, but we are told it will be for a short time.

Revelation 20:4

The Apostle John now observes thrones and people sitting on them. They have been given authority to rule and judge. Who are these people who sit on these thrones? They include the disciples of Jesus Christ as I stated in <u>Matthew 19:27-28</u>; the raptured church, as we are told in in <u>1 Thessalonians 4:16-18</u> and <u>1 Corinthians 15:51-54;</u> the martyred tribulation saints who did not worship the beast or his statue, nor accepted his mark 666 on their foreheads or their hands. They all came to life again, and they reigned with Christ for a thousand years.

These saints are rewarded by our Lord Jesus Christ to sit upon thrones during the Millennium Kingdom because they are God's chosen people. Christ made them kings and priests as we are told in <u>1 Peter 2:9</u>: *"But you are not like that, for you are a chosen people. You are a kingdom of priests, God's holy nation, His very own possession. This is so you can show others the goodness of God, for he called you out of the darkness into his wonderful light"*.

Back in <u>Revelation 5:8-10</u>, when Jesus took the scroll from the hand of God the Father, and He was about to unfold it, the four living beings and the twenty-four elders fell before Him praising Him saying: *"For you were killed, and your blood has ransomed people for God from every tribe and language and people and nation. And you have caused them to become God's Kingdom and his priests. And they will reign on the earth"*.

Revelation 20:5

The first resurrection mentioned here is in reference to the souls of those who had not worshipped the beast (antichrist) or his statue, nor accepted his mark on their foreheads or on their hands during the seven-year tribulation. The scripture says they will come back to life again, become priests of God and they will be blessed and will reign with Christ for a thousand years.

Revelation 20:6

In order to understand the meaning of the second death, I first need to explain the first death.

The first death is the physical death. It takes place when the body goes to the grave and the soul/spirit separate from the body. After death, if you are a believer in Jesus Christ, your soul/spirit goes to heaven to be with the Lord to join the souls of other saints who have passed before you. The apostle Paul tells us in 2 Corinthians 5:8 to be absent from the body is to be present with the Lord.

The second death is the spiritual death and eternal separation from God in the lake of fire as we are told in Revelation 20:14. It applies to all the people whose names are not recorded in the Lamb's Book of Life. They are the ones who rejected Christ as their Savior, and those who accepted the mark of the beast 666 during the seven-year tribulation. They will stand before our Lord Jesus Christ at the Great White Throne Judgment, which will take place at the end of the Millennium Kingdom. I will discuss this judgment in more detail in Revelation 20:11.

The prophet Malachi spoke about this judgment in Malachi 4:1: *"The LORD Almighty says, "The day of judgment is coming, burning like a furnace. The arrogant and the wicked will be burned up like straw on that day. They will be consumed like a tree -- roots and all"*.

Revelation 20:7-9

At the end of the Millennium Kingdom, Satan will be let out of the bottomless pit for a short period of time undefined in the Bible. It could be days, months, or years. Only God knows how long. Satan will be so furious from being locked up for a thousand years that he will go out to deceive many nations from every corner of the earth. He will draw them into battle compared to the war of Gog and Magog in Ezekiel 38-39.

These armies will surround God's people and Jerusalem in an attempt to destroy them for the last time. But fire from heaven will come down on the invading armies and will consume all of them, just as God brought His judgments on the enemies of Israel many times in the Old Testament.

Revelation 20:10

The Apostle John tells us Satan the devil will be permanently thrown in the lake of fire so he will no longer be able to deceive the nations. He will join the antichrist and the false prophet in the lake of fire, and they will be tormented day and night forever and ever.

Revelation 20:11-15

The Apostle John sees our Lord Jesus Christ sitting on a Great White Throne only fit for the King of kings. He is ready to execute judgment on all the unbelievers who rejected him as their Lord and Savior The scripture says the earth and sky fled from his presence, but they found no place to hide. What does this mean?

It means all people on earth and all people travelling by plane left behind after the rapture who have accepted the mark of the beast 666 will be subject to His judgment, as we are told in Matthew 16:27: "*For I, the Son of Man, will come in the glory of my Father with his angels and will judge all people according to their deeds*". I want you to know this judgment is strictly for the unbelievers. The believers who put their trust and faith in Jesus Christ will not be part of this judgment, because they were already judged right after the Rapture of the church in Revelation 4 at the Judgment Seat of Christ (2 Corinthians 5:10).

You may ask: How do I know for sure that our Lord Jesus Christ is the One who sits upon this Great White Throne as King and

Judge? The answer is found in <u>John 5:22-23</u>: *"In addition, the Father judges no one. Instead, he has given the Son absolute authority to judge, so that everyone will honor the Son, just as they honor the Father. Anyone who does not honor the Son is certainly not honoring the Father who sent him"*.

Next John sees the souls of the dead, both great and small, standing before the throne of God, and the books were opened, including the Book of Life. The dead were judged according to their works, as recorded in the books. What the Apostle John is telling us here, our Lord Jesus Christ is getting ready to judge the physically and spiritually dead unbelievers according to their works based on the record books that He maintains.

But there is another book in which our Lord keeps records of the believers' works. It is called the Book of Life, the book in which the names of all the believers are written at the moment they are saved. The New Testament refers to this Book of Life eight times, and in <u>Revelation 21:27</u> this book is referred to as the Lamb's Book of Life. Let us take a look at the passages in the Bible where the Book of Life is mentioned.

<u>Philippians 4:2-3</u>: *"Now I appeal to Euodia and Syntyche. Please, because you belong to the Lord, settle your disagreement. And I ask you, my true partner, to help these two women, for they worked hard with me in telling others the Good News. They worked along with Clement and the rest of my co-workers, whose names are written in the* **Book of Life**".

<u>Revelation 3:5</u>: *"All who are victorious will be clothed in white. I will never erase their names from the* **Book of Life**, *but I will announce before my Father and his angels that they are mine"*.

<u>Revelation 13:8</u>: *"And all the people who belong to this world worshiped the beast. They are the ones whose names were not written*

in the **Book of Life** *before the world was made—the Book that belongs to the Lamb who was slaughtered."*

Revelation 17:8: *"The beast you saw was once alive but isn't now. And yet he will soon come up out of the bottomless pit and go to eternal destruction. And the people who belong to this world, whose names were not written in the* **Book of Life** *before the world was made, will be amazed at the reappearance of this beast who had died".*
Revelation 20:12: *"I saw the dead, both great and small, standing before God's throne. And the books were opened, including the* **Book of Life**. *And the dead were judged according to what they had done, as recorded in the books".*

Revelation 20:15: *"And whosoever was not found written in the* **Book of Life** *was cast into the lake of fire".*

Revelation 21:27: *"Nothing evil will be allowed to enter, nor anyone who practices shameful idolatry and dishonesty--but only those whose names are written in the* **Lamb's Book of Life**".*

I want to take a few minutes here to review five judgments the scripture gives us that are relevant to our discussion:

1. **Judgment of the nation of Israel.** God has already judged Israel in 586 B.C. for worshipping pagan gods and falling into idolatry. Jeremiah 25:9 puts it this way:
   "I will gather together all the armies of the north under King Nebuchadnezzar of Babylon, whom I have appointed as my deputy. I will bring them all against this land and its people and against the other nations near you. I will completely destroy you and make you an object of horror and contempt and a ruin forever ".

   Even though Israel was restored back in its land as a nation in 1948, there is a time in the future when Israel will be judged again for denying Jesus Christ as the Son of God and for

315

crucifying Him. When Christians are taken out of this world at the rapture, the seven-year tribulation period begins.

The seven-year Tribulation is defined in the Bible as the time of Jacob's trouble, and it is God's way of judging the nation of Israel for the last time for denying, beating, persecuting, and crucifying His Son Jesus Christ. Jeremiah 30:7: *"Alas! For that day is great, so that none is like it; and it is the time of Jacob's trouble, but he shall be saved out of it"*.

Jesus told His disciples in Matthew 24:21: *"For that will be a time of greater horror than anything the world has ever seen or will ever see again"*. During those days, Israel will come under the terrible oppression of the antichrist, but in the end, the Jewish people who recognize Jesus as their Messiah will be saved.

2. **Judgment for our sins on the cross.** By placing our faith in Jesus Christ, we do not have to fear judgment for our sins because He took our judgment upon Himself. 1 Peter 2:23-24: *"When He was reviled, did not revile in return; when He suffered, He did not threaten, but committed Himself to Him who judges righteously; who Himself bore our sins in His own body on the tree, that we, having died to sins, might live for righteousness—by whose stripes you were healed"*.

3. **Judgment of the believers at the Seat of Christ (Bema Seat in Greek).** 2 Corinthians 5:10: *"For we must all appear before the judgment seat of Christ, that each one may receive the things done in the body, according to what he has done, whether good or bad"*.

   Romans 14:10: *"But why do you judge your brother? Or why do you show contempt for your brother? For we shall all stand before the judgment seat of Christ"*.

A common misconception among many Christian believers, which arises from misinterpreting this scripture, is God will judge the believers at the Seat of Christ for sins committed in the believer's life, and some measure of punishment for our sins will result. This is not true at all. When Jesus died on the cross for our sins, he took our place and paid the price for our sins free of charge.

This is what John 3:16 is all about. God so loved the world that he sent His only Son Jesus to die on the cross for our sins.

The judgment seat of Christ is not a place and time when the Lord will punish us for our sins. Rather, it is a place where our heavenly rewards and crowns will be given or lost depending on how we lived our lives for the Lord since we were saved.

Can you imagine standing before the magnificent throne of Jesus Christ? There, Christ will ask you these questions: "Did you put me first in your life? Did you give me the first 10% of your income and earnings? What did you do for me since I saved you? What did you do with the money I blessed you with? What did you do with your spiritual gifts and talents? What did you do with the opportunities I gave you to glorify my name and spread the Gospel?" That is what is going to take place at the Judgment Seat of Christ, and our heavenly rewards will be determined accordingly.

4. **Judgment of the Gentile nations.** This is a time when God will judge all the enemy nations of Israel. This includes all the pagan tribes that occupied the Holy Land prior to Joshua taking over those territories, the Hittites, the Amorites, the Amalekites, the Canaanites, the Perizzites, the Hivites, the Jebusites and the Philistines who lived in that region. It includes all the Arab nations in the Middle East who descended from these tribes and who are enemies of Israel. It includes member nations of the European Union and the United States of America who continue

317

to this day to put pressure on Israel to divide up its land and give it to the Palestinians.

The prophet Joel says in Joel 3:2: *"I will gather the armies of the world into the valley of Jehoshaphat. There I will judge them for harming my people, for scattering my inheritance among the nations, and for dividing up my land"*.

5. **The Great White Throne Judgment of unbelievers.** This judgment is for those who rejected Jesus Christ as their Lord and Savior. They will be resurrected from their graves and from Hades after the thousand-year reign of Christ on earth to face God's judgment.

Revelation 20:13-14 tells us their final destination will be the lake of fire where Satan and his demons reside.

Malachi 4:1: *"The LORD Almighty says, "The Day of Judgment is coming, burning like a furnace. The arrogant and the wicked will be burned up like straw on that day. They will be consumed like a tree -- roots and all"*.

Just try to visualize this scene at the end of the Millennium Kingdom: Every person on earth who put his/her faith and trust in someone other than our Lord Jesus Christ throughout the ages, whether they are emperors, kings, presidents, dictators, citizens of every nation in the world, slaves, great and small, rich and poor, Muslims, Buddhists, Hindus, Bahais, Mormons, New Age Movement followers, Scientologists, atheists, psychics, palm readers, sorcerers, devil worshippers and those who practice witchcraft, will someday bow before our Lord Jesus Christ to give an account for all their evil deeds.

This is confirmed to us in John 5:25-29: *"And I assure you that the time is coming, in fact it is here, when the dead will hear my voice -- the voice of the Son of God. And those who listen will live. The Father has life in himself, and he has granted his Son to have life in himself.*

And he has given him authority to judge all mankind because he is the Son of Man. Don't be so surprised! Indeed, the time is coming when all the dead in their graves will hear the voice of God's Son, and they will rise again. Those who have done good will rise to eternal life, and those who have continued in evil will rise to judgment".

The apostle Paul in Philippians 2:9-11 confirms this as well: *"Therefore God also has highly exalted Him and given Him the name which is above every name, that at the name of Jesus every knee should bow, of those in heaven, and of those on earth, and of those under the earth, and that every tongue should confess that Jesus Christ is Lord, to the glory of God the Father".*

Chapter Twenty-One
Making All Things New –
The New Jerusalem

The final two chapters of Revelation, twenty-one and twenty-two, present the glorious future which awaits every believer throughout the ages: Our eternal dwelling place with God, the Heavenly City, the New Jerusalem. As we shall see in the following passages of scripture, the description of this heavenly city is breathtaking and beyond imagination. This is what the descendants of Korah wrote in the book of Psalms about the New Jerusalem:

Psalm 48:1-3: *"How great is the Lord, how deserving of praise, in the city of our God, which sits on his holy mountain! It is high and magnificent; the whole earth rejoices to see it! Mount Zion, the holy mountain, is the city of the great King! God himself is in Jerusalem's towers, revealing himself as its defender"*.

Psalm 87:1-7: *"On the holy mountain stands the city founded by the LORD. He loves the city of Jerusalem more than any other city in Israel. O city of God, what glorious things are said of you! I will record Egypt and Babylon among those who know me -- also Philistia and Tyre, and even distant Ethiopia. They have all become citizens of Jerusalem! And it will be said of Jerusalem, "Everyone has become a citizen here." And the Most High will personally bless this city. When the LORD registers the nations, he will say, "This one has become a citizen of Jerusalem." At all the festivals, the people will sing, "The source of my life is in Jerusalem!"*

Revelation 21:1

Revelation 21 begins with a continuation of Revelation 20 with the word "then", which describes the events which will take place after the Great White Throne Judgment: "*Then I saw a new heaven and a new earth, for the old heaven and the old earth had disappeared. And the sea was also gone. And I saw the holy city, the New Jerusalem, coming down from God out of heaven like a beautiful bride prepared for her husband*".

The Apostle John sees a new heaven and a new earth, for the old heaven and the old earth, the ones we are living in right now, had disappeared. Does this mean in the last days this earth is going to blow up or melt away up by the sun, heaven will be rolled away, and God will create a new heaven and a new earth just like He did in Genesis 1?

It is possible, but I do not believe so. I believe what it means is the heaven and the earth will be consumed by fire on judgment day, which is God's way of purging them from all evil and sin, from all the evil spirits of the unseen world and in the heavenly realms as we are told by the Apostle Paul in Ephesians 6:12: "*For we are not fighting against flesh-and-blood enemies, but against evil rulers and authorities of the unseen world, against mighty powers in this dark world, and against evil spirits in the heavenly places*".

Afterwards the heaven and the earth will be transformed and re-created, just like our earthly bodies, when we are raptured, we will be transformed and given a new heavenly body that is sin-free.

The time and method of the disappearance of heaven and earth are described in 2 Peter 3:7 when he spoke about the changes that will take place at the start of the Millennium Kingdom: "*And God has also commanded that the heavens and the earth will be consumed by fire on the day of judgment, when ungodly people will perish*". And 2 Peter 3:10-13: "*But the day of the Lord will come as unexpectedly as a thief. Then the heavens will pass away with a terrible noise, and everything in them will disappear in fire, and the earth and everything on it will be exposed to judgment*".

This re-creation of the world was foretold by our Lord in the following passages of scripture:

Isaiah 65:17: "*Look! I am creating new heavens and a new earth, so wonderful that no one will even think about the old ones anymore*".

Isaiah 66:22-23: "*As surely as my new heavens and earth will remain, so will you always be my people, with a name that will never disappear,*" *says the Lord.* "*All humanity will come to worship me from week to week and from month to month*".

Matthew 24:35: "*Heaven and earth will disappear, but my words remain forever*".

Hebrews 12:26-27: "*When God spoke from Mount Sinai his voice shook the earth, but now He makes another promise:* "*Once again I will shake not only the earth but the heavens also.*" *This means that all of creation will be shaken and removed, so that only unshakable things will remain*".

So, there is going to be a fire cleansing in the end, just like in the Old Testament when the world was flooded and cleansed by water. God promised Noah He will never flood the earth again. However, this time He is going to do it with fire, symbolic of His judgment and cleansing.

The Lord told the prophet Jeremiah in Jeremiah 23:29:" *Is not My word like a fire?*" *says the Lord,* "*And like a hammer that breaks the rock in pieces?*"

The prophet Malachi said this in Malachi 3:2-3: "*But who will be able to endure it when he comes? Who will be able to stand and face him when he appears? For he will be like a blazing fire that refines metal or like a strong soap that whitens clothes. He will sit and judge like a refiner of silver, watching closely as the dross is burned away*".

323

The scripture tells us here in the new world the sea will be gone. There will be no oceans and seas as we know them today. Then the Apostle John sees the Holy City, the New Jerusalem coming down from heaven like a beautiful bride prepared for her husband. There are two Jerusalems mentioned in the scripture. One is Jerusalem, capital of Israel as we know it today. It will be the home of the believers during the thousand-year reign of Christ.

The other one is the New Jerusalem also known as the Heavenly City, Holy City or Eternal City, which will hover over the earth during the thousand-year reign of Christ, and then at the end of the thousand-years, after the Great White Throne Judgment and the re-creation of heaven and earth, it will come down to earth and reside there forever in the new earth.

The apostle Paul in Galatians 4:25-26 contrasts the two of them to Mount Sinai, which is symbolic of slavery to the Law of Moses, and Sarah wife of Abraham, who is symbolic of the freedom Jesus gives us from bondage to the Law: "*And now Jerusalem is just like Mount Sinai in Arabia, because she and her children live in slavery. But Sarah, the free woman, represents the heavenly Jerusalem. And she is our mother*".

The New Jerusalem is the one Christ has been preparing for us for over 2,000 years. The prophet Isaiah says this about her in Isaiah 60:1-3: "*Arise, Jerusalem! Let your light shine for all to see. For the glory of the LORD rises to shine on you. Darkness as black as night covers all the nations of the earth, but the glory of the LORD rises and appears over you. All nations will come to your light; mighty kings will come to see your radiance.*"

Hebrews 11:10 tells us the New Jerusalem is the one our Patriarch Abraham was looking for when God called him to leave home and go to another land that He would give him as his inheritance: "*Abraham did this because he was confidently looking forward to a city with eternal foundations, a city designed and built by God.*"

324

<u>Hebrews 12:22-23</u> says this about the New Jerusalem: *"No, you have come to Mount Zion, to the city of the living God, the heavenly Jerusalem, and to thousands of angels in joyful assembly. You have come to the assembly of God's firstborn children, whose names are written in heaven"*.

<u>Revelation 21:2</u>

The scripture tells us this magnificent city descending from heaven toward earth is like a beautiful bride prepared for her husband on her wedding day. I want you to know I have already made reservations for me and my wife Jacquetta for one of the mansions in that city, and if your name is written in the Lamb's Book of life, you too have a reservation. Let us look at the characteristics of this heavenly city.

This heavenly city is like a beautiful bride prepared for her husband. It parallels the scripture in <u>Revelation 19:7</u>, where one of the seven angels who held the seven bowls containing the last seven plagues came and said to the apostle John *"come with me! I will show you the bride, the wife of the Lamb"*.

<u>Revelation 21:3-4</u>

The apostle John hears a loud shout from the throne of God saying, *"Look, God's home is now among his people! He will live with them, and they will be his people. God himself will be with them. He will wipe every tear from their eyes, and there will be no more death or sorrow or crying or pain. All these things are gone forever"*.

The scripture tells us here when we become citizens of the New Jerusalem, we will live with the Triune God, God the Father, God the Son, and God the Holy Spirit. We will see Him face to face without experiencing death. Sorrow, physical pain, crying, and tears triggered by our emotions, disappointments and anger will be gone forever. Instead, the fruit of the Holy Spirit given to us in <u>Galatians 5:22-23</u> will be fully displayed in our eternal life: "*But the Holy Spirit produces this kind of fruit in our lives: love, joy, peace, patience, kindness, goodness, faithfulness, gentleness, and self-control*".

Revelation 21:5

Then John hears the voice of God saying: "Look, I am making everything new! Write this down, for what I tell you is trustworthy and true." This means everything that we are accustomed to seeing and doing here on earth will disappear, and God will create new things for us beyond our imagination, never seen before in the New Jerusalem.

The apostle Paul puts it this way in 1 Corinthians 2:9-10: "*That is what the Scriptures mean when they say, "No eye has seen, no ear has heard, and no mind has imagined what God has prepared for those who love him.*"

Revelation 21:6

John continues to listen to what God is telling him: "*And he also said, "It is finished! I am the Alpha and the Omega—the Beginning and the End. To all who are thirsty I will give freely from the springs of the water of life. All who are victorious will inherit all these blessings, and I will be their God, and they will be my children*".

In John 19:30, when Jesus was about to be crucified for our sins, he said these last words "*It is finished!*", meaning He completed the task of redemption given to Him by God the Father to atone for our sins. He conquered death and defeated Satan. Here in this passage, Jesus reminds us He is the beginning and the end, and a promise is given to all who put their trust and faith in Him: Eternal life in the New Jerusalem.

Revelation 21:7

Our Lord reaffirms to the apostle John the final destinations of the ones who put their trust and faith in Him, and the ones who rejected Him. For us believers in Jesus Christ, the overcomers, the victorious ones Jesus promises we will inherit all these blessings. Jesus will be our Father and we will be His children in the New Jerusalem.

Revelation 21:8

But the ones who reject Him and did not put their trust and faith in Him, the cowards, unbelievers, the corrupt, murderers, the immoral, those who practice witchcraft, idol worshipers, and all liars—their fate is the lake of fire, where they will be tormented forever. The second death is the spiritual death.

Revelation 21:9-10

Next the apostle John sees one of the seven angels holding the seven bowls containing the last seven plagues that are about to come upon this earth. The angel comes and says to John *"Come with me! I will show you the bride, the wife of the Lamb." the New Jerusalem descending out of heaven from God"*. He takes John in the Spirit to a great, high mountain, and he shows him the holy city, the New Jerusalem, descending out of heaven from God.

This holy city has been in the making since Jesus ascended to heaven. God is preparing it for us as our eternal dwelling with Him. After the Millennium Kingdom of Christ, it will descend from heaven to occupy the geographical area described by God to Abraham in Genesis 15:18-20:
"So the Lord made a covenant with Abram that day and said, "I have given this land to your descendants, all the way from the border of Egypt to the great Euphrates River, the land now occupied by the Kenites, Kenizzites, Kadmonites, Hittites, Perizzites, Rephaites, Amorites, Canaanites, Girgashites, and Jebusites".

This land promised to Abraham is now mostly occupied by these Arab nations: Egypt, Jordan, Saudi Arabia, Lebanon, Syria, and

Iraq. It will someday be the site of the New Jerusalem, 1400 wide x 1400 miles long x 1400 miles high, as we will see in the verses to follow.

Revelation 21:11-14

The apostle John, amazed by what he sees, begins to describe the beauty of this heavenly city. This is what he says about it.

It was filled with the glory of God and sparkled like a precious gem, crystal clear like jasper. Its walls were broad and high, with twelve gates guarded by twelve angels. The names of the twelve tribes of Israel were written on the gates. There were three gates on each side -- east, north, south, and west. The walls of the city had twelve foundation stones and on it were written the names of the twelve apostles of the Lamb.

The first thing we notice about this heavenly city is its foundation: It is based on two groups of twelve. The first group consists of His twelve disciples, excluding Judas Iscariot who committed suicide by hanging himself. He was replaced by Matthias. The second group consists of the twelve tribes of Israel, with the two tribes of Ephraim and Manasseh representing Joseph.

Here we are given a clear description of this heavenly city. Right after God expelled Adam and Eve from the Garden of Eden, He placed two cherubim angels to guard the entrance to the Garden. Here we see a repeat of that in this heavenly city. We see twelve angels guarding the twelve gates of this city. You may ask this question: Why are angels guarding the twelve gates of The New Jerusalem?

The answer is just as cherubim angels were sent by God to guard the East entrance to the Garden of Eden after Adam and Eve's fall (Genesis 3:24) to guard the way to the tree of life, so will God place cherubim angels to guard the twelve gates of the new Heavenly City. Nothing evil or impure will ever enter it as we are told in

328

Revelation 21:27; the city is reserved for all the redeemed of God. In The New Jerusalem, the redeemed will have access to the tree of life, which is symbolic of eternal life.

In John 4:10, when Jesus met a Samaritan woman at the well of Jacob near the village of Sychar, He said to her: *"If you only knew the gift God has for you and who you are speaking to, you would ask me, and I would give you living water"*. Then in vs.13-14 Jesus replied: *"Anyone who drinks this water will soon become thirsty again. But those who drink the water I give will never be thirsty again. It becomes a fresh, bubbling spring within them, giving them eternal life"*.

In this passage the living water Jesus gives is symbolic of the presence of the Holy Spirit Who indwells in us giving us eternal life.

Revelation 21:15-17

Next John sees the same angel who spoke with him earlier holding in his hand a gold measuring stick to measure the city, its gates, and its wall. When he measured it, he found it was a square, as wide as it was long.

It was in the form of a cube, for its length, width, and height, were each 1,400 miles. Then he measured the walls and found them to be 216 feet thick. Let us put this into perspective. The length of a football field in the U.S. is 100 yards or 300 feet excluding the end zones. Here we are told the thickness of the heavenly City is 216 feet, which is over two thirds the length of a football field.

The dimensions of The New Jerusalem are 1400-miles wide x 1400-miles long = 1,960,000 square miles. It is 1400 miles high. If overlaid over the Unites States of America, it will occupy two thirds of the lower forty-eight states. If overlaid over Israel and the Middle East, it will extend from Saudi Arabia to Libya (east and west) and from Turkey to Sudan (north and south).

329

But before The New Jerusalem descends from heaven, the Lord is going to recreate this earth to accommodate the size of this Holy City. This is necessary because the height of the Holy City is 1400 miles, or 739,2000 feet. Today, commercial airplanes fly at 35,000 feet, and at that level, humans cannot survive due to lack of oxygen and cold temperatures. That is one of the main reasons why it is necessary for the existing heavens and the earth to be recreated.

Revelation 21:18-20

Here is an amazing description of the New Jerusalem. The wall of the city is made of jasper, and the city is pure gold, as clear as glass. The wall of the city is built on foundation stones inlaid with twelve gems: the first was jasper, the second sapphire, the third agate, the fourth emerald, the fifth onyx, the sixth carnelian, the seventh chrysolite, the eighth beryl, the ninth topaz, the tenth chrysoprase, the eleventh jacinth, the twelfth amethyst.

If you recall from Exodus 28, these twelve precious stones were on Aaron's chestpiece in Exodus 28:15-21 as a symbol of his priestly role: *"Then, with the most careful workmanship, make a chestpiece that will be used to determine God's will. Use the same materials as you did for the ephod: fine linen cloth embroidered with gold thread and blue, purple, and scarlet yarn. This chestpiece will be made of two folds of cloth, forming a pouch nine inches square. Four rows of gemstones will be attached to it.*

The first row will contain a red carnelian, a chrysolite, and an emerald. The second row will contain a turquoise, a sapphire, and a white moonstone. The third row will contain a jacinth, an agate, and an amethyst. The fourth row will contain a beryl, an onyx, and a jasper. All these stones will be set in gold. Each stone will represent one of the tribes of Israel, and the name of that tribe will be engraved on it as though it were a seal."

Revelation 21:21

The twelve gates of the heavenly city are twelve pearls: Each individual gate is one giant pearl. The main street of the city was pure gold like transparent glass. Can you imagine living in such a magnificent city in the presence of God? I do not know about you, but I cannot wait.

A question you may be asking: Is the New Jerusalem going to be large enough to hold all the Christian believers in the world?

If we go back all the way to the beginning of the human race, and if you add up all the people who put their trust and faith in Jesus Christ, that is a lot of people. Today's world population is about 7.7 billion according to world statistics. Only thirty three percent of the 7.7 billion, about 2.5 billion, are considered Christians based on their faith, and half of all Christians are Catholic; the other half includes all other denominations. Can they all live in this heavenly city which God has created?

The answer is yes, assuming they are all born-again believers who have accepted Jesus Christ in their hearts as their Lord and Savior. But in reality, not all of them will enter this heavenly city, because there are many people in our world today who claim to be Christians, but deep inside they are not. They do not have a personal relationship with Jesus Christ. They are called nominal Christians.

Our Lord Jesus Christ said this about them in Matthew 7:21-23: *"Not everyone who says to Me, 'Lord, Lord,' shall enter the kingdom of heaven, but he who does the will of My Father in heaven. Many will say to Me in that day, 'Lord, Lord, have we not prophesied in Your name, cast out demons in Your name, and done many wonders in Your name?' And then I will declare to them, 'I never knew you; depart from Me, you who practice lawlessness!'"*

In this passage, Jesus is approaching the end of His Sermon on the Mount after He contrasted the narrow way to heaven and the wide

331

way to destruction. You may ask: Why did Jesus reject these people who called Him Lord, Lord in this passage?

The answer is they were convinced they could earn their way to heaven by performing miracles and good works in Jesus' name. What they did not admit, they were boasting about their accomplishments, glorifying themselves instead of glorifying God; they did not have a personal relationship with Jesus.

In other words, they did not put their trust and faith in Him alone. Instead, they believed it is not enough to put their trust and faith in Jesus Christ; they need to do additional good works to earn their way to heaven. This is what is taught by the Catholic church and some Christian denominations.

The apostle Paul clearly tells us by the grace of our Lord and Savior Jesus Christ, which is based on putting our trust and faith in Him alone, we are saved. Ephesians 2:8-9: *"For by grace you have been saved through faith. And this is not your own doing; it is the gift of God, not a result of works, so that no one may boast"*.

Another question you may be asking: Will we be able to communicate with each other in the New Jerusalem, or will we be speaking different languages as we do today?

The answer is given to us in Zephaniah 3:9: *"Then I will purify the speech of all people, so that everyone can worship the Lord together"*. What the prophet Zephaniah is telling us, God will purify speech and unify language so that all His people from all nations will be able to worship Him together. In other words, in The New Jerusalem, all believers will be able to understand each other; the confusion of languages at the Tower of Babel in Genesis 11 will be reversed. Now let us look at what is inside this heavenly city.

Revelation 21:22

We are told no temple could be seen in the city, for the Lord God Almighty and His Son Jesus Christ are its temple. In Jerusalem, the Holy Temple, the house of worship of the Lord which was built by King Solomon and destroyed by the Babylonians and later by the Romans, was the primary place of worship for the Jewish people. In the New Jerusalem, no temple is needed because God will be present everywhere. He will be worshipped throughout the city, and nothing will stop us from being with Him and walking with Him.

Revelation 21:23-24

We are told here the city has no need of sun or moon to shine in it, for the glory of God illuminates the city, and Jesus Christ will be its light. Jesus said in John 8:12: "*I am the light of the world. If you follow me, you won't be stumbling through the darkness, because you will have the light that leads to life*". The nations will walk by the light of the city, and the kings of the earth will bring their glory into it.

Revelation 21:25-26

The scripture tells us the gates of the city never close at the end of day because there is no night, and all the nations will bring their glory and honor to our Lord, just like the wise men from the East came to honor the Lord at His birth in Bethlehem by bringing Him gold, frankincense and Myrrh, except this time there will be need for myrrh to embalm the body of Jesus Christ.

Revelation 21:27

Here we are told nothing unclean and no one who practices idolatry and dishonesty will be able to enter the New Jerusalem. Only those who put their faith and trust in Jesus Christ, and whose names are written in the Lamb's book of life, will be allowed to enter. In Revelation 12 we are told cherubim angels will be guarding its gates just like they did after God expelled Adam and Eve from the Garden of Eden.

Chapter Twenty-Two
Jesus is Coming Soon

Revelation 22 opens with a continuation of Revelation 21 with the word "Then". In this chapter, the same angel, the one who held the seven bowls containing the seven plagues and showed the apostle John the Heavenly City in Revelation 21:9, now continues to show John what else resides in this glorious city.

Revelation 22:1

The angel shows John a pure river with the water of life, clear as crystal, flowing from the throne of God and the Lamb, coursing down the center of the main street. On each side of the river grew a tree of life bearing twelve kinds of fruit with fresh crop each month.

Our Lord Jesus Christ said in Revelation 21:6: "*To all who are thirsty I will give freely from the springs of the water of life*". What is this river of life?

The Prophet Ezekiel in Ezekiel 47:1-12 foretold about the river of life in the Old Testament which flows from the Throne of God into the New Jerusalem: "*Then the man brought me back to the entrance of the Temple. There I saw a stream flowing eastward from beneath the Temple threshold. This stream then passed to the right of the altar on its south side. The man brought me outside the wall through the north gateway and led me around to the eastern entrance.*

There I could see the stream flowing out through the south side of the east gateway. Measuring as he went, he led me along the stream for 1,750 feet and told me to go across. At that point the water was up to my ankles. He measured off another 1,750 feet and told me to go across again. This time the water was up to my knees. After another

1,750 feet, it was up to my waist. Then he measured another 1,750 feet, and the river was too deep to cross without swimming. He told me to keep in mind what I had seen; then he led me back along the riverbank. Suddenly, to my surprise, many trees were now growing on both sides of the river!

Then he said to me, "This river flows east through the desert into the Jordan Valley, where it enters the Dead Sea. The waters of this stream will heal the salty waters of the Dead Sea and make them fresh and pure. Everything that touches the water of this river will live. Fish will abound in the Dead Sea, for its waters will be healed. Wherever this water flows, everything will live. Fishermen will stand along the shores of the Dead Sea, fishing all the way from En-gedi to En-eglaim.

The shores will be covered with nets drying in the sun. Fish of every kind will fill the Dead Sea, just as they fill the Mediterranean! But the marshes and swamps will not be purified; they will be sources of salt.

All kinds of fruit trees will grow along both sides of the river. The leaves of these trees will never turn brown and fall, and there will always be fruit on their branches. There will be a new crop every month, without fail! For they are watered by the river flowing from the Temple. The fruit will be for food and the leaves for healing."

So the water of life or the springs of water of life mentioned in the scripture are both in reference to the river in the Garden of Eden in Genesis 2:8-10, and they both symbolize the presence of the Holy Spirit in our life, which becomes a perpetual spring within us giving us eternal life. Jesus explained that in John 7:37-39: "*On the last day, the climax of the festival, Jesus stood and shouted to the crowds, "If you are thirsty, come to me! If you believe in me, come and drink! For the Scriptures declare that rivers of living water will flow out from within." (When he said "living water," he was speaking of the Spirit, who would be given to everyone believing in him. But the Spirit had not yet been given, because Jesus had not yet entered into his glory*".

336

Revelation 22:2

The Tree of Life in this verse is compared to the Tree of Life in the Garden of Eden. After Adam and Eve sinned, they were forbidden to eat from the Tree of Life, because they could not have eternal life if they were sinners. But because of the shed blood of Jesus Christ on the cross, our sins are forgiven. There will be no evil or sin in The New Jerusalem.

Jesus told us that in <u>Revelation 21:27</u>: "*Nothing evil will be allowed to enter -- no one who practices shameful idolatry and dishonesty -- but only those whose names are written in the Lamb's Book of Life*". In the New Jerusalem we will be able to eat freely from the Tree of Life since we are no longer bound to sin and our eternal life with God is secure.

A question people often ask about vs. 2. Why would the nations need to be healed by the leaves of the trees if all evil is gone and there is no sickness or illness in The New Jerusalem?

The answer to this question is the apostle John is quoting here from <u>Ezekiel 47:12</u> where water flowing from the throne of God produces trees with healing leaves: "*All kinds of fruit trees will grow along both sides of the river. The leaves of these trees will never turn brown and fall, and there will always be fruit on their branches. There will be a new crop every month, without fail! For they are watered by the river flowing from the Temple. The fruit will be for food and the leaves for healing*".

The prophet Ezekiel is not implying that there will be sickness in the Heavenly City; he is telling us the water of life produces strength wherever it flows. Think about the healing leaves as eternal life herbs, natural vitamins, and supplements. Ezekiel is saying the fruit of the trees is our daily food for nourishment, and the leaves of the trees are our daily supplements that sustain us.

Revelation 22:3

In the New Jerusalem nothing will be cursed. We will worship our Lord Jesus Christ, and we will be in His presence all the time. This fulfills Zechariah's prophecy in Zechariah 14:11: "*And Jerusalem will be filled, safe at last, never again to be cursed and destroyed*".

Revelation 22:4

In the New Jerusalem God's servants will see the face of God without the fear of dying, and His name "YHWH" (see Appendix A) will be written on their foreheads. They will worship Him and praise Him. If you recall from the Old Testament, God told Moses in Exodus 33:20 "*But you may not look directly at my face, for no one may see me and live*".

Revelation 22:5

Here we see an emphasis of what the scripture said in Revelation 21:23. In the New Jerusalem, there will be no night, no moon, no lamps, no sun, for the Lord God will shine on us, and we will reign with Him forever. In John 8:12, Jesus said: "*I am the light of the world. If you follow me, you won't have to walk in darkness, because you will have the light that leads to life (eternal)*".

Revelation 22:6

In this verse, the angel reassures the apostle John that everything that was revealed to him by God, the future events yet to come, are all true and trustworthy and they will happen soon.

Revelation 22:7

In this verse, we see the sixth beatitude in Revelation: "*Look, I am coming soon! Blessed are those who obey the prophecy written in this scroll*". Our Lord is again emphasizing the importance of obeying what is written in this book just like He did at the beginning of this book in Revelation 1:3.

Revelation 22:8-9

The Apostle John, being overwhelmed by what he saw and heard, fell down at the feet of the angel to worship him just like he did before in Revelation 19:10. Again the angel told John: *"do not worship me, I am the servant of God, just like you and your brothers the prophets. Worship God!"* Here at the end of the Bible, the angel points out to the Apostle John the importance of the First of the Ten Commandments: *"Do not worship any other gods besides me"*.

Revelation 22:10

The same angel instructs the Apostle John *"do not seal up the prophetic words you have written, for the time is near"*. This is interesting especially when we compare that to the instructions the angel gave Daniel in Daniel 12:4: *"But you, Daniel, keep this prophecy a secret; seal up the book until the time of the end. Many will rush here and there, and knowledge will increase"*.

God through His angels instructed the Prophet Daniel to keep the end-times prophecy sealed and not share any of it with the Israelites, as its timing is not yet according to God's plan, and they would not have understood its meaning. However, the apostle John was instructed to share the end-times prophecy with everyone, because the time is near when these events will take place.

If you recall the Apostle John wrote the book of Revelation around 95 A.D. Since the angel told him the time is near for these events to take place, think how much nearer the time is today for these events to take place over nineteen hundred years later. That is why it is so important to repent of your sins, turn to God and ask Jesus to come into your heart before it is too late.

Revelation 22:11

As Christ's return draws closer and closer, we see a greater separation in our world today between the followers of Jesus Christ and Satan's followers. That is why the angel says to the apostle John "*Let the one who is doing wrong continue to do wrong, the one who is vile, continue to be vile, the one who is good, continue to do good, and the one who is holy continue in holiness*".

In <u>Daniel 12:9-10</u>, the heavenly messenger that appeared to Daniel gave him the same message "*Go now, Daniel, for what I have said is for the time of the end. Many will be purified, cleansed, and refined by these trials. But the wicked will continue in their wickedness, and none of them will understand. Only those who are wise will know what it means*".

Revelation 22:12

In this verse Jesus again emphasizes he is coming soon to judge the believers, and His reward is with Him.

Revelation 22:13

The Lord reminds us here of His infinite wisdom, His omnipotence (all powerful nature of God), and His Omnipresence (His ability to be always everywhere).

Revelation 22:14

Here we see the seventh and last beatitude in Revelation: "*Blessed are those who wash their robes so they can enter through the gates of the city and eat the fruit from the tree of life*". Those who washed their robes are the ones who put their trust and faith in Jesus Christ. They can enter through the gates of The New Jerusalem and eat the fruit from the Tree of Life. In other words, they will be given eternal life with God.

Revelation 22:15

Here we see a repeat of what the angel told the apostle John in Revelation 21:8: *"But cowards, unbelievers, the corrupt, murderers, the immoral, those who practice witchcraft, idol worshipers, and all liars—their fate is in the fiery lake of burning sulfur. This is the second death"*. According to this passage, the final destination of the sinners is the Lake of Fire, and they have no access to the Holy City. The emphasis here is nothing evil and no sinner will be in the presence of God. Only holy people will be in His presence.

Revelation 22:16

Jesus is referred to here as the source of David and the Heir to his throne. What this scripture is telling us, as the Creator of the universe, Jesus existed long before King David. That is what the Apostle John tells us in John 1 and Revelation 5:5.

John 1:1-3: *"In the beginning was the Word, and the Word was with God, and the Word was God. He was in the beginning with God. All things were made through Him, and without Him nothing was made that was made"*.

Revelation 5:5: *"But one of the elders said to me, "Do not weep. Behold, the Lion of the tribe of Judah, the Root of David, has prevailed to open the scroll and to loose its seven seals."*

However, as human, Jesus is one of David's direct descendants as the prophet Isaiah tells us in Isaiah 11:1-5: *"Out of the stump of David's family will grow a shoot -- yes, a new Branch bearing fruit from the old root"*.

Then Jesus declares Himself to be the bright morning star. We see references to Jesus as the morning star in the following two passages:

341

2 Peter 1:19: *"You must pay close attention to what they (the prophets) wrote, for their words are like a lamp shining in a dark place--until the Day dawns, and Christ the Morning Star shines in your hearts"*.

Revelation 2:26-28: *"To all who are victorious, who obey me to the very end, to them I will give authority over all the nations. They will rule the nations with an iron rod and smash them like clay pots. They will have the same authority I received from my Father, and I will also give them the morning star!*

The contrast here is a morning star appears just before dawn when the night is darkest. As the Messiah, Jesus is the light to this world which has fallen into darkness.

Revelation 22:17

Here we see the Great Invitation "The Holy Spirit and the bride (the church) are heard saying "come, let the thirsty ones come and drink freely the water of life". When Jesus met the Samaritan woman at Jacob's well in John 4:1-15, He told her of the living water that he supplies. Here this image is used again as Christ invites anyone to come and drink the water of life.

Today we live in a world that is desperately thirsty for living water, and many people are dying of thirst. The water Jesus gives (His Holy Spirit) takes away thirst altogether. It becomes perpetual spring with us giving us eternal life.

Revelation 22:18-19

Jesus gives a warning to those who might purposely add or subtract from the message in this book. Moses gave a similar warning in Deuteronomy 4:1-2: *"And now, Israel, listen carefully to these laws and regulations that I am about to teach you. Obey them so that you may live, so you may enter and occupy the land the LORD, the God of your ancestors, is giving you. Do not add to or subtract from these commands I am giving you from the LORD your God. Just obey them"*.

Proverbs 30:5-6 warns about tampering with the Word of God: *"Every word of God proves true. He defends all who come to him for protection. Do not add to his words, or he may rebuke you, and you will be found a liar"*.

We too must handle the Book of Revelation and the Bible with care and great respect so that we do not distort or delete from its message. God warns if we do, He will send the plagues on us described in the Bible, and He will take away our share in the tree of life and in the Holy City, the New Jerusalem.

Revelation 22:20

We should take note here. Our Lord reaffirms to us that he is coming quickly and soon. Quickly or soon means "at any moment", and we must be ready for Him, always prepared for His return.

In 2 Timothy 4:8, the apostle Paul promised the Crown of Righteousness for the believers who live their lives eagerly looking forward to the glorious return of Christ: *"And now the prize awaits me -- the crown of righteousness that the Lord, the righteous Judge, will give me on that great day of his return. And the prize is not just for me but for all who eagerly look forward to his glorious return"*.

No one knows the day or the hour of Jesus' return, but Jesus is coming soon and unexpectedly. This is good news to those who put their faith and trust in Him, but bad news for those who have rejected Him.

The book of Genesis describes Adam and Eve walking in the Garden of Eden and talking with God. The book of Revelation describes the overcomers, the faithful seeing the Lord's face for the first time and worshipping Him face to face without the fear of dying. Genesis describes a beautiful garden with evil disguised in a serpent.

Revelation describes a perfect Heavenly City without sin or evil. In Genesis 3 God placed a curse on the earth, and He told Adam he will struggle and sweat all his life to earn a living. In Revelation 22, the curse is lifted and replaced with blessings. In Genesis, paradise was destroyed by sin, but it is re-created in The New Jerusalem without sin.

The Lord planted all sorts of trees bearing delicious fruits in the Garden of Eden and three rivers to water the garden. Revelation describes a pure river with the water of life clear as crystal flowing from the Throne of God. On each side of the river grew a tree of life bearing twelve crops of fruit with a fresh crop each month.

In closing, Revelation is a book of hope. It is not about the antichrist; it is not about the wrath of God that will come upon this earth; it is not about the loss of life that will take place during the seven-year tribulation. This book is about the Revelation of our Lord Jesus Christ in His majesty and sovereignty. It shows no matter what happens on this earth, God is still in control. He created the universe, and He alone controls human history and destiny. He forgives sin and brings everlasting peace.

Revelation depicts the wonderful rewards awaiting those who put their faith and trust in Jesus Christ. The Apostle Paul gives us this promise about the New Jerusalem in 1 Corinthians 2:9: *"No eye has seen, no ear has heard, and no mind has imagined what God has in store for those who love Him"*.

May the Lord bless you as you read my book and we await His return at the glorious rapture! To get in touch with me or to comment on my book, please visit me online at www.christinrevelation.org.

Appendix A
The Titles of God the Father in the Bible

Hebrew Title	Meaning	Scripture
Adonai	The Master	Genesis 15:2
El Elohe Israel	The God of Israel	Genesis 33:20
El Elohim	God the Creator	Deuteronomy 10:17
El Elyon	God the Most High	Genesis 14:20
El Roi	God Who Sees	Genesis 16:13
El Shaddi	The All-sufficient One	Genesis 17:1-8
El Olam	The Everlasting God	Genesis 21:33
El Qanna	The Lord is jealous	Exodus 20:4
Jehovah	The Lord God	Genesis 2:4
Jehovah-Jireh	The Lord provides	Genesis 22:14
Jehovah-Rapha	The Lord Who Heals	Exodus 15:26
Johovah-Nissi	The Lord my Banner	Exodus 17:15
Jehovah-Mekoddishken	The Lord Who sanctifies you	
		Exodus 31:13
Jehovah-Shalom	The Lord is Peace	Judges 6:24
Jehovah-Sabaoth	The Lord of hosts	1Samuel 1:1-11
Jehovah-Raah	The Lord my Shepherd	Psalm 23:1
Jehovah-Tsidkenu	The Lord our Righteousness	
		Jeremiah 23:6
Jehovah-Shammah	The Lord is there	Ezekiel 48:35
Jehoshaphat	The Lord Judges	Joel 3:2 & 3:12
Peniel or Penuel	The Face of God	Genesis 32:28
YHWH	The One who existed	Exodus 3:13-14
	I Am Who I Am	John 8:58

Appendix B
The Titles of God the Son in the Bible

Title	Meaning	Scripture
Alpha & Omega	Jesus is the First & the Last, the Beginning and the End of all things created	Revelation 1:8 Revelation 22:12-13
Branch	Branches out like a tree	Zechariah 6:12
Bread of Life	He strengthens us	John 6:35
Bright Morning Star	The Light of the world	Revelation 22:16 Matthew 2:9-10
Deliverer	The One who saves us	Psalm 18:2
Everlasting Father	Our Eternal Father	Isaiah 9:6
Faithful & True	Jesus is the Way, the Truth, and the Life He is faithful and True	John 14:1-6 Revelation 19:11
Fortress	The strength in our life	Psalm 18:2
Good / Great Shepherd	He lays down His life for His sheep	John 10:11; Hebrews 13:10
Heir to David's Throne	Descendant of David	Revelation 22:16
Immanuel	God with us	Isaiah 7:14; Matthew 1:23
Jesus Christ	God is salvation, our Savior	Matthew 1:20-21
King of Kings	His Name at His second coming	Revelation 19:16
Lamb of God	He is the Passover Lamb	Genesis 22:7-8; Exodus 12-13; John 1:29
Light of the World	He enlightens us with the Holy Spirit and gives us wisdom to see the truth	John 1:1-9; Revelation 21:23

Living Water	He cleanses us with His Holy Spirit	John 7:37-39;
	We no longer thirst for sin	Revelation 22:1-2
		1 Corinth.10:1-4
Lord of lords	His Name at His second coming	Revelation 19:16
Mighty God	Omnipotent God	Isaiah 9:6
Prince of Peace	The One Who gives us peace	Isaiah 9:6
Scepter	Symbol of authority	Genesis 49:10
Redeemer	One Who provides salvation	Isaiah 59:20
Rock	The solid Foundation of our Christian life	
		Psalm 18:2; 78:35
		1 Corinth.10:1-4;
		Matthew 16:18
		Exodus 17:6
Savior	One Who saves us from sin	1 John 4:14
Son of David	Descendant of David	Matthew 1; 21:9
Source of David	Descendant of David	Revelation 22:16
Star Risen from Jacob	His roots are in Israel	Numbers 24:17
	He is our Guardian	1 Peter 2:25; 5:4
Stone; Cornerstone	The solid Foundation of our Christian life	
		Isaiah 2:11
		Ephesians 2:19-20;
		1 Pet 2:6-8
The Lion of the tribe of Judah		
	His Name at His second coming	Revelation 5:5
The True Vine	He branches out to everyone	John 15:1-8
Wonderful Counselor	Gives us wisdom	Isaiah 9:6
Yeshua	Joshua in Hebrew	Zechariah 6:9-13
		Revelation 14:1-2

Appendix C
The Titles of God the Holy Spirit in the Bible

Title	Scripture
Breath of the Almighty	Job 33:4; John 3:6
Comforter	John 14:16
	John 14:26; 15:26
Eternal Spirit	Hebrews 9:14
Free Spirit	Psalm 51:12
God the Spirit	Acts 5:3-4
Good Spirit	Nehemiah 9:20
	Psalm 143:10
He knows God's Thoughts	1 Corinthians 2:11
Our Helper	John 14:16; 15:26
Our Seal for the day of redemption	Psalm 51:11
	Luke 11:13
	Ephesians 1:13; 4:30
Power of the Highest	Luke 1:35
Spirit of the Lord God	Isaiah 61:1
Spirit of God moving over the surface of the waters	
	Genesis 1:2
Spirit of the Father	Matthew 10:20
Spirit of Christ	Romans 8:9; 1 Peter 1:11
Spirit of the Son	Galatians 4:6
Spirit of life	Romans 8:2;
	Revelation 11:11
Spirit of grace	Zechariah 12:10
	Hebrews 10:29
Spirit of prophecy	Revelation 19:10
Spirit of adoption	Romans 8:15
Spirit of truth	John 14:17; 15:26
Spirit of holiness	Romans 1:4
Spirit of revelation	Ephesians 1:17
Spirit of judgment	Isaiah 4:4; 28:6

Spirit of burning	Isaiah 4:4
Spirit of glory	1Peter 4:14
The Spirit	Matthew 4:1
	John 3:6
	1Timothy 4:1

The seven Spirits who are before His throne (Revelation 1:4 and Isaiah 11:2):

1. Spirit of the Lord
2. Spirit of wisdom
3. Spirit of understanding
4. Spirit of counsel
5. Spirit of might
6. Spirit of knowledge
7. Spirit of the fear of the Lord

Sources: My Sunday school teachings, Northeast Baptist Church, Ponca City, OK; First Baptist Church, Owasso, OK; Friendship Baptist Church, Owasso, OK.
Source: www.biblestudytools.com